Stereotyping as Inductive Hypothesis Testing

European Monographs in Social Psychology
Sponsored by the European Association of Experimental Psychology

Series Editor:
Professor Rupert Brown, Department of Psychology, University of Kent, Canterbury, Kent CT2 7NP

The aim of this series is to publish and promote the highest quality of writing in European social psychology. The editor and the editorial board encourage publications which approach social psychology from a wide range of theoretical perspectives and whose content may be applied, theoretical or empirical. The authors of books in this series should be affiliated to institutions that are located in countries which would qualify for membership of the Association. All books will be published in English, and translations from other European languages are welcomed. Please submit ideas and proposals for books in the series to Rupert Brown at the above address.

Published

The Quantitative Analysis of Social Representations
Willem Doise, Alain Clemence, and Fabio Lorenzi-Cioldi

A Radical Dissonance Theory
Jean-Léon Beauvois and Robert-Vincent Joule

The Social Psychology of Collective Action
Caroline Kelly and Sara Breinlinger

Social Context and Cognitive Performance
Jean-Marc Monteil and Pascal Huguet

Conflict and Decision-Making in Close Relationships
Erich Kirchler, Christa Rodler, Erik Hölzl, and Katja Meier

Stereotyping as Inductive Hypothesis Testing
Klaus Fiedler and Eva Walther

Intergroup Relations in States of the Former Soviet Union
Louk Hagendoorn, Hub Linssen, and Sergei Tumanov

Forthcoming Title

The Passionate Intersection of Desire and Knowledge
Gregory Maio

Stereotyping as Inductive Hypothesis Testing

Klaus Fiedler and Eva Walther

University of Heidelberg, Germany

LONDON AND NEW YORK

First published 2004 by Psychology Press

Published 2016 by Routledge
2 Park Square, Milton Park, Abingdon, Oxfordshire OX14 4RN
711 Third Avenue, New York, NY 10017, USA

First issued in paperback 2016

Routledge is an imprint of the Taylor & Francis Group, an informa business

Typeset in Times by Keystroke, Jacaranda Lodge, Wolverhampton
Cover design by Amanda Barragry

British Library Cataloguing in Publication Data
A catalogue record for this book is available from the British Library

Library of Congress Cataloging-in-Publication Data
Fiedler, Klaus, 1951–
Stereotyping as inductive hypothesis testing / Klaus Fiedler & Eva Walther.
p. cm.
Includes bibliographical references.
ISBN 0-86377-832-1
1. Stereotype (Psychology)—Research—Methodology. 2. Social sciences—Research—Methodology. I. Walther, Eva, 1964– II. Title.
BF323.S63F54 2003
303.3′85′072—dc21

2003010529

ISBN 13: 978-1-138-88309-3 (pbk)
ISBN 13: 978-0-86377-832-2 (hbk)

Contents

List of tables

List of figures

1 The topic of social hypothesis testing

At the end of a recently held seminar on the topic of this volume, social hypothesis testing, some ambitious students confessed that they had been initially threatened by the seminar announcement, expecting mainly formal statistics and methodology. Although they learned, later on, that models borrowed from statistics were indeed not irrelevant, they nevertheless discovered an extremely exciting topic behind the title. Research on social hypothesis testing is at the heart of many intriguing phenomena that have occupied scholars in social psychology, cognitive psychology, and decision making for many decades. It tells stories about cognitive fallacies and shortcomings, collective illusions, and sources of stereotypes and superstition, but also stories about adaptive cognition and amazing subtleties of information processing and communication.

Moreover, seminar participants ought to have noticed, as a side effect, that being concerned with the psychology of *social* hypothesis testing in everyday settings raises critical thinking and emancipation with regard to *societal* hypothesis testing. As one begins to understand the formation and persistence of stereotypes (e.g., about ethnic groups, gender, mentally ill people, homosexuals, etc.) as a consequence of hypothesis testing, one inevitably becomes more skeptical in judging how political, economical, and educational hypotheses are treated in public. An emancipated student of hypothesis testing may begin to reconsider the epistemological status of such societal issues as: the enhanced criminality rates of fugitives, the alleged superiority of boys over girls in mathematics and science, the impact of salary level on economic growth, the influence of highway speed restrictions on ozone intoxication, or many beliefs about stigmatized or marginalized groups such as gay people, physically handicapped, or psychotics. Note that many of these everyday hypotheses refer to ill-founded beliefs lacking any strong evidence or solid ground: Some of these hypothetical beliefs may even turn out to be completely false and misleading, reflecting a collective bias in hypothesis testing. In the remainder of this volume, however, we are mainly concerned with hypothesis-testing processes in the context of social stereotypes

Last but not least, participants in our seminar may have noticed that the same lesson can be expanded to *scientific* hypothesis testing. After all, the way in which researchers favor, or even fall in love with, certain hypotheses, while ignoring others, is only slightly different from the symptoms of the everyday lay hypothesis tester. The history of many theories covered by the present book provides vivid examples for this claim. Just like a persistent, hard to abolish stereotype, many common claims and theories would persist for decades, often in the face of strong contradictory evidence, simply because researchers are reluctant or sometimes even resistant to consider alternative hypotheses

In the present volume, to repeat, we delineate the common characteristics of hypothesis testing with special reference to the formation and maintenance of social stereotypes. The overarching theme connecting all following chapters is the claim that *social hypotheses appear to have a built-in device for verification*. Merely considering or focusing on a hypothetical attribute suggested by a stereotype will often increase the belief that the focused attribute is really there (Fiedler, 2000c; Gilbert, 1989; Snyder, 1984). Considering one explanation for an observed phenomenon often entails blindness to other possible explanations. Let us illustrate this phenomenon with a well-known experiment conducted by Mark Snyder and his colleagues (Snyder, Tanke, & Berscheid, 1977) on the *what-is-beautiful-is-good stereotype* (Dion, Berscheid, & Walster, 1972). Male college students were shown a photograph of an unknown female student with whom they would supposedly have a telephone conversation. In one condition, participants were shown a highly attractive woman, whereas in another condition the woman on the picture was less attractive. In actuality, both groups held a telephone conversation with a randomly paired female student. Later analyses of the phone calls demonstrated that those men who thought they were interacting with an attractive woman behaved in a more sociable, outgoing, self-confident, and warm fashion than men in the other group. Interestingly, the women in turn matched the positive interaction style when they interacted with a partner who *thought* they were attractive, in contrast to those who talked with men who *did not think* they were attractive.

The genuinely social nature of this experimental setting highlights the interplay of several factors that can potentially contribute to the process of hypothesis testing and verification. On the one hand, the hypothesis testers' *stereotypical expectations* and his *one-sided information search* (i.e., looking for sympathetic properties in allegedly attractive females) may play an important role. Moreover, the hypothesis tester's *need to form a consistent impression* may lead him to discount disconfirming (i.e., unfriendly) reactions and observations. On the other hand, the behavior of the female target is no less important. Being flattered by the charming utterances of the male, females will often cooperate and reciprocate the style of the interaction partner. In doing so, they *comply with conversational norms and situational demands*. However, interestingly, even when the female target does not confirm the male's expectations, *merely imagining and mentally simulating* how an attractive person *might* behave will provide surrogate evidence for the guiding stereotype that attractive people are high in social skills.

Apparently, then, the reasons why social interaction will often end up with hypothesis confirmation are manifold. Some of these reasons are intuitively plausible and not very surprising. Other reasons, however, are not visible at first sight and would hardly be discovered without experimental research—and without a clearly spelled out theoretical framework. What Snyder and colleagues demonstrated in their experimental setting holds true for scientific inquiry and everyday reasoning alike. Researchers do not like to face alternative hypotheses that could challenge their preferred hypothesis; likewise, politicians, physicians, decision makers, or jurors would rather avoid and suppress alternative hypotheses than face them.

Don't round up the usual suspects

However, it is quite interesting that under certain conditions we are not that blind for alternative hypotheses, suggesting that we are not concerned here with an absolute restriction of the human mind. People who are trained in "hypothesis-testing games" may develop a problem-solving set that makes them sensitive to alternative, sometimes even far-fetched, hypotheses. For example, somebody whose primary hobby is solving detective-story puzzles may have acquired a chronic strategy not to believe in the most plausible, best-fitting hypothesis. Such an individual would rather look out for uncommon solutions that often require to abstract from salient but misleading features of the story. Indeed, one goal of the present book is to encourage the reader to take a similar perspective as the whodunit reader and look out for alternative hypotheses—both in science and everyday encounters. Thus, we want to impart a perspective that goes beyond the usual suspects. Maybe, this was also the take-home message that the seminar participants gained from the course in social hypothesis testing.

The mentioned experiment on social perception and attraction clearly speaks to social psychological process of stereotyping. How can we carry over the essence of such experimental studies to more natural settings in which hypothesis testing is an even more complex endeavor? The reader is invited to recognize various analogies to the above experiment in the following short story. The narrative style of a short story will offer a more refined and embellished sketch of the many traps and misleading paths of hypothesis-testing processes in real life.

A short story

Professor Johnson was a little tense as he approached the huge porch of the building. After all, this was the first interview after he received tenure from his home university more than 15 years ago. He was well aware that he was neither attracted by the salary (which was only slightly higher than what he gets right now), nor by the busy atmosphere created by all these extremely young colleagues (actually, all these clever and ambitious young guys frightened him a little). No, after his divorce last year he just wanted to demonstrate to himself that he was not too old for a change, that he was still able to compete for a job, that he was still flexible enough to adapt to a different working place. He also held the tacit hope that a new start in a different city might help him to cope with the loneliness he experienced since Alice left him.

While all these thoughts were running through his mind, he was now waiting in the secretary's room to meet the dean of the department who was supposed to be his first interview partner. Looking at his wristwatch for the third time in the last 2 minutes Professor Johnson nervously realized that he had to visit the bathroom. Because of construction work on this wing of the building, the secretary explained that he must leave the building, turn to the right, then to the left, walk for approximately. . . . Mr. Johnson tried to concentrate on this apparently endless description, but knowing that he was never good at spatial orientation he stopped listening after the fourth "to the left" and stumbled through the door. There he tried hard to remember at least the beginning of the description, and followed the sidewalk between two smaller buildings which he did not dare to enter because he was afraid that someone would realize that he was lost. Unfortunately, he met nobody to ask and after a while he desperately decided to relieve himself behind a bush. It was the same moment he was seen by Dr. Higgins, the new chief psychiatrist, who showed some members of the donation around the hospital. Fumbling at his trousers and trying to hide himself behind the thicket with an anxious expression in his eyes in the midst of the clinic bungalows, Professor Johnson presented the prototypical picture of a lunatic, who tries to steal away from the hospital.

"Hello, I'm Dr. Higgins, who are you?" Dr. Higgins cried in his most friendly voice with which he wished to impress the donation members. "I'm Professor Johnson," Professor Johnson yelled back at him. "Of course you are, here are several professors and also kings and popes," Dr. Higgins replied, and provoked a collective laughter in the group. "What are you doing Professor?" Dr. Higgins asked, now sure that this would be one of his more entertaining patients.

"I have an appointment with the Dean," Professor Johnson answered faithfully. Laughter again,

"I'll take you there," Dr. Higgins promised after he briefly excused himself and guided Mr. Johnson to the ambulance. There Dr. Higgins handed over Professor Johnson to the nurse on duty. "Here is a new patient, I think paranoid-schizophrenic. Make the usual tests, I'll take a look at him later," he told the nurse, and left the room.

Ten minutes later Mr. Johnson tried to defend himself against the two male nurses who led him away to a small room. "I am Professor Johnson," he shouted. "I have a very important appointment with the Dean. Let me go," he yelled.

"You are in good company," one of the male nurses remarked. "We have two other professors here on the ward." "Yes," the other one giggled, "you can hold conferences."

One hour later, an exhausted-looking Professor Johnson was sitting vis-à-vis the diagnostician in the interview room, a nurse bending over her memo-pad behind him. "If I cooperate and answer all questions truthfully, they *must* realize that I am a real Professor and let me go," Prof. Johnson said to himself, feeling new hope that this horror would end soon.

"Who are you?" the diagnostician started the interview.

"I repeat it for the thirteenth time, I am Professor Johnson," he answered, hardly able to suppress his impatience. "I am Professor Johnson and I have a very important appointment right now with Dean."

"Do you often lose your temper, Mr. Johnson?" the physician asked.

The—admittedly far-fetched, but not at all unrealistic—short story about the sane person in an insane place illustrates a number of important points concerning the vicissitudes of social hypothesis testing. First, we can see the distinction between three roles, or participants in the social interaction: the *agent* (diagnostician) who runs the hypothesis test; the *target person* (Professor Johnson) whose behavior is the focus of the test; and the passive *observer* (the nurse), who perceives the agent's interaction with the target. All three roles participate in a characteristic fashion. The agent promotes the confirmation of the hypothesis that the target person is psychotic in the way he conducts the interview, interprets the patient's utterances, retrieves information from memory and from inferences shaped by prior knowledge. The target himself facilitates the confirmation process in that he provides responses that match (though they try to disconfirm) the assumptions underlying the question, and by his own self-doubts and reactions to the psychiatric terror. Last but not least, the nurse who only kept the record in the observer role cannot help but adopt a similar impression, namely that this person is obviously of the same kind as most other mad patients in the hospital. After all, that's why this person was sent to hospital. Madness is thus a suitable baseline hypothesis in the given environment. Notably, however, the nurse does not remain totally passive. Eventually, she also takes on an active role in that she communicates with other people (e.g., staff) and thereby spreads the confirmed hypothesis that has now become social reality.

The story also conveys a sketch of the psychological process stages that determine the outcome of hypothesis testing. First and foremost, the whole process of *information search* is guided by the suspicion that the target person is psychotic. Although Professor Johnson's behavior is sort of unusual, it would not have instigated the impression of a lunatic in a context different from a psychiatric hospital. But the mere context of behavior provides cues that lead to a certain hypothesis. Based on this starting hypothesis, the diagnostician asks test questions, figuring out whether the target is irritated, mentally confused, or paranoid. One might have also asked questions about his sufficient characteristics, assets, or skills, but for pragmatic reasons the clinical staff cannot pursue all plausible hypotheses and have to confine themselves to the one hypothesis that is most plausible in the given context. As time and resources are restricted in a hospital, and as the goal of this institution is to diagnose psychiatric illness rather than adaptive behavior or social skills, it is very likely that agents concentrate on psychiatric hypotheses. Thus, concentrating on information that matches the focal hypothesis—a process called *positive testing* (Klayman & Ha, 1987)—is not even irrational or narrow-minded; it is a natural consequence of the institutional environment.

Second, the agent engages in *schema-consistent encoding* of the target's utterances and behaviors. Based on the agent's prior knowledge (i.e., psychiatric education), he interprets very common and harmless utterances as constituents of pathological episodes, going way beyond the information given. Such inferences need not be driven by negative motives or instrumental goals. Drawing inference is what all experts are expected to do; that is, a professional diagnostician has to interpret observed behaviors as symptoms of pathological laws. Of course, another agent, with a different objective in mind and with different background knowledge (e.g., whodunit reader), might have drawn different inferences, being attentive to the rather unlikely hypothesis that sometimes a sane person happens to intrude a psychiatric hospital. However, from the psychiatrist's point of view, the pathological inferences drawn from the present patient's behavior suggest themselves, and may even be justified.

A third process is *accentuation*. The perceived difference between the target under focus and the comparison standard of a normal person is accentuated, because the target person not only deviates in his behavior but also in his appearance, his language, and his biography. Such a coincidence of several distinctive features serves to increase the perceived distance of the target from other persons, even when the correlated distinctions as such are of restricted diagnostic value (Corneille & Judd, 1999; Eiser & Stroebe, 1972; Krueger & Rothbart, 1990; Tajfel,1957).

Another characteristic process is the tendency to discount, or interpret away many observations that are incompatible with the picture of a psychotic person. For example, the target's apparent insider information about psychiatry and his normal responses on a projective test might be compatible with the notion that he is a normal patient. But it was quite easy to maintain the hypothesis, assuming that this patient belongs to a subtype of psychotics who exhibit many normal intellectual functions. This type of discounting or immunization from disconfirming evidence is commonly referred to as *subtyping* in research on stereotyping (Johnston & Hewstone, 1992; Kunda & Oleson, 1995; Rothbart & John, 1985; Maurer, Park, & Rothbart, 1995).

As time passes by and the agent meets the target again the next day, *selective memory* comes into play. For several reasons, it may happen that the agent can remember more details of yesterday's interview that fit the hypothesis than details that do not fit. In the meantime, the evidence was even enriched with *constructive memory intrusions*. For instance, the agent has thought about the new patient overnight and considered some interview questions he might have asked, but did not. In doing so, the agent has thought of potential answers that the target may have given, and these self-generated fantasies have also been integrated in the overall memory representation. Later on, the agent was no longer sure which part of this representation was based on actual observations and which part was due to constructive intrusions.

A related, very serious source of bias in hypothesis testing is the agent's *meta-cognitive blindness* for external constraints. For example, that the target speaks about his success as a "professor" is counted as further evidence for a psychotic cause, although the agent himself has solicited this topic, asking a direct question about the target's job experiences. This inability to understand the consequences of one's own biased information search may also contribute to the process of *perseverance* (Ross, Lepper, & Hubbard, 1975). This concept refers to the tendency to adhere to an erroneous inference once the error has been clarified. Thus, even after the diagnostician learns later that the whole episode was a mistake, it is rather likely that he will continue to believe that this person is in fact latently psychotic.

What is even worse, the target himself appears to show perseverance, questioning whether he is really a sane person. Why else did anybody believe in this hypothesis for such a long time? To some degree at least, the dangerous experiment in the hospital has become a *self-fulfilling prophecy* (Jussim, Eccles, & Madon, 1996). Being treated like an insane person for some time, and having shown many reactions that fit this expectancy, the target cannot totally erase this experience, which continues to impact his self-image.

The process by which a hypothesis becomes social reality is rounded up by the way in which observers communicate to others what they have seen. (Of course, not only passive observers, but agents and targets can also be in the communicator role.) It is not only important that observers communicate, but also what *linguistic tools* they use for communication. The *linguistic expectancy bias* (Maass, 1999; Wigboldus, Semin, & Spears, 2000) implies that communicators tend to use particularly abstract words (e.g., adjectives such as "weird", "unrealistic", "anxious") when conveying expected, hypothesis-confirming information. As these abstract utterances are too vague and detached from factual behaviors to be tested critically, this tendency further supports the maintenance and immunization of confirmed hypotheses.

It should finally be noted that even though the short story results in an extreme case of illusion, or self-fulfilling prophecy, it does so without ever presupposing any motive or prejudice in the three participating roles: the agent, the target, and the observer. Thus, the storywriter obviously did not want to attribute to the diagnostician any goal, desire, or vested interest to classify the patient as psychotic; nor was the agent (diagnostician) characterized as sloppy, superficial or cognitively lazy. Likewise, the target person was not described as ill-motivated, and observers were not lacking the cognitive capacity or resources necessary to make accurate judgments based on a careful account of the observed stimulus information. For the short story to work, it was also not necessary to assume any severe cognitive shortcomings or irrational biases in the persons' perception and memory. Rather, it was presupposed that all people are motivated to be realistic and accurate. Nevertheless, a severely biased outcome arose in the absence of biased processes, just as a consequence of people's interaction in a complex environment, with its own interaction rules.

This latter point is essential for the *cognitive-environmental approach* that guides the present monograph. We do not contest that stereotypes are sometimes the result of severe biases, personal motives, wishful thinking, capacity constraints, self-presentation concerns, or vested interests in the individual persons involved. Ignoring such motivational and irrational influences on the stereotyping process would be completely out of touch with reality. While we take these influences for granted, we do not believe that reiterating this prominent point can add much beyond what is already well established in stereotype research (Hamilton & Sherman, 1994; Hilton & von Hippel, 1996; Spears, Oakes, Ellemers, & Haslam, 1997). Rather, we believe that it is particularly interesting to consider unmotivated, incidental processes of environmental learning that often happen to support stereotypes as a side effect. Even in the absence of stereotype-congruent goals or motives, stereotypes arise as a by-product of the individual's normal interaction with other people, groups, tasks, and institutions. We believe that investigating these "innocent", unmotivated sources of stereotyping will lead to more new insights and innovative theoretical perspectives than searching for corresponding motives and goals.

2 Stereotyping as a cognitive-environmental learning process

Delineating the conceptual framework

The two examples used in the opening chapter have illustrated, plausibly and vividly, how stereotypical hypotheses can become social reality. Many similar demonstrations have been obtained in controlled experiments and field settings. The social psychological literature is replete with research findings demonstrating how easily hypotheses are confirmed in the absence of supportive evidence. Prominent examples include: teachers who succeed in finding unjustified support for the allegedly lower achievement of working-class than middle-class children (Rosenthal & Jacobson, 1968); experimenter biases verifying erroneous expectancies that some experimental rats are superior to others (Rosenthal, 1966); the influence of starting hypotheses on interview results (Zuckerman, Knee, Hodgins, & Miyake, 1995), and survey outcomes (Blau & Katerberg, 1982); the impact of expectancies on medical diagnoses (Ledley & Lusted, 1959); false eyewitness memories induced by leading questions (Loftus, 1979); innuendo effects in the mass media (Wegner, Wenzlaff, Kerker, & Beattie, 1981); and the impact of starting hypotheses on group decision making (Schulz-Hardt, Frey, Lüthgens, & Moscovici, 2000), to list but a few pertinent findings.

Let us now try to raise the discussion from a mere listing of familiar examples to a more comprehensive analysis of the underlying psychological processes. With this goal in mind, the purpose of the present chapter is:

- to outline the basic research paradigm for studying stereotype verification
- to provide an introduction to some representative research findings
- to spell out the psychological assumptions that have been offered to explain those findings
- to introduce a common terminology
- to illustrate the fertility of treating stereotyping as a hypothesis-testing process.

Locating the present approach in a theoretical framework

Aside from these objectives, the first and foremost purpose of this chapter is to develop a theoretical framework in which the present research approach is anchored. Explaining the theoretical underpinnings, and setting the present approach apart from previous ones, entails the twofold question of what our approach is and what it is not. To unfold the answer, we can start with an outline, and with a suggested name, for two different meta-theories that in our opinion represent the contrast between the traditional approach to stereotyping and the goal of the present approach. To sensitize the reader for the ideas we want to convey in the present monograph, we may somewhat overstate the contrast between these two different meta-theories that may be called an *animistic approach* to stereotyping and a *cognitive-environmental learning approach* (CELA). Whereas the term "animistic" is pertinent to many (though certainly not all) traditional theories of stereotyping, the most important characteristic of CELA is its reliance on normal rules of environmental learning.

The traditional, animistic approach to stereotyping

What the term "animistic" conveys—we believe correctly—can be understood as a kind of fundamental attribution bias (Ross, 1977) in psychological theorizing —a metaphor also recently used by Bond and Kenny (2002). Just as everyday attributions by naive people tend to explain behaviors in terms of internal causes or dispositions within animate beings, rather than situational conditions or abstract system features, past research on social stereotypes during the last half-century has exhibited a marked preference for animistic explanations that point to internal causes within individual people's *beliefs* and *desires*. These two prominent constituents of animistic theories correspond to cognitive expectancies and motivational goals, respectively, as the major determinants of stereotypes. Theories of stereotyping and lay explanations of social behavior share the central role assigned to beliefs and desires.

To illustrate the force and extent of animistic explanations, let us once more consider the Snyder et al. (1977) study. How could the finding be explained that female communication partners that were expected to be attractive were found to be more sociable than allegedly less attractive women? No doubt, most reasonable explanations that come to mind begin with the male participant's *expectancy* that the female communication partner was attractive or not. In fact, this was the focus of the major experimental manipulation, which guaranteed that expectancies or beliefs were the crucial independent variable. In addition to beliefs, of course, desires or motivational factors may also be at work. At least part of the richer and more positive interaction with attractive rather than less attractive partners may reflect the hedonic *motive* to build up a positive relationship with attractive people, or the need to attain a sense of control in an expectancy-congruent world.

Most of the other subprocesses we mentioned in the first chapter can be understood as factors that mediate the impact of beliefs and desires as the two major constituents. Thus, once the belief in the assets and the desire to get along with attractive people has been elicited, it seems natural that the participant will treat attractive partners in a selective fashion. Participants may raise pleasant topics while conversing with persons they expect to be attractive. The same verbal statement by the target may be perceived as more charming than it would be perceived in a less desired person. Rude behavior in an attractive person may be overlooked, discounted, or subtyped as exceptional, or non-serious, humorous behavior. Observations that disconfirm the relationship between attraction and social skills may tend to be forgotten. The relative contribution of these factors —selective information search, biased perception, selective memory, subtyping— may vary with the specifics of the task situation. In any case, however, the implicit assumption is that these factors can be explained in terms of the individual's expectancies and motives, beliefs and desires. Without this assumption, there would be no sound explanation for why somebody should solicit pleasant rather than unpleasant behaviors in attractive people, or why somebody should forget information that disconfirms rather than confirms the stereotype.

Theory formation within the animistic approach might be characterized as involving a theoretician who empathizes with the individual (i.e., the stereotype holder) and reconstructs her behavior in terms of reasons and motives. To be sure, animistic theories do not deny environmental factors. After all, the attractive female's nice and sociable behavior is supposed to be solicited by the hypothesis tester's actual behavior, and researchers would hardly contest that context factors can moderate the behavior. However, the crucial theoretical constructs used to explain the behavior in question are the animistic factors (beliefs and desires) within the individual, which are assumed to mediate the impact of any environmental stimuli or context factors.

Introducing the cognitive-environmental approach (CELA)

Indeed, the animistic approach has been so influential that we can hardly imagine how this sensible story could *not* be true. Would anybody contest that beliefs and desires can have a strong impact on the way in which we treat and perceive other people? Of course, nobody would seriously come to doubt that the kernel of the animistic interpretation that stereotypes reflect interaction partners' beliefs and desires is realistic. Human individuals do shape their interaction processes as a function of beliefs and desires; contesting this truism would appear to be cynical. And so we do not seriously contest the plausibility or importance of animistic factors such as needs, goals, wishes, beliefs, expectancies, attitudes, cognitive representations, and shortcomings within the individual. When we nevertheless contrast our own approach against the animistic meta-theory, we do not refute these potential influences, but we take them for granted as common ground among contemporary scientists interested in stereotyping. We don't even want to claim that the theoretical potential of the animistic approach has been fully exhausted. However, we do claim that another, much less noted, non-animistic approach— that can be named "cognitive-environmental"—can add a number of fundamentally new insights beyond animistic forces, and therefore deserves to be pursued as well.

The general message to be conveyed in this approach is that even when beliefs and desires are ruled out or controlled for, the inclination of hypotheses and stereotypes to be verified and maintained continues. In other words, stereotypical biases may even persist when the psychological processes within subjects are completely unbiased, or uncontaminated by selective information processing due to beliefs and desires. Environmental factors alone may explain that stereotypes are likely to be confirmed in hypothesis testing. Let us assume, for example, that participants in the Snyder et al. (1977) experiment did not fall prey to the suggestion that their conversation partner is attractive and did not hold the belief that attractive people score high in social skills. Rather, participants start to interact with their discussion partners in a fully unbiased way, and those partners do not selectively respond to the way they are treated. Nevertheless, the task environment may facilitate or inhibit the confirmation of social skills in the target, and cause an upward or downward bias in subsequent judgments, according to completely normal rules of environmental learning. To explain how this works, let us assume that most interaction partners in Western cultural environments are high in sociability and gregariousness, regardless of appearance. Thus, while attractive and unattractive individuals are treated the same and react similarly, the only difference between experimental conditions might lie in sample size, or the *number of observations* solicited from allegedly attractive versus unattractive targets (for whatever reasons). Given a stimulus environment that renders information about attractive people particularly visible, the ecologically prevalent tendency towards sociability and gregariousness will receive more support for an attractive target than for a less attractive target for whom information is more scarce. As the next four chapters will show, this is a typical example of a seemingly trivial but actually very powerful theoretical aspect of the information environment.

Note that sample size does not matter in the animistic approach. No motives and cognitive biases are required for an influence of large versus small stimulus samples, or rich versus poor environments, to impact on subsequent judgments. A cognitive inference process that is influenced by sample size is by no means irrational, or biased. Any effective information-processing device should be sensitive to sample size, or amount of information. Normative models of hypothesis testing, such as the Bayes theorem or student's t-test, would draw stronger inferences about the target's sociability and gregariousness if the information base is large rather than small. The resulting impression of the target may therefore differ markedly, as a function of the amount of information that the stimulus ecology renders accessible. The amount of information about the target, in turn, may depend on such diverse factors as spatial distance, observation time, sensory modality (text, auditory, audio-visual), degree of acquaintanceship, salience of target, activity level of target, and so forth.

Interestingly, among the factors that determine amount of information may also be factors that are normally in the focus of animistic explanations. For instance, there are good reasons for assuming that social ecologies (e.g., media, attended part of the social world) tend to provide richer information about attractive than unattractive people. As we have just seen, with increasing amounts of information the target's social skills (sociability, gregariousness) will become more apparent. However, note that in this case the resulting judgment bias in favor of an attractive person will only mimic a genuine influence of attraction, or associated beliefs and desires. In fact, in this scenario, attraction is but one of many factors that influence the crucial environmental variable of information amount or richness, which is the true cause of the judgment bias. In this way, a purely non-animistic, abstract and "innocent" property of the information environment can contribute to the hypothesis confirmation bias, and to the maintenance of the stereotype that attractive people are high in social skills.

Let us now assume that the experimental instructions to test specific hypotheses are manipulated. Rather than testing whether the target is sociable and gregarious, the instruction could focus on whether the target shows serious *deficits* in sociability and gregariousness. Granting that the participant's attention will now focus on deficits, it is possible that judgments of social skill will now decrease, or become more negative, as the amount of information increases. Attractive people, who are salient targets of attention, may suffer particularly from this reversed focus manipulation. Again, such a disadvantage that attractive people might now suffer need not result from a reversed expectancy or belief induced by the reversed instruction. It might again reflect the impact of the hypothesis direction on information search and on the amount of information gathered, thus illustrating a genuine interaction of cognitive (looking for deficits) and environmental factors (access to target information)—which is at the heart of any CELA.

Let us consider still another case. There might be two targets that are equivalent in social skills but different in terms of attractiveness. Participants are instructed to test the hypothesis that the *less* attractive person is higher in social skills. Thus, the task instruction supposed to guide the cognitive-environmental interaction runs against the intuitive tendency to attend more to the attractive person. In such a setting, environmental factors and animistic factors are pitted against each other. If it can be demonstrated that acquiring richer information about the less attractive person will serve to confirm the impression that the unattractive person is higher in social skills than the attractive person, in spite of the opposite stereotype, then the distinctive implications of the CELA can be set apart from the animistic approach. To be sure, CELA's implications need not always be distinct from, or opposite to, the predictions derived from common animistic explanations. Across many empirical phenomena, environmental factors operate in the same direction as beliefs and desires, thus affording alternative explanations in terms of confounded influences. However, those intriguing cases in which the implications diverge are particularly important to substantiate the original potential of cognitive-environmental processes.

Table 2.1 gives an overview of the features that distinguish the CELA from the traditional animistic approach and, thus, of the specific insights that can be expected from CELA. To begin with, one major difference corresponds roughly to the difference between causes and reasons, or *third-person and first-person explanations*. Animistic accounts in terms of beliefs and desires refer to subjective reasons that give meaning and intention to the subject's behavior, relative to personal goals. Theoretical explanations of behavior—considered from a meta-theoretical perspective—involve taking the perspective of, or empathizing with, the individual and looking for the motives and knowledge structures that match the observed behavior. The resulting first-person accounts sometimes run the danger of being

Table 2.1 Comparison of characteristic features of the animistic and the cognitive-environmental meta-theory

Animistic approach	*Cognitive-environmental approach (CELA)*
Explanation refers to reasons within the individual (first person explanation)	Explanation refers to causes in the environment (third person explanation)
Explanatory construct meaningful, personal, and sometimes tautologically close to the phenomenon to be explained	Explanatory construct abstract, systemic, and remote from phenomenon to be explained
Locus of stereotyping: intrapsychic	Locus of stereotyping: more inclusive environment
Causal conditions: Cognitive and motivational biases	Causal conditions: Stimulus distribution in learning environment
Enabling conditions: Reduced mental resources	Enabling conditions: Lack of control over environmental stimulus generation
Chief factors manipulated: Expectancies and motivational states; cognitive load	Chief factors manipulated: Hypothesis; stimulus distribution; active information search
Emphasis on maintenance of already existing stereotypes in natural domains	Emphasis on acquisition of new stereotypes in artificial domains

tautological (Brandtstädter, 1982; Greve, 2001; Wallach & Wallach, 1994), as the explanatory constructs remain too close to the phenomenon to be explained.

For example, the explanatory statement "*Attractive conversation partners received enhanced judgments in social skills because a stereotype says that attractive people can be expected to be high in social skills*" is logically correct, and hard to refute. However, the price for the disarming plausibility—and perhaps the popularity—of such expectancy accounts is that they run the risk of getting circular. For assessing the stereotype and assessing the behavior towards attractive people is probably hard to distinguish operationally. Of course, this is not to suggest that all animistic theories fall into this trap. However, avoiding this trap is certainly a problem for theories of this kind.

One interesting corollary of first-person explanations is that they have to be reasonable; that is, beliefs and desires have to be consistent with the behavior to be explained. They do not allow for empirical reversals of a-priori gestalts. Thus, it is permissible to say that the judgment of an attractive person's social skills was high because the judge expected attractive persons to be high in social skills. However, the a-priori restrictions of animistic theories would hardly permit an explanation stating that social skill was judged to be high because social skill was expected to be low. Just as it would be impermissible to explain that a judge exaggerated the social skills of attractive persons because he tried hard to be fair and accurate. Or, when explaining actions in terms of intentions, as in Fishbein and Ajzen's (1974) theory of reasoned action, it makes sense to explain charming behavior towards an attractive woman in terms of the intention to please her. But the animistic notion of intentional action could hardly be used to explain an opposite empirical outcome, namely, that an intention to please her produces disgusting behavior. It is because the reversal or falsification of many animistic theory assumptions creates anomalies, rather than meaningful falsifications, that their empirical status has been questioned (cf. Brandtstädter, 1982; Wallach & Wallach, 1994).

To be sure, all these paradoxical reversals are possible, psychologically. High judgments of social skill may indeed reflect a contrast effect due to pretentious expectancies (Helson, 1964; Sherif & Hovland, 1961); trying hard to be accurate may indeed result in inaccuracy (Wilson & Schooler, 1991); or intending to please somebody may fail and cause unpleasant behavior (Steele & Aronson, 1995). Strictly speaking, animistic approaches do not have these cases in their repertory of normal behavior. To the extent that animistic theories, like the theory of reasoned action (Fishbein & Ajzen, 1974), are formulated as universal nomological theories with an unrestricted domain, such demonstrations falsify the logical cogency of the underlying instrumental rationale—that beliefs and desires *explain* congruent behavior. Of course, this rationale does not really explain behavior of the opposite behavior. To be sure, animistic theories can still cope with reversals by inventing auxiliary assumptions, such as assuming that the failure to charm the attractive woman caused uncertainty, or frustration, which in turn led to aggression, etc. However, regardless of how well the counterintuitive findings can be dealt with by additional assumptions, the intuitive plausibility of animistic explanations should not be confused with its scientific value. In contrast, the CELA focuses on third-person explanations that refer to external causes in the environment more than to internal reasons. These explanations would often appear less self-explanatory and less intrinsically related to the phenomenon. Thus, explaining the judgment advantage of an attractive person in terms of a larger sample does not appear to capture the essentialist core of attractiveness as a social property. For esthetic reasons alone, such an explanation should not gain the same popularity as essentialist explanations in terms of approval, instrumental motives, or self-presentation goals. To be sure, it is a well-established fact from a century of behaviorist research that learning increases with amount of information, or number of trials. So it seems clear that learning about the social skills of a target will increase with the number of trials. And if there are more exposures to attractive than unattractive persons, learning about the social skills of the former will be more complete. However, even though the stereotype phenomenon can be subsumed under a very basic, simple law of learning, the resulting parsimonious explanation is unlikely to be accepted as psychologically satisfactory or "sexy" at first sight.

Nevertheless, upon closer inspection, the explanations provided by CELA may turn out to be at least as intriguing and "sexy" as the familiar animistic explanations. Once the simple learning law is considered worthwhile, it may turn out to offer exciting new alternative explanations for numerous phenomena, and it may inspire new avenues of research that have not been realized before. In this regard, another purpose of the present volume is to demonstrate that seemingly pallid rules of environmental learning can open exciting new perspectives and formerly unknown phenomena.

To continue the discussion of Table 2.1, it seems justified to say that animistic approaches attribute the locus of stereotyping to the individual's intrapsychic processes, whereas CELA would locate source of stereotyping in the interaction of cognitive and environmental processes. This distinction may appear somewhat arbitrary because environmental conditions, such as information overload, are also quite common in the animistic approach. However, even when external conditions are varied, the fact remains that the *abnormal conditions* that are given causal status (Hilton & Slugoski, 1986; Mackie, 1974) are typically located within the individual person's cognitive and motivational biases. Thus, an ecologically given overload of information is not conceived as a causal condition, but only as a relevant boundary condition that renders the causal factors within the individual (e.g., limited capacity) observable.

Conversely, CELA may also draw heavily on cognitive and motivational biases within the individual, especially because these biases may affect the individual's information search process and interaction with the social and physical environment. However, the abnormal condition that is considered causal in the entire process is not this intrapsychic bias but the resulting sample of information, which reflects a genuine interaction with environmental factors. For example, even when the enhanced stimulus sample for an attractive target originates in a male judge's biased attention, driven by his motive to date her, this does not really *explain why* gathering a large sample influences judgments of social skill. The crucial feature for the explanation of this phenomenon lies in a principle of learning—namely, that an increasing number of observations will make the existing social skills more and more visible. Thus, for the meta-theory underlying CELA, the causal conditions are sought in the stimulus environment, whereas the individual's beliefs and desires are merely exchangeable examples from a much broader class of factors that can influence the stimulus environment.

In accordance with this subtle but important difference in the roles assigned to intrapsychic and ecological conditions, the chief experimental manipulations of the two approaches refer to similar but slightly different factors. In the animistic approach, the crucial manipulations pertain to specific cognitive and motivational states within the individual. Environmental conditions (such as distracters or overload) serve the secondary role of context factors supposed to moderate the impact of the primary intrapsychic factors. In contrast, in CELA, specific distributions of stimuli provide the primary manipulation, whereas cognitive or motivational states or biases fulfill the secondary role. Consistent with this different focus, the main research emphasis is on stereotype maintenance or stereotype learning, respectively. In the animistic approach, already existing cognitive structures and motives are used to explain biases in judgments (Bodenhausen, Kramer, & Suesser, 1994; Kunda, 1990; Neuberg & Fiske, 1987), decisions (Mummendey & Schreiber, 1983; Tajfel & Turner, 1986), and behaviors (Bargh, Chen, & Burrows, 1996), which serve to maintain the underlying stereotype structures that participants have typically possessed prior to the experiment. In CELA, as in other notable examples of environmentalist approaches (cf. Hoffman & Hurst, 1990; McArthur, 1981), new structures have to be abstracted from a series of stimulus observations, and pre-existing stereotypes are typically eliminated or controlled statistically, to isolate pure, unconfounded learning rules that might explain the genesis of stereotypes under controlled experimental conditions.

Explicating the theoretical assumptions of CELA

It was already mentioned that the juxtaposition of two idealized meta-theories in the last section might have exaggerated the actually existing difference between the present framework and the research on social stereotyping. The intention here was merely to highlight the distinct theoretical perspective that connects the experiments to be reported in the following chapters. The intention was neither to oversimplify the distinction nor to misuse the so-called animistic approach as a strawman. Perhaps most investigations or investigators could not be classified as purely belonging to one of the two contrasted meta-theories, but represent some mixture of elements from both approaches. However, we do insist on the claim that previous research has shown a clear-cut bias towards animistic accounts, and a neglect of those ideas that will be emphasized in the CELA. Regardless of whether this appraisal is correct or not, we hope that contrasting CELA against animistic notions has helped to clarify the present perspective.

Let us now leave this comparative discussion behind us and turn to a positive description of CELA. In this section, we try to delineate the theoretical assumptions required to study stereotyping as an environmental learning process, within a hypothesis-testing framework. Here is a synopsis of the theoretical assumptions to be substantiated by empirical evidence in the remaining chapters. Premises and domain:

> CELA affords a framework for the study of the antecedent inductive-learning processes that underlie social stereotypes.

Although our CELA focuses on the inductive acquisition of stereotypes, other situational accounts that are mainly concerned with the activation of already existing concepts through external stimuli (e.g., priming accounts) can in principle be subordinated to our approach. However, CELA's interface with the empirical world, or domain, is the inductive-statistical learning process through which stereotypical knowledge structures are confirmed or disconfirmed. Only within this inductive interface, it makes sense to conceptualize stereotyping as a hypothesis-testing process.

> A stereotype, in its elementary form, is conceived as a knowledge structure that represents a hypothetical contingency between two variables, such as the contingency between social groups and their behavioral attributes.

This definition is largely congruent with a common definition that is—explicitly or implicitly—adopted by many other researchers. As explicated by McCauley and Stitt (1978), a stereotype involves the comparison of two conditional probabilities. The probability p(A/G) of an attribute A in a target group G has to be different from the probability p(A / not-G) of attribute A in another group not-G, or the overall probability p(A / G or not-G). Formally, such a comparison of two conditionals makes up a contingency that describes the degree to which the target group G differs from others in terms of attribute A. The standard way to represent such a contingency, in the dichotomous case, is in a 2 × 2 contingency scheme (see Figure 2.1).

> Learning or updating of stereotypical knowledge takes place as stimulus information is encountered that confirms or disconfirms the hypothetical contingency.

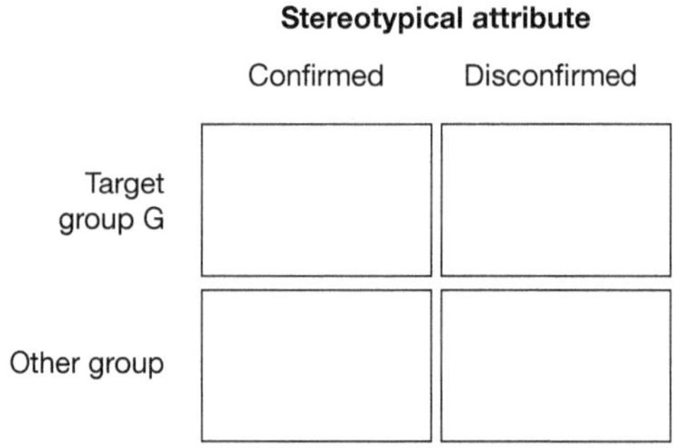

	Stereotypical attribute	
	Confirmed	Disconfirmed
Target group G		
Other group		

Figure 2.1 Social stereotype defined as a contingency to be tested through environmental learning. The degree to which the stimulus information provides confirming vs. disconfirming evidence for a stereotypical attribute in target group G, as compared to other groups or people in general.

Relevant information for testing the stereotypical hypothesis can originate in different sources (external environment, internal memories), modalities (raw observations, oral communication, written reports), and appear in different formats (sequential observations, statistical summary statements). The most convenient paradigm to study stereotype learning is one in which an experimental stimulus series is presented sequentially, with each elementary observation showing either the presence or the absence (or opposite) of attribute A in group G, or in another group not-G. This paradigm—which treats stereotypes as (illusory) correlations—will be the focus of Chapter 3.

Ordinary laws of environmental learning can explain accurate acquisition of contingencies under many circumstances as well as stereotypical biases under specific conditions. These biased outcomes need not reflect irrational or selective processes (i.e., motivational or cognitive distortions) but are often side effects of adaptive behavior in a probabilistic environment.

As already emphasized in the present chapter, we suggest that due to certain motives and cognitive restrictions people do not always process information accurately and in an unbiased fashion. There is common ground to assume that people can engage in wishful thinking, biased perception, motivated forgetting, or guessing based on prior beliefs. CELA does not contest these apparent facts but adds new sources of bias that continue to bias the outcome of stereotypical hypothesis tests when selective processing is ruled out.

Among the learning rules which can bias stereotypical hypothesis testing, the following are most important:

- Learning in a probabilistic world means to infer latent properties (e.g., the true rate of attribute A in group G) from a limited sample.
- Learning of latent properties depends on the size of stimulus samples.
- Learning depends on the reliability of stimulus samples.
- Learning depends on the perspective from which samples are drawn.
- As the samples for different groups and attributes can differ in all these respects, samples can lead to divergent inferences about the same latent property.
- People lack an understanding of the sample-dependence of their learning input.
- In particular, people lack a meta-cognitive understanding of the degree to which differing pictures of the same latent properties can emerge from the interaction of cognitive and environmental processes.

We do not make an attempt here to fill these abstract rules with concrete contents. The empirical studies reported in Chapter 3 will do a much better job in illustrating all these abstract points than further comments can do at the moment. By the end of the next chapter, the reader will understand the full meaning of these rules and what they can contribute to stereotype learning and social hypothesis testing. Before we turn on to these empirical studies, however, one final assumption has to be presented and commented on:

> The very samples of stimulus information, which mediate stereotype learning, are the emergent product of a dynamic interaction of the individual with his or her social and environment. This interaction involves (at least) three participants: the judge, the target, and the observer (or community).

The remainder of this chapter is devoted to describing this triadic interaction (see Figure 2.2) in some more detail. Starting in the center of the diagram, we recognize the 2 × 2 scheme representing the stereotype hypothesis. All investigations revolve around learning problems of this kind, in which the relative strength of conditional probabilities has to be assessed and compared, such as the conditional distribution of an attribute in different groups. Problems may vary in content and complexity; that is, the hypothesis guiding the learning problem may not be restricted to a 2 × 2 structure but extend to more complex contingencies involving more variable levels (5 × 5) or more variables (2 × 2 × 2). Towards the end of the volume, we shall even deal with contingencies as complex as 16 × 8 × 2 which

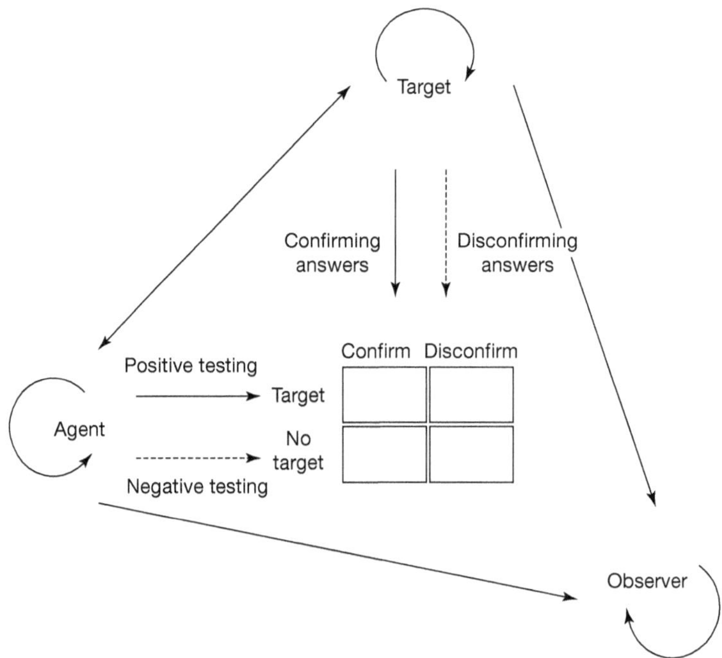

Figure 2.2 Triadic relation among the roles involved in stereotypical hypothesis testing. The agent (hypothesis tester) and the target (person or group) cooperate in generating confirming or disconfirming stimulus observations relevant to the hypothesis (accrued in the contingency table in the centre of the triad). The resulting information may also elicit judgments in passive observers who are not directly involved in hypothesis testing.

are still manageable for the CELA approach, obeying the same ordinary learning rules as the elementary 2 × 2 case, which is most convenient for presentation purposes.

Traditionally, the stimulus series in a learning experiment is fully under the experimenter's control. Accordingly, we also start to investigate stereotype learning in a series of experiments in which participants passively observe group-attribute contingencies across an experimentally controlled stimulus series. Experiments from such a paradigm are commonly known as illusory-correlation experiments—which is the topic of Chapter 3.

However, although a stimulus series provided by the experimenter allows for maximal control, the task situation of an experimental participant whose role is restricted to passively receiving input is hardly typical of real-life hypothesis testing situations. In reality, hypothesis testers often play a much more active role. The information input is at least partly determined by the individual's own information search and selective exposure (Frey, 1986). When this feature is built into the experimental task, such that participants can actively select or search for relevant stimulus data, the illusory-correlation paradigm is turned into a typical hypothesis-testing paradigm, which is in the focus of Chapter 4.

Of the three roles depicted in Figure 2.2, the *agent* (or hypothesis tester) is clearly the protagonist in this paradigm. On one hand, the agent's active search and selective exposure determines the stimulus sample from which the contingency has to be evaluated. This influence is reflected in the arrow from the agent to the contingency table in the center of Figure 2.2. On the other hand, however, a characteristic feature of social hypothesis testing is that the agent solicits behavior in the *target*, as indicated by the arrow pointing from agent to target.

However, the target itself is not confined to playing a passive-object role either. Rather, target and agent determine the stimulus input together. While the agent's information search determines the hypothesis-test questions being asked, as it were, the target's behavior is responsible for the responses given. An arrow from the target to the contingency represents this impact of target behavior on the stimulus input. Moreover, an arrow back from the target to the agent symbolizes a direct influence of the target on the agent's further information search and final judgment, in addition to the indirect influence mediated by the contingency.

Finally, an *observer* of the agent-target interaction may also witness the hypothesis test and may be influenced by the result, as in a vicarious-learning experiment. To the extent that the presence of an observer influences the agent's and the target's behavior (e.g., thorough information search, socially desirable responses, etc.), the very existence of the observer may also impact on the information gathered about the contingency. Thus, Figure 2.2 also includes arrows to indicate the possible direct and indirect influences of the observer on the contingency and on other persons in the triad.

One role of observers in social reality testing is to provide an audience or a "community" that witnesses and evaluates the interaction and the outcome of the hypothesis test. This function also highlights the importance of communication for stereotype learning and change. Most of the time, social stereotypes are not learned from first-hand information, in direct contact with the stereotyped targets or groups, but from communicated second-hand information, in the media, in rumors, or other people's idiosyncratic reports. In other words, verbal and non-verbal communication provides an important part of the social information ecology. The manner in which communication rules and collective-memory exchange can affect the environmental learning of stereotype contingencies will be examined in Chapter 5.

Two other chapters are devoted to the complications, but also the enrichment and new insights, that arise when stereotypes are embedded in more complex knowledge structures. Chapter 6 deals with trivariate contingencies of the order 2 × 2 × 2, which occur whenever an elementary stereotype (e.g., the 2 × 2 contingency of attraction and social skill) changes with the social context (e.g., in private vs. professional life). Experimental approaches to study these trivariate problems are particularly likely to open new theoretical perspectives. In Chapter 7, we will be concerned with the most extreme levels of complexity that can be found in social hypothesis testing, such as the teacher's task to learn the contingency between many different students in various disciplines or subject matters, distinguishing several performance aspects (e.g., motivation vs. ability). Empirical evidence for this highest level of complexity comes from a number of experiments in a simulated school-class environment. The purpose of this chapter is not only to emphasize the generality of the CELA approach, but also to highlight its external validity using a research paradigm that shares many features with a naturalist environment.

Finally, Chapter 8 will provide a theoretical synopsis of the empirical findings reported in all previous chapters. It will outline the essentials of a cognitive-environmentalist learning theory that integrates the major empirical findings, that provides alternative explanations for a number of prominent phenomena, and that has already motivated completely new findings and suggested new testable predictions which have not been noticed in the traditional, animistic approach to stereotyping.

Locating CELA in relation to modern stereotype research

To introduce CELA, we have drawn on the comparison with the *traditional* approach, which we have characterized as animistic. To locate CELA in the theoretical landscape, however, we also have to consider the leading paradigms of *modern* stereotype research, which can be hardly reduced to the kind of first-person theories, revolving around the core concepts of beliefs and desires that we have termed animistic. What prominent topics of stereotype research would an up-to-date review article, or textbook chapter, reveal? A literature review of the last decade would be probably centered on the following most frequent research topics:

- *Cognitive resource limitations as a crucial condition of stereotyping*. As short-term memory is limited and cognitive capacity is depleted, stereotypes are interpreted as the individual's attempt to reduce information processing to simplifying stereotypes and other primitive heuristics (Bodenhausen, 1990; Macrae, Milne, & Bodenhausen, 1994).

- *Priming and activation of stereotypical knowledge*. Granting that all available knowledge cannot be activated at the same time, stereotypes are assumed to reflect the subset of accessible knowledge activated by recent prime stimuli (Bargh et al., 1996; Devine, 1989).
- *Stereotype use and suppression*. Alternatively, crucial to stereotyping may not be what knowledge is activated but what activated knowledge is actually used (Wittenbrink, Judd, & Park, 2001), or cannot be suppressed or controlled volitionally (Gollwitzer & Schaal, 1998; Kawakami, Dovidio, Moll, Hermsen, & Russin, 2000).
- *Expectancies, self-fulfilling prophecies, and stereotype threat* (Jussim, 1989; Steele & Aronson, 1995). Stereotypes are supposed to reflect culturally learned expectancies, or the failure to overcome stigmatizing expectancies.
- *Memory representations based on categorical versus individuating information*. Stereotypes are assumed to be facilitated by memory representations of people and groups in terms of abstract categories rather than specific behavioral examplars (Fiske & Neuberg, 1990).
- *Categorization and recategorization*. The impact of stereotypes can be ameliorated when behaviors are understood as belonging to more than one category, or when persons belonging to different groups are recognized as also belonging to superordinate categories (Dovidio, Gaertner, Validzic, Matoka, Johnson, & Frazier, 1997; Gaertner, Rust, Dovidio, Backman, & Anastasio, 1994).
- *Role-based approaches to stereotyping*. The social roles served by individuals and groups determine the stereotypical traits they are attributed (Eagly, 1987; Hoffman & Hurst, 1990).

How can CELA be compared to these prominent topics of modern social psychological research? In order to locate CELA in the theoretical landscape of these topics, we keep two major questions in mind. First, is there any overlap between approaches, such that CELA can supplement or complement those modern paradigms, or such that those paradigms can enrich and improve CELA? Second, what is CELA's potential in terms of stereotype change and possible influences that can be exerted on the stereotyping process, in comparison with other recent approaches?

We believe that the emphasis on ordinary learning mechanisms is one of the major assets of CELA, because learning entails the potential of education and change. Moreover, to the extent that stereotypes are largely governed by *ordinary*, as opposed to exceptional, misguided, or pathological learning, one need not resort to unusual learning mechanisms to explain the formation, maintenance and change of stereotypes. This basically optimistic, or active, perspective of CELA stands in obvious contrast with the emphasis on basically uncontrollable factors in the focus of most popular paradigms, such as insurmountable capacity constraints, automatic association processes, inability to suppress, inability to overcome stereotype threat, or motives and expectancies outside the realm of volitional action. The individual is caught and imprisoned in this powerful field of forces, which afford the ultimate *independent variables* of contemporary stereotype research. The main research goal seems to lie in the optimization of the *dependent variables*—that is, direct and indirect measures of stereotype strength, using priming procedures (Fazio, Jackson, Dunton, & Williams, 1995; Lepore & Brown, 1997; Macrae et al., 1994; Wittenbrink et al., 1997), non-blatant (Swim, Aikin, Hall, & Hunter, 1995) and indirect measures of stereotypes and prejudice (Greenwald, McGhee, & Schwarz, 1998), dual-task paradigms (Bless, Clore, Schwarz, Golisano, Rabe, & Woelk, 1996), assessment of memory structure (Linville & Fischer, 1993; Park & Hastie, 1987; Park, Judd, & Ryan, 1991), statistical-bias paradigms (Hamilton & Gifford, 1976; Schaller, 1992), person and group-judgment paradigms (Wänke, Bless, & Igou, 2001), and even computer-simulation measures (Kunda & Thagard, 1996; Smith, 1991).

While the methodological precision and scientific scrutiny of the measurement procedures for the dependent variables are flourishing, the independent variables that force people into stereotyping seem to be taken for granted. Capacity constraints are simply given, such as automatic association structures, or motivational forces. Here we are still on the firm ground of animistic restrictions located within the individual. There is surprisingly little research interest in the question of how the associative structures are learned that are used for hundreds of priming experiments, when expectancies are acquired ontogenetically, how stereotype threat was acquired, whether capacity restrictions must really result in impairment under realistic conditions, or the extent to which the concept of automaticity contributes to practical questions of stereotype genesis and change. We believe that complementing the current prominent research topics with an environmental learning approach has the potential of filling this obvious gap, and we believe that this constitutes a major asset of our approach. Let us, for the rest of this chapter, elaborate on this point, with reference to all of the aforementioned research topics.

Cognitive capacity restrictions as a crucial condition of stereotyping

No doubt all information processing has to be selective because the quantity and density of information in the complex world exceeds our cognitive capacity. Moreover, not all information that is stored in long-term memory can be accessible and used at the same time. Therefore, when cognitive load is induced experimentally, or specific parts of long-term memory are made accessible under experimental conditions, systematic effects on subsequent memory tests or social judgments can be obtained. Accordingly, the literature is replete with demonstrations that stereotypical responses are facilitated, when cognitive capacity is reduced or occupied (Bodenhausen, 1990) or when stereotypical knowledge is made accessible through priming procedures (Lepore & Brown, 1997; Wittenbrink et al., 1997).

However, does this imply that resource limitations always lead to stereotyping, or that all stereotypical behavior requires resource limitations? There is evidence that individuals have a highly flexible and adaptive way with capacity constraints.

Social observers sometimes use powerful structures or smart heuristics to cope with an enormous amount of information. Moreover, capacity that is missing for one task can be taken from another task that is done routinely and economically. Several chapters speak to the capacity restriction issue, from the distinct perspective of CELA. Chapter 3, next to the present section, will be concerned with illusory correlations—one of the most prominent experimental paradigms of stereotype research during the last 25 years. The illusion to observe a correlation that actually did not exist in the stimulus input (e.g., between attractiveness and social skills; cf. Snyder et al., 1977) has been often explained by selective attention to particular event combinations and failure to attend to others. The stimulus-learning approach to this phenomenon in Chapter 3 will demonstrate that selective attention is neither a necessary nor a sufficient condition for illusory correlations. In Chapter 7, empirical findings from a simulated classroom environment will be presented where multiple illusory correlations occur at the same time (viz., one correlation between each pair of students and their respective achievement level).

A sensible explanation for the pattern of results in this complex, semi-natural environment has to take learning principles into account. Moreover, in spite of the notorious overload of information—when a teacher has to assess 16 students' performance in 8 different disciplines, as in Chapter 7—one is impressed with the remarkable degree of accuracy that characterizes judgments of boys and girls in science and language disciplines. Apparently, then, inductive learning and judgment in complex environments allows for adaptive compensation mechanisms. That is, by allocating the cognitive resources, judges appear to be able to compensate for restricted capacity. Accuracy and stereotyping may coexist in such a framework. Conversely, simple fast and frugal heuristics (Gigerenzer & Todd, 1999) may lead to more accurate and more adaptive judgments than exhaustive strategies using maximal capacity. In any case, pointing to overload alone neither appears to provide a sufficient nor necessary explanation for the specific deviations from accuracy that are observed—or the residual biases in judgment.

Priming and activation of stereotypical knowledge

Due to the advent of modern computer technology and an increasing interest in automatic rather than controlled psychological processes, a huge number of recent experiments have employed *priming* procedures (Bargh, 1997). Just as semantic priming can be used to activate any kind of knowledge structure, it can also be used to activate stereotypical knowledge. For instance, priming of the concept BLACK can activate stereotypical knowledge about black people or, to keep within the continuous example of this chapter, priming of the concept ATTRACTIVE could automatically activate schematic knowledge associated with attractive individuals. Note that within our nomenclature priming does not refer to an animistic approach. Similar to CELA, automaticity models imply that the individual's (stereotypic) responses are under the control of environmental stimuli rather than due to intrapsychic cognitive or motivational processes. Moreover, priming effects can go unnoticed, undetected by the realm of conscious beliefs and desires.

Thus, both automaticity accounts and CELA focus on external stimuli (i.e., cues, primes, samples) in predicting (stereotypic) judgments. In their purest version current priming models even assume the complete absence of any higher cognitive mediation, by merely supposing a direct perception-behavior or perception–judgment link (Bargh, 1997).

In spite of these similarities, there are important differences between both, CELA and priming accounts. First, whereas priming accounts describe the *activation* of already existing concepts, schemas, and knowledge structures, learning approaches like CELA refer to the inductive *acquisition* of these concepts. While CELA can therefore account for *long-term stationary differences* in the assessment of incoming information, the priming paradigm is by definition a *state account* that describes transient influences of the momentary situation on existing knowledge structures. In as much as priming effects can be easily obtained by presenting sub- or supraliminal cues, other contextual or self-generated cues can exert or even override the influence of the original prime. Priming models and a CELA go together well, because they address different parts of the variance that should be explained.

Second, as the remaining chapters will illustrate, the CELA is a robust account that can be applied to a variety of *different experimental paradigms*, procedures, timings, and settings. In other words, CELA is not restricted to a particular paradigm at all. In contrast, most priming effects are *extremely time sensitive*: procedures differing in some milliseconds may lead to assimilation, no effect, or contrast effects (Stapel, Koomen, & Ruys, 2002). Third, within CELA there is in principle no *difference between active and passive information, implicit or explicit, between conscious and unconscious effects of sampling*. Within the priming paradigm, however, these differences matter a lot. For instance, there is strong evidence that *awareness of the prime leads to contrast* rather than to assimilation effects (Lombardi, Higgins, & Bargh, 1987; Strack, Schwarz, Bless, Kübler, & Wänke, 1993). Thus, the most fascinating aspect in priming is also its weakness; the absence of mediational assumptions makes it sometimes hard to predict a priori whether assimilation, contrast or no priming effects at all will occur (Mussweiler, in press; Schwarz & Bless, 1992; Stapel, Koomen, & van der Pligt, 1996). However, there are some regularities. Subsequent judgments are contrasted away from primed information when the priming is recognized consciously, memorized explicitly, or when the prime becomes the target of cognitive elaboration (Lombardi et al., 1987). In different situations, especially when priming remains subliminal and undetected or when primes are attributed to internal states, assimilation can be expected. This means that the relationship between primed stereotypical knowledge and behavioral consequences is complex rather than simple and monotonous.

The effects of priming can be easily subordinated in a CELA because priming models account for the momentary transient influence external stimuli might have on learning and internal representations. Some of the vicissitudes of priming influences will be dealt with in Chapter 5, which focuses on constructive memory effects. Although we are not concerned with the typical questions of automaticity and subliminality that are in the center of current priming research, we will nevertheless show how priming-like processes can instigate self-generated learning and constructive memory intrusions. However, priming is not under the experimenter's control but conceived as an integral part of social interaction, conversation, and hypothesis testing. Within a CELA approach, many social-interaction games afford natural priming treatments. In Chapter 6, too, the temporal priority with which stimulus episodes are presented will be shown to impact the process of stereotype-related learning. However, it has to be emphasized again that although we do not ignore this major research tool of priming, we are using it from a distinct learning perspective—quite different from most other recent priming research. Most importantly, perhaps, we do not use the word "priming" as an explanatory construct, as if it could explain precisely the occurrence of one stereotype influence, rather than its opposite.

Stereotype use

Turning to stereotype use, the question of what the individual does with a stereotypical hypothesis, and what the psychological outcome is, depends on several factors. Chapter 5 will emphasize the role of schematic structures that mediate the impact of activated knowledge. For instance, the valence of a behavior may be attributed either to the sentence subject or to the sentence object, depending on the verb used to describe the behavior (Brown & Fish, 1983; Fiedler & Semin, 1988). Or the clinician's diagnostic knowledge may determine his or her constructive inferences about behaviors that a patient actually did not show. Another possibility, covered in Chapter 7, is that teachers' naive personality theories—that is, their tendency to infer ability from motivation—depends on whether prior learning in the classroom setting associates high or low motivation with high ability. Last but not least, whether the activation of a stereotypical hypothesis in the agent leads to stereotype maintenance or change depends on dynamic interaction with the target, and on the target's responses (see Figure 2.2). Once more, CELA reveals a number of ways in which stereotype use can be learned, moderated, and controlled—and is by no means predetermined by structural constraints and automatic processes.

Expectancies and self-fulfilling prophecies

In Chapter 4, 6, and 7, various experiments will be reported in which participants are asked to observe or to actively seek information about a target or group, in an explicit hypothesis-testing paradigm. Prior research on social hypothesis testing has emphasized the importance of prior expectancies, which are turned into self-fulfilling prophecies (Kukla, 1993; Rosenthal & Rubin, 1978; Snyder, 1984)—the premise being that self-fulfillment is predetermined in the individual's stereotype expectancies. For instance, expecting attractive persons to be socially skilled and satisfactory will lead agents to treat attractive targets in a manner that serves to fulfill the expectancy. CELA can enrich and modify this prevailing view in several ways. In several experiments, ordinary learning principles have been shown to override expectancies.

Moreover, what appears to constitute expectancy effects, can often be explained alternatively in terms of ordinary stimulus learning because expectancies are constantly reproduced by the stimulus world. This point is strongly evident in Eagly's (1987) social-role approach to gender stereotyping, which anticipates many aspects of the CELA approach. Accordingly, gender stereotypes are created, and can be recreated all the time, from the social roles served by male (breadwinners) and female (child raisers) people. To the extent, however, that gender roles built are constantly visible in the stimulus ecology, an "expectancy" is no longer a top-down bias triggered by beliefs and desires.

Memory representations based on categorical versus individuating information

Central to several so-called dual-process theories (Brewer, 1988; Chaiken, Liberman, & Eagly, 1989; Fiske & Neuberg, 1990; Petty & Cacioppo, 1986) is the assumption that information can be processed in two different modes, systematically (with high capacity demands, driven by accuracy motivation) and heuristically (with low capacity demands, driven by goal motivation). A related assumption is that resulting memory representations are based either only on categorical information or include plenty of individuating information about specific details. Within this rationale, stereotyping belongs to heuristic processing and refers to categorical or prototypical representations, whereas systematic processing and sensitivity to piecemeal information are considered the key to overcoming stereotypes.

CELA is in direct opposition to the dualism proposed in dual-process theories. CELA is essentially based on the assumption that a constant set of learning rules can account for a variety of findings. The very goal of CELA is to provide a theory that does not need to postulate different processes to account for different phenomena, but that can explain many phenomena by the same process rules. In this respect, it is consistent with a recently advocated position by Kruglanski, Thompson, and Spiegel (1999), who provide theoretical and empirical argumemts for a *uni-model* that explains most prominent findings of dual-process research without postulating two qualitatively different processes. All empirical chapters contribute to conveying this basic message. Particularly in Chapter 8, evidence will be presented for the claim that information processing is never really systematic. It is always heuristic, even under highest accuracy motivation and most auspicious capacity conditions. A strong point will be made for the claim that there is no cogent evidence at all in the research literature that people ever manage to process information truly systematically—if that means logically correct, according to an analytical calculus, and under stringent meta-cognitive control.

Categorization and recategorization

Much recent work on social stereotyping revolves around the concepts of *social identity* (Tajfel & Turner, 1986) and *self-categorizations* (Turner, Hogg, Oaks, Reicher, & Wetherell, 1987). Accordingly, people are motivated to achieve positive social identities, especially on those typical attribute dimensions that are important for their personal identity. Two major classes of empirical findings are explained in terms of this striving for positive social identity: the ingroup-serving bias, and the outgroup-homogeneity effect (Park & Rothbart, 1982). The former refers to the tendency to peceive one's own group in more favorable ways than other groups, whereas the latter is the tendency to form more simplified, less differentiaed representations of outgroups than ingroups.

As the social-identity motive is universal, and shared by all people, this approach again highlights an unavoidable source of stereotyping, that one cannot resist or change through information or re-education. In the next chapter, a much less rigid picture of intergroup biases will be conveyed from a CELA perspective. Ingroup-serving biases and outgroup homogeneity—that appear to reflect genuinely motivational factors—will be explained in terms of the richer learning environment for ingroups than outgroups, in line with ordinary rules of ordinary environmental learning. At the same time, CELA suggests specific conditions under which intergroup biases can be eliminated or even reversed, following the same common learning rules. Once more, CELA cannot pretend that social identity motives and self-categorization effects do not exist and cannot exert a strong influence on behavior. However, inspection of environmental learning processes may reveal that these influences may not be as unavoidable and inextricable as those universal animistic theories suggest.

Summary

In this chapter, we have tried to explicate and illustrate the conceptual framework that characterizes the present approach to stereotyping as a hypothesis testing process. To highlight the distinct features of the present approach, we have first contrasted our cognitive-environmental learning approach (CELA) against the animistic meta-theory, which has guided traditional research on social stereotyping. The animistic research program emphasizes intrapsychic factors within the individual's cognitive (beliefs) and motivational (desires) processes as major sources of stereotyping and biased hypothesis testing. In contrast, CELA starts from the premise that in order to understand cognitive functions within the individual, one first has to understand the distribution of stimulus information that provides the input to all cognitive processes. From this perspective, stereotypes arise as a normal by-product of cognitive-environmental interaction, governed by ordinary learning principles—even in the absence of cognitive and motivational biases.

The remainder of this chapter was devoted to discussing CELA in the context of prominent topics of modern stereotype research, such as cognitive capacity constraints, priming and stereotype activation, stereotype use and suppression, expectancies and self-fulfilling prophecies, categorical versus piecemeal representations, and social categorization approaches. Whereas many of these contemporary research topics are based on the assumption of uncontrollable, automatic processes, CELA's reliance on ordinary learning rules opens an even broader and richer research domain, and a more optimistic view on stereotype change, re-learning, and environmental control.

3 Learning social hypotheses

Stereotypes as illusory correlations

In this chapter, we begin to present an empirical research program that reflects the shift from an animistic theory approach to a genuinely cognitive-ecological approach. The purpose is twofold. First, empirical demonstrations within one particular research paradigm—illusory correlations—will render the various assumptions provided in the last chapter much more concrete. Second, by applying the two contrasted approaches—the animistic and the CELA—to the same concrete research questions, it will be shown that the difference is not just a matter of taste, or different wording, but clearly distinct experimental predictions. In particular, in the present chapter:

- we make a point for the importance of stereotype learning as distinguished from the consequences of existing stereotypes;
- we present a learning analog of illusory correlations, one of the most prominent paradigms of current stereotype research;
- contrast the CELA account of illusory correlations with a popular animistic approach;
- we then present a series of studies conducted in our own lab to demonstrate that simple learning rules alone can explain the genesis of illusory correlations in the absence of any processing bias;
- we will locate illusory correlations in the context of a number of seemingly different phenomena that are all covered by the same simple learning rule, thus emphasizing the theoretical potential of the CELA approach.

A case for studying stereotype acquisition before measuring the consequences

One asset of a deliberate emphasis on the stimulus ecology is that it suggests an answer to the question of where the hypotheses come from which provide the basis of stereotyping. In most previous research, the hypotheses driving stereotypes are given as a pre-existing aspect of social reality. Black people are aggressive, females are emotional, male pupils are good in mathematics, and the ingroup is superior to the outgroup. The existence of these starting hypotheses is usually taken for granted, and the stereotyping process consists of the affirmation and perpetuation of these social clichés, the origins of which are rarely studied empirically.

Consider, once more, the Snyder et al. (1977) example that attractive women are more socially competent than unattractive women. That interaction partners who are allegedly attractive versus unattractive actually end up being judged as different in social competence is a nice demonstration of how hypothesis can become social reality. However, the origin and the direction of the hypothesis itself is not considered much of a problem; it is simply plausible. When forced to provide a psychological foundation for this hypothesis, most psychologists would content themselves with an explanation in terms of expectancies (it is commonly expected that attractiveness and competence go together). Others would say that attraction and social competence are semantically related concepts, suggesting semantic similarity as an origin of stereotypical hypotheses (Camerer, 1988; Shweder, 1977). Quite a few theorists of the animistic approach would largely equate the two answers silently, feeling that expectancies and semantic proximities are the same.

However, a moment of reflection shows that merely alluding to expectancies and similarities is less than satisfactory, for several reasons. First, these notions only defer the problem of where the hypotheses come from and how they have been acquired. Saying that attractive people are expected to be competent, or that the two concepts are related, only means that the person (or other people or cultures) must have learned a corresponding correlation. After all, not every similarity is based on mystical or superstitious associations (such as black panther—dangerous). Rather, the relationship between *attractive* and *competent, obese* and *funny, female* and *talkative*, must have been learned in the first place—whether veridical or illusory. This initial learning process has to be covered by a comprehensive theory of stereotyping.

Second, it is easy to demonstrate that expectancies and semantic similarities are conceptually independent. Somebody may share with other language users much knowledge about semantic connotations, suggesting that *attractiveness* and *social competence* have many semantic features in common, and yet be convinced that attractive people are *incompetent*, because attraction prevents people from efficient social learning. Having disentangled similarity (i.e., the features determining word meaning) and expectancies (i.e., beliefs of what goes together), the question remains what the relative importance is of these two components. Finally, a third reason for not being satisfied with the common allusion to expectancies and similarities is that other, less plausible, explanations exist based on less commonsensical theories, as we shall see below.

Within a cognitive-ecological approach, one need not resort to expectancies and similarities, but many hypotheses are determined naturally by the problem environment. In the courtroom, the hypothesis being tested is about the defendant's guilt, not about the defendant's merits, or another person's guilt. It is only of secondary importance whether the defendant is black or white, male or female, and whether his appearance resembles the meaning of the crime he is accused of (although the latter is clearly not irrelevant). Likewise, in medical diagnosis, the hypothesis is about one particular patient's disease, not about another person's illness, or the given patient's attractiveness. In product advertising, the hypothesis is about the advantages of one focused product. From a theoretical point of view, these examples of environmentally determined hypotheses do not appear to be particularly surprising, but they highlight that judgments and decisions based on fully arbitrary hypotheses may obey the same rules as meaningful relations based on expectancies and similarities.

The present chapter constitutes an attempt to identify some of the origins of hypotheses leading to stereotypes, without pretending of course to provide a full answer. It is about basic processes of learning and conditioning in normal stimulus environments that create initial hypotheses and stereotype targets in a fully unbiased learning process, in the absence of any initial expectancies and similarities (or other animistic concepts, such as intentions, goals, or motives). To illustrate this basic learning mechanism, consider the following thought experiment: A puppy is born on a farm and the dog's ordinary learning environment consists of the identification of various reinforcement agents. There are two persons on the farm who used to bring food, Person A and Person B (we intentionally refer to abstract symbols, A and B, avoiding any relation to sex, appearance, or prior expectancies). For both agents, the reinforcement rate is, say, 70%; that is, on 70% of the occasions when the young dog sees these persons, they will bring food. However, Person A appears twice as often as B. Thus, while the reinforcement rate is the same, the dog is exposed to twice as many learning trials involving A than trials with B. Which person is likely to become a more potent conditional stimulus, A or B?

Hardly any psychologist with only basic knowledge in learning and conditioning will contest that at most points in time during the learning period A is a stronger reinforcer than B. When given a choice between A and B, the dog will presumably choose A, all other things being equal. Any plausible learning model (i.e., Rescorla & Wagner, 1972) predicts that learning increases with the number of trials. As the dog is exposed to more A than B trials, the learning process for A should be ahead of the learning process associating B with the same probability of food. So we have identified a very basic learning principle that suggests which stimuli are likely to become the target of an initial hypothesis. Assuming an equal reward for different targets, the most frequently met target is likely to become the focus of an initial hypothesis, linking the target to positive expectations. Conversely, assuming an equal punishment ratio for several targets, the one target with the highest number of exposures is likely to become the focus of an aversive hypothesis.

Stereotype learning in the illusory correlation paradigm

Obvious and simplistic as this learning account may appear, it was persistently ignored in one of the most popular social psychological approach to stereotype learning, namely, the illusory correlation approach. In the seminal research by Hamilton and Gifford (1976)—the starting point of hundreds of related experiments—human participants were exposed to the same stimulus environment as the dog in the example above. Stimulus experiences with members of two groups, A and B, were predominantly positive (providing in this case a 69% reinforcement schedule). However, there were twice as many behavior descriptions for group A (the "majority") than for group B (the "minority"), yielding 18 positive and 8 negative items for A as compared with 9 positive and 4 negative items for B. As the positivity ratio was the same for both groups, $18/(18 + 8) = 9/(9 + 4) = 69\%$, the correlation between groups (A vs. B) and behavior valence (positive vs. negative) was zero.

However, the challenging result of these and many other experiments (see meta-analysis by Mullen & Johnson, 1990) is a more positive impression of the majority group A than of the minority B. This kind of illusory correlation is manifested in more favorable trait ratings of A than B, in frequency judgments associating less negative items with A than B, and in a cued-recall test in which judges, when asked to reproduce the association of behaviors to groups, tend to assign relatively more positive behaviors to A and relatively more negative behaviors to B.

This bias in favor of the majority, and against the minority, is especially noteworthy as the stimulus distribution used by Hamilton and Gifford (1976) reflects the distribution that can be expected to hold in natural environments. Majorities are, by definition, more frequent than minorities, and positive (norm-conforming, socially desirable) behavior is typically the rule, whereas negative (norm-deviant, undesirable) behavior is the exception (Gigerenzer & Fiedler, 2003; Kanouse & Hanson, 1972; Parducci, 1965). Given such a realistic assumption about the social environment, the present variant of illusory correlations suggests a general advantage of majorities over minorities in the absence of any real differences—a truly challenging result of psychological research.

Distinctiveness versus differential learning account of illusory correlations

However, although the analogy to the dog example and animal conditioning is compelling, social-cognitive research on this intriguing phenomenon did not notice that analogy for a long time. The most preferred account that still dominates most textbooks was in terms of the alleged distinctiveness, extra salience, and memory advantage of the least frequent event category, negative behavior of the minority. Theorizing concentrated almost exclusively (cf. Hamilton & Sherman, 1989) on the notion that the infrequent group's (B) infrequent (negative) behavior receives most efficient memory encoding because this event category should appear most distinctive or outstanding. Thus, quite in line with the preference for animistic explanations, it was taken for granted that the illusory correlation must originate within the human mind, that a biased outcome (devaluation of the minority) must reflect a biased cognitive process (selective memory for negative minority behavior), and that any variance not explained by this cognitive bias must be due to residual expectancies (e.g., the more positive connotations of category "A" as compared with "B"; Schaller & Maass, 1989; Spears, van der Pligt, & Eiser, 1985). The alternative possibility that the advantage of the majority group A could be explained in terms of completely normal, unbiased rules of associative learning (i.e., the higher number of "reinforcements" for A than B), was virtually never considered over many years.

That possibility was not mentioned before the early 1990s (Fiedler, 1991), and although our animal learning example sounds extremely plausible if not trivial, this alternative account was met with extreme resistance. How could a judgment bias in favor of a majority and against the minority not be due to a cognitive processing bias? How could it not be somehow related to the psychological surplus meaning of "minority" as something rare and exceptional? Within these confines of animistic theory formation, the distinctiveness account advanced by Hamilton and colleagues (Hamilton, Dugan, & Trolier, 1985; Hamilton & Gifford, 1976; Hamilton & Sherman, 1989) would fit the frame of a sensible theory much more than the parsimonious but less animistic learning account. Only the distinctiveness account entered social psychological textbooks (see Aronson, Wilson, & Akert, 1998; Brehm, Kassin, & Fein, 1999), and it was treated like a well-established theory, without convincing evidence for its memory assumptions (Klauer & Meiser, 2000) and without seriously considering alternative accounts (cf. Hamilton & Sherman, 1989).

A notation for experiments on illusory correlation and hypothesis testing

In this section, we consider empirical evidence on illusory correlations in the Hamilton–Gifford paradigm, its boundary conditions, and new insights gained from a cognitive-ecological perspective. In presenting this evidence, we again refer to the 2 × 2 contingency scheme that was already introduced in Chapter 2. In Figure 3.1, we have adapted the contingency table to fit the case of hypothesis testing in the illusory-correlation paradigm. The two rows in Figure 3.1 denote Group A and B and the columns represent the valence of behavioral evidence on an attribute related to the target objects (positive as opposed to negative behaviors). Using standard notation of 2 × 2 tables, lower-case letters *a, b, c*, and *d* denote the frequencies of observations representing the four event combinations: positive (*a*) and negative (*b*) behaviors of Group A and positive (*c*) and negative (*d*) behaviors of Group B.

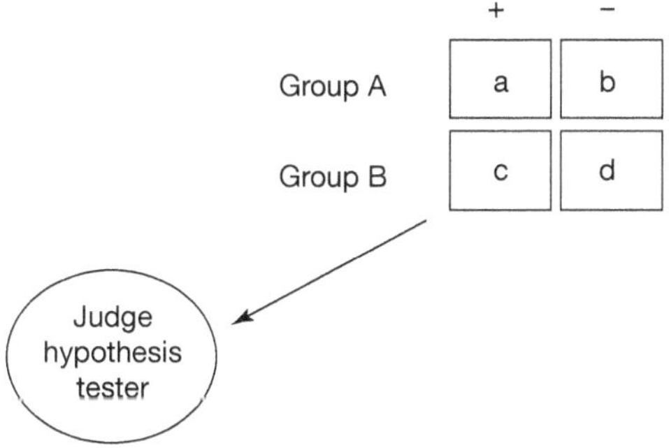

Figure 3.1 Graphical illustration of the illusory correlation paradigm of stereotype learning.

An alternative way of framing the 2 × 2 table would be to say that the left column represents confirming evidence for the predominant positive attribute (with frequencies *a* and *c*), whereas the right column represents disconfirming evidence (with frequencies *b* and *d*). In the learning paradigm, one would refer to *a* and *c* as numbers of reinforced trials and to *b* and *d* as numbers of unreinforced trials. Thus, the notation is flexible enough to deal with several, slightly different task situations. Likewise, the 2 × 2 frame is also compatible with the even more elementary case in which only one target object (e.g., only Group A) is present and the task is to evaluate the degree to which a single attribute is present in a single target object. Even in this seemingly more elementary case, we need four cells to represent the problem structure. To test the hypothesis, say, that Group A behaves in a desirable fashion, we have to allow for positive (*a*) and negative (*b*) evidence about Group A. Moreover, to test a hypothesis about A's desirability, we need some standard of comparison to examine, for instance, whether the desirability of A is above 50%, or above 0%, or above the global average of desirability in the culture. Thus, in the one-target case, the (implicit) second target in the second row of the contingency table is the standard of comparison (characterized by some norm distribution of *c* confirmations and *d* disconfirmations). Thus, we can treat our 2 × 2 scheme as a generally applicable format for the analysis of (an elementary case of) social hypothesis testing.

The other element in Figure 3.1 is the agent judge, or hypothesis tester; an arrow pointing from the stimulus distribution in the 2 × 2 table to the judge indicates that, in the standard illusory correlations paradigm, the judge is influenced by the stimulus information presented by the experimenter. The judge does not actively influence the search and acquisition of information, as indicated by the absence of an arrow pointing from the judge to the stimulus table. As already mentioned, the figure will be elaborated in subsequent chapters to include more errors, representing more complex relations, or hypothesis-testing paradigms.

Empirical tests of theoretical predictions

With reference to this notation and graphical representation, the above two theories of illusory correlations can be clearly distinguished. Central to the distinctiveness account is the joint infrequency of the *d* observations about negative minority behaviors. Accordingly, observations from this rare category should be particularly salient and distinctive during encoding. As a consequence, these observations should have a memory advantage. In developing this prediction, Hamilton and Gifford (1976) borrowed the distinctiveness concept from Chapman (1967) that actually goes back to the old von-Restorff (1933) effect. Hedwig von Restorff, a student of the famous gestalt psychologist Koehler, had demonstrated that an outstanding item in a list of learning items (e.g., a number in a list of letters) is memorized better than the rest of the materials. By analogy, Hamilton and colleagues reasoned that the joint infrequency of negative minority behaviors should gain from the same memory advantage and thereby determine the illusory correlation effect.

By contrast, simple associative learning in a probabilistic environment has fully distinct implications. In general, learning from a single presentation of 36 stimuli (18 + 8 + 9 + 4 = 36) that positive behavior prevails and that the positivity rate is about 69% (i.e., 18/(18 + 8) = 9/(9 + 4) = 18/26 = 9/13 = 0.69) should be less than perfect. Part of the information should thus be lost from the objectively presented stimulus distribution to the final subjective judgments. Such information loss in a probabilistic environment is typically evident in regressive judgments; that is, judgments should underestimate the actually existing difference between high and low frequencies. Thus, without prior expectancies, judges have to find out gradually that the positivity rate is above 50% and the negativity rate is below 50%. (The reverse holds in another experimental condition in which negativity prevails.) However, learning the actually existing difference of 69% positive behaviors versus 31% negative behaviors takes time, and as long as learning is imperfect, judgments should arrive somewhere in between (between 50% and 69% positivity and between 31% and 50% negativity). Importantly, however, as there are fewer trials to learn about B than A, more information should be lost and regression should be more severe for B than A. That is, the actually existing prevalence of positive over negative information should be extracted to a lesser degree for Group B than for the larger Group A (as illustrated in Figure 3.2). Unlike the distinctiveness account, which implies enhanced memory and increased accuracy for cell *d* information, the environmental learning approach predicts less efficient learning and memory and reduced judgment accuracy for Group B.

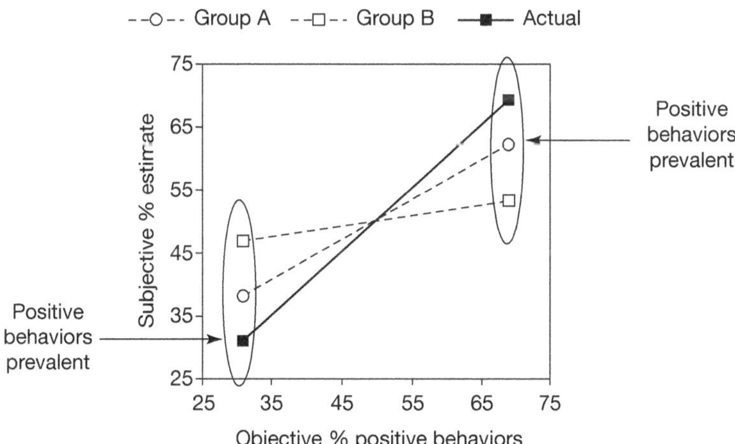

Figure 3.2 Regressiveness of subjective estimates. Due to the smaller number of observations, the regression is stronger for the minority Group B than for the majority Group A. Thus, an objectively high positivity rate (data points on the right) is underestimated for Group B more than for Group A. When the actual positivity rate is low (data points on the left), positivity is more overestimated for B than for A. In general, frequency differences are learned less well for B than A.

Given the clarity of these conflicting predictions, it should be easy to draw a decision empirically. Indeed, proponents of the distinctiveness account have interpreted many findings as supporting evidence for the claim that cell *d* information is actually recalled better and judged more accurately than information belonging to other cells. However, many of these arguments are logically and methodologically flawed in that they mistake inaccurate overestimation of cell *d* for enhanced memory. Thus, the very fact that the number of negative behaviors in Group B is (erroneously) estimated to be higher than the number of negative behaviors in Group A was taken as evidence for a memory advantage of cell *d*, much like the cued-recall finding that many negative items are erroneously attributed to Group B whereas relatively more positive items are assigned to Group A. However, in actuality, these findings merely demonstrate that negative items are erroneously associated with Group B (complementary to the fact that too few positive items are associated with B). The neglect of B's positivity and the emphasis on B's negativity must not be taken as evidence for a memory advantage for items that have been originally paired with group B.

To test the alleged recall and accuracy advantage of cell *d* and to disentangle exaggerated *d* judgments from accurate *d* judgments, we conducted several series of experiments that will be reported now. The first experiment reported by Fiedler (1991) was in essence a replication of the original Hamilton and Gifford (1976) paradigm, with a few modifications. One notable difference in the data analysis was that the judges' estimates of frequencies *a, b, c*, and *d* were not converted to phi coefficients (as an overall measure of the correlation between groups and positivity). Instead, the frequency estimates were analyzed in terms of the judged proportions of positive items for Group A (i.e., the frequency *a* divided by the sum $a + b$) as compared with the judged proportion of positive items in B (*c* divided by the sum $c + d$). One noteworthy side effect of this modified analysis is that it makes the actual accuracy of the judged positivity proportions transparent, relative to the objective proportions presented. In one experimental condition, 69% of the stimulus behaviors were positive ($a = 18$, $b = 8$, $c = 9$, $d = 4$), whereas in another condition the negative behaviors were prevalent (i.e., 69% and only 31% positive) in both groups ($a = 8$, $b = 18$, $c = 4$, $d = 9$). The mean judged proportions of positive and negative items for Groups A and B are given in Figure 3.3, as a function of experimental conditions, along with the objective proportions.

In fact, it is justified to conclude that the strongest bias is evident in the overestimation of the least frequent behavior valence in Group B. However, interpreting this deviation in terms of enhanced accuracy of cell *d* information would appear to be strange. Although judgments of cell *d* appear augmented, this augmentation effect is a consequence of inaccuracy and information loss for Group B, rather than enhanced memory. While the actually present difference between positive and negative items (69% vs. 31%) is at least partially discovered for Group A (60% vs. 39%), due to a sufficiently large number of learning trials, information about the smaller group is almost totally lost. The close to chance (i.e., 50% vs. 46%) judgments of positive and negative items in Group B indicate an extreme degree of regression, or information loss, suggesting that the prevalence of positive

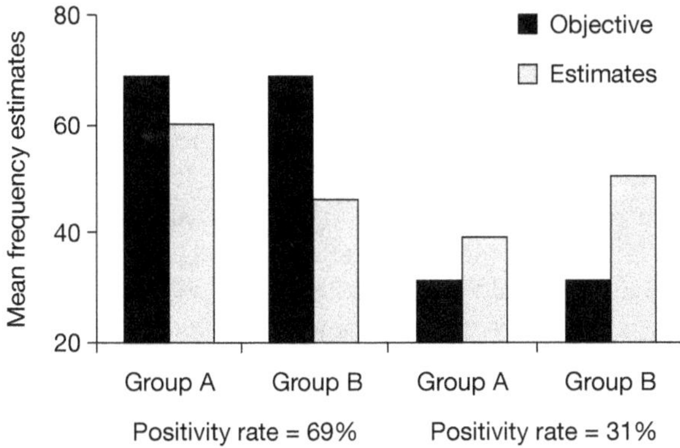

Figure 3.3 Frequency estimates as compared with objective stimulus frequencies in an experiment reported in Fiedler (1991). Estimates for the smaller group (B) are much more regressive than estimates for the larger group (A).

items (or negative items in the other condition) went unnoticed in the minority. In other words, the seeming accentuation of infrequent items in Group B (cell *d* information) is but one aspect of a complete pattern that reflects severe information loss of Group B.

A similar picture arises from the cued recall test, where judges are presented with all behavior descriptions once more, and they have to recall the group with which each description had been associated. Again, the deficit in Group B learning is manifested in an exaggerated proportion of negative items assigned to Group B. However, again, this increased tendency to recall negative items as belonging to Group B does not provide cogent evidence for enhanced cell *d* memory but it only reflects the fact that the preponderance of positive items was only detected for Group A, but not for B. Inferring a cell *d* recall advantage from the proportion of items assigned to cells *a, b, c,* and *d* on the cued-recall test is logically inappropriate, to be sure. Logically appropriate would be to analyze the proportions of correctly assigned items *stemming from each cell,* rather than assigned to each cell. Thus, if cell *d* information is in fact distinctive and salient and is therefore encoded more efficiently, the negative items originally paired with Group B in the stimulus series should be recalled better on the cued recall test.

It is noteworthy that such an analysis of cued-recall accuracy was virtually never done by proponents of the enhanced memory claim. If it is done—as in the Fiedler (1991) study—there is no evidence whatsoever for enhanced memory of cell *d* items. However, the data are fully in line with the regular learning account. At the level of individual items, there is no evidence of biased processing, that is, items from all cells are encoded equally well and are therefore equally likely to be recalled. At the group level, however, more systematic information is extracted about the larger group, as manifested in more accurate positivity rates reproduced for Group A than Group B.

More direct evidence on the role of memory performance in the formation of illusory correlations comes from an investigation by Fiedler, Russer, and Gramm (1993). Signal detection analyses were applied to separate genuine discrimination (i.e., actual recall of the group association of positive and negative items) from response bias (i.e., guessing tendency to associate positive or negative items with one group more than the other). If there is actually a selective recall advantage for negative behaviors associated to the minority, Group B, then cued-recall responses should correctly assign many negative items to Group B if and only if these were originally paired with B. But they should not incorrectly assign other negative items to B that have in fact been paired with A. Such genuine *discrimination* performance should be clearly distinguished from a *response bias*, or guessing tendency to assign any negative items to Group B, whether originally paired with B or A.

The results of this signal detection analysis of cued recall data in the illusory correlations paradigm are summarized in Figure 3.4 (pooled over several other conditions manipulated in this investigation). Most importantly to the crucial theoretical question, the discrimination index (sensitivity) is not higher for negative than positive items. If items stemming from cell *d* had a memory advantage, discriminating between cell *d* and *c* should be facilitated, and this should be manifested in enhanced cued recall of negative stimuli (distributed over *c* and *d*). However, if anything, cued recall discrimination of *positive* items is slightly superior. (This reversal is actually not expected and not found in other studies.) In any case, our signal detection analysis clearly did not support the contention of a processing bias towards infrequent, allegedly distinctive information.

In the analysis of the response bias index (a measure of the tendency to assign items to the larger group, A, regardless of their actual pairing), judges exhibit a significant bias to ascribe positive items to Group A, as evident here in a bias index

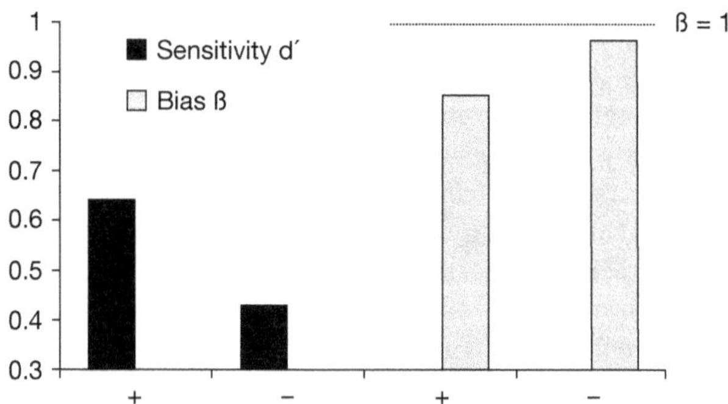

Figure 3.4 Signal detection analysis of memory performance for positive and negative items in an illusory correlation experiment (pooling over various conditions of Fiedler et al., 1993). Apparently, sensitivity d′ is not higher for negative than for positive items. The bias index β decreases well below 1 for positive items, which in this anaysis reflects a response tendency to attribute positive behaviors to group A rather than B.

clearly lower than 1. In comparison, for negative items, a bias index close to 1 indicates the lack of a similar response tendency to assign negative items to Group A (see Figure 3.4). This means that, regardless of item-specific memory, judges have acquired general knowledge that Group A behavior tended to be positive, but they have acquired little distinct impression of Group B. Together, this pattern of results suggests that there is virtually no evidence for selective memory of cell *d* information to cause illusory correlations. However, the illusory association of the larger Group A with the predominant positivity can explain the response bias on the cued recall test.

Further support for this interpretation is obtained in regression analyses, using the degree of illusory correlation (in frequency estimates and in evaluative trait ratings) as criteria and the proportions of items from the four cells of the contingency table that were assigned to Group A as predictors. (Note that the assignment rates for two cells, which actually belong to Group A, are hit rates, whereas the assignment rates for the other two cells are false alarms.) From the mean standard regression weights β in Figure 3.5, it is apparent that the degree of the illusory correlation effect is not primarily determined by the least frequent cell, corresponding to negative B behaviors (B–). Rather, the strongest (negative) predictor of the illusion is due to A–, reflecting a failure to assign negative A items to A. The general pattern means that the size of the illusion is a function of two response tendencies, to ascribe positive items to A and to ascribe negative items to B (i.e., not to A), regardless of where these items actually come from.

Analogous results were recently reported by Klauer and Meiser (2000), using multinomial modelling of cued recall responses. An algorithm proposed by Hu and Batchelder (1994) was used to decompose cued-recall data according to a three-step decision tree. Accordingly, the assignment of, say, a positive stimulus to Group

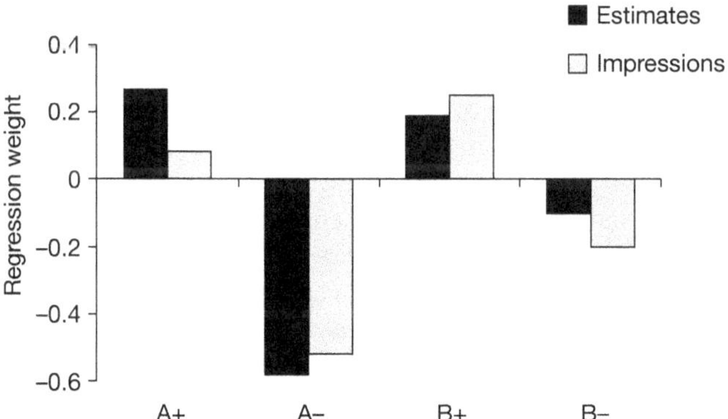

Figure 3.5 Regression analysis of the contribution of the four cells of the contingency table to the prediction of illusory correlations. The regression weight of B– information is negligible. The strongest predictor of the illusion is the failure to correctly assign negative A items to Group A. In general, the pattern means that the illusion reflects a respone tendency to assign positive but not negative items to A.

A can arise from: (1) actually recalling the original pairing; (2) deriving the A assignment from the fact that Group A was mostly positive; (3) mere guessing if neither (1) nor (2) provided the basis for a decision. Using this methodological tool for cognitive modelling, Klauer and Meiser (2000) again found no evidence for better encoding and genuine recall of cell *d* information, but a significant response bias, or judgment tendency at the group level, to associate Group A with positive behaviors. These findings converge with our own evidence in supporting the environmental-learning account: Even though stimuli from all cells are processed equally (i.e., in the absence of a memory bias), the larger number of Group A than Group B trials creates a stronger association of Group A with the predominant valence (positivity).

In conclusion, only a few studies have applied state-of-the art memory analyses to the illusory correlation, and the results of these studies do not support the animistic account that a biased cognitive process has to be assumed to explain the biased judgment outcome. Rather, assuming a constant, unbiased learning process, the learning environment provides more A than B trials and thereby produces a fully "innocent bias"—one that would also occur in an unbiased, rational device like a computer. Indeed, several computer simulation studies have demonstrated learning mechanisms or connectionist algorithms (Fiedler, 1996; Smith, 1991; Slugoski, Sarson, & Krank, 1992) that are sensitive to number of learning trials. That is, without assuming selective processing of different events these models can produce illusory correlations of the Hamilton–Gifford type.

It has to be mentioned that some researchers have reported other findings which they interpreted as evidence for a cell *d* advantage. For example, Johnson and Mullen (1994) found that self-determined encoding times for negative minority behaviors were higher than for information from the other, more frequent cells. However, such evidence is inconclusive because increased latencies need not indicate improved encoding or recall. Analyses of latencies are of little worth unless speed–accuracy tradeoffs are controlled for, and unless the ultimate recall performance is really measured. Unfortunately, Johnson and Mullen (1994) did not report recall accuracy data. The studies reported above (and many others we examined for recall accuracy in our own lab) strongly suggest that they would not have found the crucial recall or memory advantage of cell *d*.

In one experiment (Hamilton et al., 1985), cell *d* information was superior in *free recall*, but this finding is hard to replicate. Even if it is valid, it only refers to recall of item contents but not to the association of item valence with particular groups. Ordinary memory models (such as Smith & Graesser's, 1981, schema pointer plus tag model) predict that the first few items from each category should be encoded at a more specific level than further items. As there are only 4 cell *d* items, free recall of these items should profit from such a tendency. Because of the uncontrolled impact of such set-size effects, these and several other pieces of evidence are hard to interpret and cannot be counted as cogent evidence for the claim that illusory correlations are mediated by the distinctiveness and memory advantage of jointly infrequent items (cell *d*).

Other evidence for an ordinary-learning account from related paradigms

Perhaps the most unequivocal evidence for the independence of illusory correlations of the distinctiveness of infrequent stimuli comes from experiments in which the frequency of the most infrequent category is zero. If no stimuli are presented, they cannot be distinctive and they cannot dominate the memory representation. However, regressive judgments resulting from imperfect learning can still account for the fact that zero frequencies are overestimated, much like high frequencies are underestimated.

Pertinent evidence for this variant of an illusory correlation was provided in another experiment reported by Fiedler (1991). Participants saw a series of stimuli describing male versus female people who were interested in four different topics: politics, study, traveling, and sports. The actually presented stimulus distribution is given in Table 3.1, along with the memory-based frequency judgments. Quite in line with the usual regression effect that holds for all frequency learning in a probabilistic environment (Greene, 1984; Sedlmeier, 1999), the actual frequency differences were blurred in the subjective estimates. Higher frequencies were underestimated whereas low frequencies were overestimated. However, notably, and also in line with a normal regression effect, this tendency was most pronounced for extreme frequencies. In particular, the overestimation effect was strongest for zero-frequency categories which received estimates of over 16% on average. Thus, the same tendency to overestimate low frequencies (as a consequence of incomplete learning) that holds for a minority group can also be demonstrated, and more radically so, for an event of zero frequency, where distinctiveness is ruled out completely.

In a similar vein, Shavitt and Sanbonmatsu (1999) have recently demonstrated an effect of the number of learning trials when there is but one group. When a single group is characterized by more positive than negative behaviors and the positive–negative ration is held constant, just increasing the number of observations will also increase the positivity of the resulting group judgments. Clearly, this

Table 3.1 Regressiveness of frequency judgments (after Fiedler, 1991)

Topic	*Gender*	*Objective presentation frequency*	*Objective proportion*	*Mean judged proportion*	*Over/under-estimation*
Politics	Male	4	25.0	28.3	+3.3
	Female	4	14.3	21.2	+6.9
Study	Male	8	50.0	37.6	–12.4
	Female	16	57.1	32.7	–24.4
Traveling	Male	0	0.0	16.0	+16.0
	Female	8	28.6	39.0	+8.4
Sports	Male	4	25.0	22.5	–2.5
	Female	0	0.0	16.1	+16.1

demonstration of a gradual learning curve (more and more extracting the dominance of positive behaviors with an increasing sample of observations) cannot be explained by the distinctiveness of another group's negative behavior.

However, this finding again nicely fits the simple learning account. By the way, a similar pattern of findings was long known from research in the information integration paradigm (Anderson, 1967; Kaplan, 1981), showing that increasing the absolute number of predominantly positive or negative stimulus traits leads to more polarized judgments. Again, the failure to consider this obviously relevant evidence in the explanation of the Hamilton–Gifford effect is indicative of the strong preference of contemporary social psychology for animistic forces (distinctiveness, salience, memory bias) and the relative lack of interest in simple, ordinary laws of associative learning. Nevertheless, we intend to demonstrate in the chapters to follow that such a simple, disillusionary account can be as intriguing and adventurous as an animistic account. Furthermore, the ecological learning approach will lead to many new phenomena and alternative explanations of old phenomena that would not have been found without such a theoretical approach.

Note that the regular, unbiased learning account, or information loss account of illusory correlations, has a very wide range of applications. It applies to all situations where the density or frequency of stimulus distributions cannot be expected to be equal or rectangular. This can indeed be expected to be the case most of the time. As we move through the social environment, we are more likely to be exposed to observations about ourselves than about others, more about ingroups than outgroups, more about friends and colleagues than about foreigners, more data about proximal than distal objects, and more information about our own car, house, or profession than about other people's cars, houses or professions (Fiedler, 1996). In all these cases, the number of learning trials can be expected to be higher for the proximal, familiar, self-referent targets than for the distal, unfamiliar, other-referent targets, and we should expect illusory correlations of the same type as in the Hamilton–Gifford paradigm.

The associative learning approach is particularly applicable to the Snyder et al. (1977) finding that attractive females end up being experienced as more socially competent than less attractive females. Now we see that even in the absence of expectancies and semantic similarities, the learning approach to illusory correlations suggests a different, alternative account. It might be—although this has to be tested of course—that attractive women merely attracted more questions or behavioral prompts, because of their higher hedonic value (or for any other reason), and thereby created a larger sample of observations. Assuming a constant proportion of socially competent responses (say 70%), the virtually higher number of effective learning trials for attractive targets may be responsible for the fact that their social competence was learned more effectively.

We shall return to this alternative explanation of the Snyder et al. (1977) results in terms of the amount of attention or the number of questions asked in the next chapter, when we shall apply the illusory correlation concept to active social hypothesis testing. In this chapter, we shall describe experiments in which participants not only receive experimenter-provided information passively, but ask questions and search for information actively when testing a given hypothesis. Before we turn to this new paradigm, however, we should recapitulate the specific insights gained from the empirical results reviewed so far in the present chapter.

Distinctive assets of an environmental-learning approach

In this chapter, we have reviewed two competing theoretical approaches to the explanation of illusory correlations in the Hamilton–Gifford paradigm—one of the most prominent paradigms of stereotype learning in the last 25 years. A moment of reflection is in order to figure out the specific innovations gained from an environmental-learning approach—as contrasted with the traditional, "animistic" approach that highlights cognitive and motivational factors within the individual. The first distinctive feature of the cognitive-environmental framework, considered from a meta-theoretical point of view, is the insight that an analysis of the stimulus environment is as important as an analysis of the cognitive and emotional processes within the individual. In fact, one cannot describe—nor even understand—the latter before the former is accomplished.

Focus on the analysis of the environment

For example, to understand a cognitive illusion such as the one first studied by Hamilton and Gifford (1976), it is essential to describe the distribution of stimuli in the environment that impinges on the individual. This distribution is by no means flat; rather, it is extremely heterogeneous, multi-modal, and consisting of numerous peaks and gaps. Stimuli in different parts of the environment, or experienced from different perspectives, differ in frequency, proximity, and accessibility. Minorities are by definition rare, although from the perspective of a minority member, the frequency of encountering minority-related information may be rather high. In any case, one group is more prominent than another, affording more opportunity to learn. At the same time, norm-conforming behaviors are usually more frequent than non-conforming, deviant behaviors. Granting that norms prescribe desirable, positive behaviors, this means that the conjoint occurrence of positive behavior and members of majorities constitutes a high-density source of stimulation. Given such a stimulus environment, the possibility suggests itself that illusory correlations may be already explained by the environment itself. No processing bias within animate human beings has to be postulated to account for the illusion.

To illustrate this point, imagine that a robot system—without any cognitive or affective biases—might be used to figure out whether the rate of positive behavior in different groups is above some threshold. For statistical reasons alone, such a robot system is more likely to find "significant" evidence for tendencies in large groups than for small groups, just as in statistical significance testing (using binomial tests, Bayesian inference, etc.) the same ratio of positive to negative behavior is more significant in a large sample than in a small sample.

However, notably, the cognitive-environmental approach does not stop at this point of analysis. It is not a purely environmentalist approach. Rather, it takes for granted—as a matter of principle—that the same environment looks different when observed and experienced from different perspectives. As already mentioned, the minority group (e.g., religious minorities, gay people, handicapped, ethnic minority) may not be unusual or rare from the perspective of minority members. Deaf people, for instance, may be quite unknown and hardly accessible for most of us, but somebody who is herself deaf will go to school with other deaf people and will have many deaf friends and acquaintances. Moreover, regardless of the objective number of direct encounters, deaf persons will be inclined to think about and memorize episodes involving deaf people. So the effective stimulus distribution that provides the ultimate input to the cognitive system is not confined to externally encountered stimuli but includes internally generated (memorized, imagined, mentally fabricated, attentionally selected) stimuli as well.

In other words, as a matter of principle, it is the interaction of the individual and the environment that determines the effective stimulus input. A minority, such as deaf people, may be rare in general, but it may not be rare, and not evade extensive learning, for members of the minority. Similarly, the overall prevalence of positive, norm-conforming behaviors may be inverted for somebody particularly interested in deviant behavior as, for instance, an expert in criminology or pathology. In any case, the effective stimulus ecology is not fixed but changes flexibly and drastically with the perspective of the viewer, much like the view of the world that is captured by a camera changes with the direction, the focus, the zoom factor, and the adjusted illumination of the camera. Chapter 8 will provide a deeper elaboration on this notion of psychological relativity.

The second feature that characterizes the cognitive-environmental approach to stereotyping is its emphasis on basic laws of learning, as opposed to ad-hoc laws specifically tailored to explain particular stereotype illusions. In the traditional approach, minority-related illusory correlations—that is, the relative underestimation of positive behavior in minorities—is explained by the specifically tailored assumption that positive minority behaviors are encoded less effectively in memory than negative minority behaviors. Thus, the explanation remains very similar and close to the phenomenon to be explained—so close that there is always the danger of circularity. Within an environmental learning approach, only very basic, general, parsimonious assumptions are required to explain the phenomena. Nobody would come to doubt a law of learning as basic as the assumption that learning increases with the number of trials. By implication, it can be predicted and explained that, given the same prevalence of positive behavior, the prevalent positivity should be recognized more reliably and more quickly in the effective majority than in the effective minority. Applying a fully normal, universal law of learning to an emergent stimulus environment can explain a specific phenomenon such as the devaluation of minorities in a parsimonious, non-circular fashion.

Innovative potential and original implications

The resulting theoretical explanations are not peculiar to the specific phenomenon under focus, but structurally similar explanations and predictions can be carried over to seemingly different phenomena. The same basic learning principle that larger samples make predominant tendencies in the ecology more visible than small samples can not only explain the devaluation of minorities but a number of other prominent findings in social psychology as well (see Table 3.2). In this way, the cognitive-environmental approach turns out to be fruitful and broad in scope. For example, the so-called *self-serving bias* which looms prominently in the literature on motivational judgment biases could arise quite independently of any motivational bias. Assuming the same relatively high proportion of positive behaviors in the Self as in others, more favorable judgments of the Self may be simply due to the fact more information is available about the Self than about others. Given the central status of the self-serving bias in research and theorizing, it seems more than surprising that this obvious possibility is hardly ever considered in the pertinent literature (Kunda, 1990; Pyszczynski, & Greenberg, 1987; Zuckerman, 1979).

In a similar vein, the simplistic learning rule can be applied to the *ingroup-serving bias* (Brewer, 1979). Assuming more frequent observations, or learning trials, about ingroups than outgroups, the prevalence of positive, norm-conforming

Table 3.2 Synopsis of social psychological phenomena that can result from different number of learning trials alone, without selective processing

Phenomenon	*Description*
Illusory correlation	Prevailing tendency in a group is more readily extracted for large than for small groups
Self-serving bias	Predominantly positive, desirable behavior is more visible for the Self than for others
Ingroup-serving bias	Predominantly positive, desirable behavior is more visible for the ingroup than for the outgroup
Outgroup homogeneity effect	A greater number of descriptive aspects recognized in the ingroup than the outgroup, due to differential richness of information
Set-size effect in impression formation	Holding the ratio of positive to negative attributes constant, the extremity of resulting impressions increases with the absolute number of attributes
Mere thinking effect	Extremity of an attitude increases as the number of relevant thoughts increases through extended thinking
Group-polarization effect	Group decisions become more extreme as the number of relevant arguments increases through group discussion

behavior should be detected more reliably and more significantly for the ingroup. Again, regardless of whether this alternative interpretation is in fact responsible for all sorts of ingroup favoritism, it seems remarkable that such a self-evident account was virtually never considered. Once more the example shows the fertility of the environmental-learning approach, which opens a number of new perspectives on old phenomena.

Take, for another example, the phenomenon of *outgroup homogeneity*, that is, the tendency to judge outgroups in a less differentiated, more simplified fashion than ingroups (Judd & Park, 1988; Linville, Fischer, & Salovey, 1989). In operational terms, judges are more willing to generalize attributes over outgroup members than over ingroup members. Common interpretations involve the assumptions that people are motivated to present their own group as distinct from others, or that ingroup-related information is encoded in memory in more piecemeal, exemplar-based fashion than outgroup information, which is represented in terms of abstract prototypes (Park & Rothbart, 1982). Again, the traditional explanations are sought within the individual. From a cognitive-environmental point of view, however, it would be worthwhile at least to think of the simple learning rule. If an environment feeds people with more ingroup-related than outgroup-related information, the social learning process should discover more ingroup aspects than outgroup aspects, thus arriving at more differentiated ingroup than outgroup impressions.

This possibility is consistent with the finding that the outgroup-homogeneity effect is sometimes reduced or even reversed in minority members. From a minority perspective, the outgroup is often a majority that affords more learning opportunities than the ingroup. Consequently, the learning rule predicts that minorities might acquire relatively more differentiated outgroup impressions than majority members. In a recent computer simulation study (Fiedler, Kemmelmeier, & Freytag, 1999), a whole variety of empirical variants of outgroup homogeneity could be simulated by a single algorithm that is sensitive to the number of learning trials, without assuming any processing bias.

Exactly because the environmental learning rule is more general than, and logically detached from, the phenomenon itself that it was originally meant to explain (i.e., illusory correlations), it raises several surprising, insightful theoretical analogies. Just as doubling the number of stimulus attributes in an impression formation experiment (e.g., 4 positive and 1 negative trait doubled into 8 positive and 2 negative traits) can intensify the resulting impression (Anderson, 1967; Shavitt & Sanbonmatsu, 1999; see above), increasing the number of attitude-relevant arguments could as well lead to a more intense, polarized attitude. Conceiving of an attitude as an impression of an attitude topic, such as the Greenpeace organization, for instance, a moderately positive attitude (based on, say, 6 pro and 2 contra arguments) should become more extremely positive when the informational basis increases (e.g., to 12 pro and 4 contra arguments). In this way, our simple learning rule offers a noteworthy but formally fully ignored explanation for another well-known phenomenon in social psychology, attitude polarization through *mere thinking* (Tesser, 1978). If merely thinking about an attitude object increases the number of activated arguments in the attitude holder's memory, the predominant attitude tendency should become more pronounced, or polarized (Fiedler, 1996). Note that no selective processing of attitude-consistent or extreme arguments is assumed in this argument. All that has to be assumed is that the number of attitude-related learning trials increases through mere thinking. Even the mere repetition of arguments is sufficient for the phenomenon to occur, as demonstrated by Downing, Judd, & Brauer (1992). A novel aspect here is that learning relies on self-generated information sought in memory—a very important part of the social individual's environment.

When mere thinking does not occur within individual people's minds but in a collective group discussion, the same principle lends itself to the explanation of the *group polarization* phenomenon (Moscovici & Zavalloni, 1969; Myers, 1978). The very modest assumption that group discussions will increase the number of arguments about an attitude or judgment topic implies that the predominant tendency will be enhanced through extended learning. No selective, one-sided tendency to utter confirming arguments has to be assumed. Merely increasing the number of learning trials or relevant pieces of information should be sufficient to strengthen the dominant tendency. Such a theoretical implication receives actual support by empirical research showing that mere repetition of statements in group discussions is sufficient for group polarization to occur (Brauer, Judd, & Gliner, 1995). No selective processing or biased group discussion is necessary. To be sure, the selective coverage of particular topics in group discussion—such as the well-established bias towards redundant information shared by many discussants (Stasser & Titus, 1985)—may also contribute to polarization effects and constitutes an exciting research topic in its own right. However, an even simpler principle, based on the number of learning trials, is already sufficient to cause a more basic and primitive variant of the same polarization effect.

A synopsis of the reviewed phenomena that can be explained by the same parsimonious learning rule—number of trials—is given in Table 3.2. The emphasis here is on highlighting the theoretical innovations that can be gained from a cognitive-environmental perspective, which supplements other ecological approaches to social psychology (Eagly & Steffen, 1986; McArthur & Baron, 1983). Unexpected theoretical analogies between seemingly unrelated phenomena become apparent, and new implications and explanations can be derived, testifying to the theoretical fertility of the approach that has been the focus of the present chapter. Other evidence pertaining to more complex learning environments will be presented in Chapter 7.

Similarity-based stereotype learning

Up to here, the amount-of-learning principle has been illustrated and operationalized almost exclusively in terms of the *frequency distribution* of learning trials. Within such a simplifying statistical model, only the number of learning trials are counted, as if all learning trials were equally important and contributed the same amount of learning. Drawing on the universal law that learning increases with the number of trials, we could account for a variety of stereotype-learning phenomena. Accordingly, the stereotype that women tend to be more emotional than men could arise even when the actual proportion of emotional (rather than cool) is the same for both gender groups, simply because women are more often involved, and can be more often observed in emotionally relevant situations. In the last section of this chapter, we shall briefly touch another universal law of learning to supplement the primitive statistical model, if only to remind the reader that the cognitive-environmental approach is not restricted to a singular rule. In this section, a concrete reason, or mechanism, will be depicted to show that the statistical frequency model is too simple because learning trials vary in other aspects than frequency. In particular, learning depends on *similarity*. In the learning and conditioning literature, this is well-known as preparedness (Seligman, 1971) or belongingness (Garcia & Koelling, 1966). Not all pairings of a conditional stimulus (CS) with an unconditional stimulus (US) are equally effective. Learning is often more efficient when CS somehow resembles US. An olfactory stimulus is more readily paired with sickness than an electric shock (Garcia & Koelling, 1966). A negative facial impression is more readily paired with an aversive stimulus than a pleasant facial impression (Orr & Lanzetta, 1980).

In the traditional, animistic approach to stereotype learning and change, the similarity principle is commonly reflected in the role attributed to subjective beliefs and preconceptions, as evident in concepts like naive theories (Schneider, 1973), expectancy-based illusory correlations (Hamilton & Rose, 1980), or the representativeness heuristic (Kahneman & Tversky, 1972). Accordingly, the stereotype that women are emotional would be explained by the assumption that people have a corresponding expectation, or naive theory, or that the meaning of the attribute, emotional, is more representative of women than men. Again, the proximity of the explanatory construct (expectancy of the female-emotional link) to the phenomenon to be explained (stereotypical belief in the female-emotional link) is striking, and conspicuous. The expectancy (explanans) and the stereotypical illusory correlation (explanandum) may be but two different measures of the same underlying propensity—too close to provide a satisfactory scientific account.

Once again, an analysis of the stimulus environment in which stereotype learning occurs affords a less empty explanation of the cognitive process underlying the similarity effect, both in stereotyping and in the more general domain of learning and conditioning. This explanation is an essentially *semiotic* one—that is, based on assumptions about the operation of sign systems in the social environment—and logically independent of the phenomena to be explained. Consider the above example again: What are the cognitive-environmental conditions under which people learn the association of femininity and emotionality?

Reminiscent of the maxim that an informed analysis of cognitive processes presupposes an analysis of the stimulus environment, we must first of all describe the nature and structure of relevant stimulus observations. One crucial insight to start with is that meaningful attributes, like femininity and emotionality, cannot be observed immediately. That is, we have no sense organs to literally perceive if somebody is feminine or emotional, just as most other meaningful attitude, judgment, and decision targets (e.g., risk, danger, intelligence, humor, attraction) are not amenable to direct perception. Rather, these meaningful attributes have to be inferred, or construed, from more proximal cues that are often only loosely related to the distal attribute. To "perceive" emotionality, we may use such cues as pupil size, verbal activity, degree of self reference, reactivity to particular stimuli, emotion-related words, etc. Each of these cues, when considered in isolation, is not very diagnostic as a valid index of the construct to be assessed, emotionality; empirical correlations would turn out to be modest, if not lousy. Only through the aggregation of information coming from multiple probabilistic cues can the brain make an inference with reasonable validity, just as a personality test reaches a reasonable reliability only when aggregating over a number of items. Thus, number of available cues (underlying individual observations) is as important an aspect of the information environment as the number of different observations.

This essentially Brunswikian sketch of socially meaningful perception (Brunswik, 1956) can be generalized to most stereotype problems: The stimulus surface that really enters the cognitive system is not the attribute of interest, but a vector of cues that are more or less useful for inferring the attribute. In the present example, what we see is not emotionality but a set of more or less relevant cues. Even the perception of an attribute like femininity is not based on biological sex alone but contaminated with a number of cues related to gender roles and differences between more or less typical examplars of the female category. Within such a multiple-cue framework, similarity can be conceived as *cue overlap*. The cues that mediate the assessment of emotionality overlap with the cues that mediate the assessment of femininity, rendering these two attributes semiotically confounded (i.e., relying on the same diagnostic signs). The situation is analogous to two personality tests measuring independent traits but consisting in part of the same items. Due to such overlap, one attribute cannot be assessed independently of the other. Similarly, to the extent that emotionality and femininity depend on the same cues, the "observation" of one attribute is artificially correlated with the "observation" of the other. Thus, imagine in a thought experiment that the "true" values of a number of targets on emotionality and femininity (assuming they were known) are uncorrelated across persons. Because these uncorrelated attribute values have to be inferred from confounded cue systems, they would nevertheless appear to be correlated. The sign system will support the assessment of the joint occurrence of persons who are high in both emotionality and femininity or low on both attributes, because any cue system that indicates high (low) emotionality will tend to indicate high (low) femininity as well. Conversely, evidence for the joint occurrence of high emotionality and low femininity (or vice versa) will be reduced artificially because any cue pattern that indicates a high value on one attribute will interfere with the assessment of a low value on the other.

In this way, overlapping or confounded cue systems afford an explanation of similarity-based illusory correlations (Fiedler, 2000a). The illusion that two meaningfully related, similar attributes correlate higher than they actually do may arise from the fact that they cannot be measured or assessed independently. Thus, the common stereotype that foreign people are dangerous may reflect the fact that foreignness and dangerousness are defined psychologically by highly overlapping cue systems. The same may hold for many other similarity-based illusory correlations, such as the Snyder et al. (1977) example of attraction and social skills we have used at the outset.

It is important to note that this semiotic account of similarity effects is conceptually different from expectancy-based illusory correlations (Fiedler, 2000a). Thus, even when there is no prior expectancy at all regarding the co-variation of X and Y, but X and Y are based on overlapping cues, the present account predicts an illusory correlation. This was recently demonstrated for an illusory correlation between artists and painting styles across a series of paintings, consisting of composed sets of abstract symbols (Plessner, Freytag, & Fiedler, 2000). When the graphical cues of an artist named "Greve" overlapped with the cues defining a particular style, "Wenturalism", participants believed erroneously to have observed that Greve pictures were often painted in Wenturalism style. Only when both attributes were defined by separable cues, could their independence be assessed accurately.

Once more, the cognitive-environmental analysis of similarity effects leads to uncommon insights and new theoretical perspectives. A novel semiotic approach to explaining similarity-based illusory correlations is suggested. A ubiquitous source of potential stereotypes based on overlapping cues becomes apparent. Similarity-based illusory correlations turn out to be conceptually different from expectancy-based illusory correlations—that have been treated synonymously before. Formerly unknown parallels between seemingly unrelated phenomena become visible—such as expectancy-based illusory correlations in social psychology and item overlap artifacts in test theory (i.e., trait measures correlate artificially because similar or identical items appear in questionnaires supposed to measure different traits).

Summary

The double purpose of the present chapter was to render our environmental learning approach to social stereotypes more concrete than the theoretical statements in the preceding chapter, as well as to point out the various distinctive predictions of our approach. Following the chronological course of our own research, we chose the illusory correlation paradigm for this initial demonstration. Starting from a simple conditioning analogy, we reasoned that no processing bias or selective memory has to be postulated to explain less positive judgments of minority than majority groups, when the same rate of positive behaviors prevails in both groups. To explain the illusive difference, all we have to assume is that more learning trials are available for a larger than for a smaller group to find out the dominant tendency. Further analyses showed that selective encoding (of negative minority behavior) can not only be dismissed as a necessary condition. Rather, when memory performance is analyzed empirically, selective memory does not appear to contribute to the genesis of illusory correlations in the standard paradigm. Ordinary learning rules not only proved to provide a more parsimonious account, but also a more powerful one, covering a number of other phenomena as well. Self-serving biases and ingroup-serving biases, the outgroup-homogeneity effect, the set-size effect in impression formation, the mere thinking effect, and the group polarization effect are all related by the simple rule that extended learning makes latent trends more and more visible. In the following chapter, still other implications and applications of the same idea will now be presented with respect to another experimental paradigm, hypothesis testing through active information search.

4 The auto-verification of social hypotheses

In the last chapter, we addressed the question of how stereotype-related hypotheses are acquired through mere observation. We drew on experiments in which participants were passively exposed to a series of stimulus observations, or learning trials, about target persons or groups. The learning process started from zero and was not guided by any prior expectancy or instruction focus. In these situations, learning served to create hypotheses about the target persons or groups. In the present chapter, the analysis of stereotype learning is carried one step further. Taking the existence of a guiding hypothesis for granted—which is induced by explicit experimental instructions—we examine what people do when they put a social hypothesis to an empirical test in direct interaction with target persons or groups. Participants in these experiments are not restricted to observing a series of stimuli passively but can actively determine the process of information search. Indeed, an analysis of their information search strategies is of equal interest in these experiments as the analysis of the outcome of social hypothesis testing.

How can the domain of the hypothesis-testing paradigm be defined? According to Klayman and Ha (1987), we may define hypothesis testing as any task "that requires the acquisition of evidence to determine whether or not a hypothesis is correct" (Klayman & Ha, 1987, p. 211). This includes hypotheses about the past ("Did I ever hit my little sister?"), about causation ("Punishment increases neurotic behavior"), and predictions ("A tough childhood leads to depression"). Also, hypotheses can vary in strength and precision; that is, they can refer to vague ideas as well as to strongly held specific beliefs. In general, the hypothesis-testing paradigm covers *all situations in which empirical evidence is required to judge the veridicality of a given hypothesis.* In the present chapter we will investigate hypothesis-testing processes in an active information search paradigm and in a setting that is relevant to social psychology. More concretely we address the following questions:

- Which principles guide information search in hypothesis-testing processes?
- Is confirmation bias an explanation for biased outcomes in hypothesis testing?
- What is the autoverification principle and why is this principle an alternative explanation for biased outcomes out of hypothesis-testing processes?
- Is there empirical evidence for sampling processes that lead to autoverification?

- How does autoverification contribute to the stereotype literature?
- Can sampling processes provide a remedy against stereotypes?

Hypothesis testing in the active information-search paradigm

As already mentioned, within this hypothesis-testing paradigm, we are particularly interested in one influential processing stage, namely *active information search in the environment.* Within a sequence of information processing stages that starts with the acquisition and perception of the empirical stimuli and ends with a final judgment, information search clearly belongs to a very early stage. It can therefore have a critical impact on all subsequent processing. Whereas all later stages can influence the cognitive process only gradually—through perceptual interpretation and disambiguation, encoding inferences, selective memory—the information search strategy determines radically what information will be considered at all. Information search can therefore be conceived as a crucial interface between the environmental reality and the theory tester's cognitive representations and goals. The prevailing hypothesis-test strategy is thus extremely important, not only for scientific decision processes but also for mundane judgments outside the laboratory. Getting-acquainted episodes, legal proceedings, or diagnostic investigations are only some of the most prototypical hypothesis-test settings in the social world.

Although scientific norms demand falsification rather than confirmation of hypotheses (Popper, 1959), a vast amount of empirical and anecdotal evidence indicates that the search for disconfirming evidence occurs rarely, in real life as well as in scientific research itself (Mynatt, Doherty, & Tweney, 1977). It even seems to be the case that scientists, who are, or at least should be, well aware of the normative principles of hypothesis testing, are no less tendentious than non-scientists: They focus on one hypothesis while neglecting others, and they are often more interested in hypothesis-confirming rather than disconfirming information. On a theoretical level, immunization against alternative accounts rather than falsification is the predominant strategy in the development of theories. The underlying reasons may often be motivational: wishful thinking, desire to be correct, avoidance of cognitive dissonance, or suppression of unwanted alternative perspectives. However, apart from such motivated aspects of the hypothesis testing process, the point we want to make is that hypotheses have a built-in device for *auto-verification* anyway, independent of vested interests or other kinds of motivated reasoning. We try to argue logically, and demonstrate empirically, that hypotheses tend to become true regardless of whether cognitive or motivational biases distort information processing. This auto-verification is just a consequence of the stimulus input resulting from information search in the environment. To explain this phenomenon, and to elucidate why biased outcomes are not contingent on any biased processes, we first of all have to consider people's predominant hypothesis-testing strategy.

Positive testing

A pioneer in the investigation of hypothesis testing was Wason (1968), who analyzed test strategies in a rule discovery task. In these studies, participants were told that a series of numbers, for example: 2, 4, 6, confirmed a unitary rule. The task was to discover this underlying rule by generating sample series. After proposing the next number to continue the series, participants received feedback whether the proposed number conformed to the rule underlying the experimenter's series (e.g., numbers of increasing magnitude) or not. At any time, participants were also invited to indicate the rule they believed to have discovered, and the experimenter would inform them whether their suggested solution was correct. The study ended when the correct rule was announced, or when 45 minutes had elapsed. However, unlike most other concept attainment tasks, the primary aim of theses studies was not to investigate rule discovery performance. Rather, the main point was to study participants' problem-solving behavior when their hypotheses were confirmed or disconfirmed by new evidence. In response to negative feedback suggesting that an assumed rule was incorrect, one might have expected from a logical point of view that participants would revise their hypothesis and cease to use the old rule for predicting the next elements of the series. For instance, if feedback showed the rule "increasing even numbers" to be incorrect, rationality would demand for a series which is inconsistent with the rule just disconfirmed. However, Wason found that this rarely occurred. His findings suggest that "subjects were either unwilling or unable to eliminate their hypothesis in the task" (Wason, 1968, p. 169). In other words, most participants did not give up a hypothesized rule that was disconfirmed. They failed to use the procedure appropriate for a negative proof through falsification. Further studies demonstrated that neither financial incentives nor the explicit demand to falsify the generated rule were sufficient to improve performance (Wason & Johnson-Laird, 1969).

Although one might object that Wason's rule discovery task is relatively artificial or misleading (Wetherik, 1962), there is convergent evidence from many studies that one-sided hypothesis testing is a robust phenomenon. Of most influence to social psychology, Snyder and Swann (1978) investigated hypothesis testing using a less artificial, more meaningful paradigm. In their studies, participants were assigned the role of an interviewer who either had to test the hypothesis that their interview partner was extraverted or, in another experimental condition, that the target person was introverted. In order to test the corresponding hypothesis, interviewers were required to select questions from a list that included items referring to both extraverted and introverted behaviors. Results indicated that the majority of questions asked by the interviewers matched the hypothesis focused in the instruction. That is, they selected more questions about the target's extraverted behaviors when they had the hypothesis of an extraverted target in mind, but they raised more questions about introverted behaviors when testing the hypothesis of an introverted target. For instance, in the extraversion condition, participants raised questions such as "What kind of situation would you seek out if you wanted to meet new people?" In contrast, when testing the introversion hypothesis they asked more questions referring to introverted behaviors, such as "What things do you dislike about loud parties?" Snyder and Swann (1978) called this overall tendency to raise predominately hypotheses-consistent questions a *confirmation bias.*

However, Klayman and Ha (1987) recognized that the term "confirmation bias" is strictly speaking a misnomer for the process described by Snyder and Swann because confirmation cannot be derived from hypothesis-matching questions, but only from hypothesis-supporting answers. After all, one-sided questions do not guarantee confirming answers given by the target (for a similar point, see Gadenne, 1982). Even when an interviewer uses unfair communication tools such as leading questions or presuppositions (not asking *whether* but only *what* the target undertakes to meet people), the interview partner is in principle free to deny the question and to provide disconfirming answers. Thus, more than the reference to one-sided questions is needed for a logically sound explanation of a confirmation bias. For a more appropriate term for the dominant information search strategy, Klayman and Ha (1987) referred to *positive testing,* denoting the tendency to search information in categories that match the hypothesis under focus. Another way to define positive testing would be to say that people look out for observations that are more likely to occur under the focal hypothesis than under an alternative hypothesis. The diagram in Figure 4.1 relates this common search strategy to our schematic representation of hypothesis testing in a 2 × 2 contingency table. Positive testing means to concentrate information search from the first row referring to the focused hypothesis, rather than the second row for alternative hypotheses. To round up an explanation of auto-verification—that social hypotheses tend to be verified rather than falsified—it also has to be assumed here that targets tend to provide positive, confirming answers, independent of the target's real attributes.

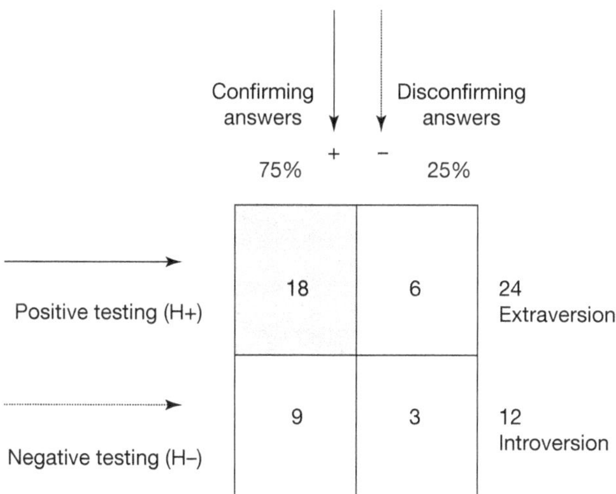

Figure 4.1 The gray cell shows the effects of positive testing in an affirmative environment. The contingency between traits and confirmation rates remains zero ($\Phi = 0$).

Thus, imagine an introverted target person who is asked a question about an extraverted theme (e.g., "In what situations are you most talkative?"), because the interviewer is testing an extraversion hypothesis. It would appear to be natural for such a target to provide a negative answer, making clear that she is actually not talkative. However, filling a missing link in the explanation of the above notion of a "built-in device for auto-verification," the assumption in Figure 4.1 is, obviously, that targets of hypothesis testing would probably cooperate in the process of confirmation.

Indeed, there is strong evidence in various parts of the research literature (for an early review, see Snyder, 1984) that social targets do cooperate in the interpersonal "confirmation game." Empirical evidence suggests that targets of stereotypical hypotheses often contribute actively to self-fulfilling prophecies (Jussim, 1992; Kukla, 1993; Rosenthal & Rubin, 1978; Zebrowitz, Voinescu, & Collins, 1996) or show impairment due to stereotype threat (Steele & Aronson, 1995). An additional source of confirmation is cooperative communication (Grice, 1975). Targets may simply behave as if they were just playing the complementary role in a social game started by the hypothesis tester (e.g., the extravert communication game; it's about jokes, friends, and parties rather than loneliness and serious topics). On a more general level, a common research finding says that targets are apt to respond in the affirmative, irrespective of the question contents. Thus, regardless of whether an individual is asked about extraversion or introversion, it is more likely that she responds Yes rather than No (Zuckerman, Knee, Hodgins, & Myake, 1995). In interview and survey research, this generalized Yes-response tendency has long been noted and is commonly referred to as an *acquiescence bias* (Jackson, 1979; Lenski & Leggett, 1960).

But why are people more likely to respond "yes" rather than "no," independent of the question's content? There are at least three explanations for the acquiescence bias. First, yes-saying may constitute a type of deferential behavior (Lenski and Leggett, 1960). Second, targets may be more interested in satisfying the interviewer than they are in being truthful. Third, most people's self is complex enough to include at least some positive evidence for either hypothesis. Almost everyone is likely to find evidence for extraverted as well as for introverted behavioral episodes due to one-sided information search in memory.

Positive testing + acquiescence = confirmation?

Putting positive testing and the acquiescence bias together, Zuckerman et al. (1995) concluded that hypothesis confirmation reflects the joint influence of both components indicated in Figure 4.1, the hypothesis tester's positive testing and the target's acquiescence. From this perspective, hypothesis confirmation appears to be an inevitable consequence of the double fact that hypothesis testers predominantly raise one-sided questions and targets in return give more yes than no answers. Both components together appear to imply and to explain a confirmation bias in social interaction (cf. Snyder, 1984). If one partner asks many extraverted questions and the other partner tends to affirm, then the argument seems to be closed and the confirmation cycle seems to be fully explained. Plausible as this line of reasoning may appear, however, a closer inspection of this equation reveals that the co-occurrence of positive testing and acquiescence bias does not logically account for hypothesis confirmation.

Imagine a case (cf. Figure 4.1) in which a hypothesis tester follows a positive test strategy and asks twice as many questions about the target's extraversion than about her introversion. This skewed information search might result in 24 questions about extraversion and 12 questions about introversion. Imagine further a target with an acquiescence response set that gives 75% "yes" and 25% "no" answers. Figure 4.1 clearly shows that the resulting contingency does not confirm the hypothesis at all; that is, the contingency between traits and confirmation rates remains zero: p("yes"/introversion question) = p("yes"/extraversion question) = 75%, implying $\Phi = 0$. Therefore, on a logical-statistical level, the mere concatenation of positive testing and predominantly affirmative answers does not constitute a conclusive explanation for the hypothesis confirmation phenomenon.

The auto-verification of social hypotheses

CELA does provide a sufficient and rather simple explanation, suggesting that a positive test strategy may lead to hypothesis confirmation even when the confirmation rate is constant (i.e., a zero correlation). Even though the proportions in our example (cf. Figure 4.1) are the same, the two samples (i.e., for extraverted and introverted behavior) resulting from positive testing are not equivalent, psychologically. As we have repeatedly seen, larger samples are from an environmental learning perspective psychologically more significant than the small samples, because larger samples lead to stronger associations between the target and the respective trait. In our example, the larger sample leads to a stronger association between extraversion and the target than between the target and introversion.

Note that the same simple logic of unequal sample sizes that served to explain illusory correlations and a number of other judgment biases (cf. Table 3.2) in Chapter 3 turns out now to be applicable to the case of active hypothesis testing. One way to interpret the analogy is to say that positive testing generates the very kind of skewed frequency distributions that have been shown to result in illusory correlations in Chapter 3. However, within CELA it matters little whether skewed frequency distributions originate in a passively observed stimulus list provided by the experimenter, or in the hypothesis tester's active information search in the environment. Given the same prevalent tendency in a large and in a small sample of observations, the tendency will loom larger in the former. Unequal sample sizes alone—independently of the source of information—are therefore sufficient to predict the common confirmation effect. The learning principles underlying this outcome were sufficiently explained in the preceding chapters: larger samples dominate judgments simply because there are more trials to learn from. As already noted in Chapter 3, a rat that experienced 16 electrical shocks in 24 trials in a yellow Skinner box would learn that this yellow box is more aversive than the blue box, in which she got only 12 shocks.

We called this phenomenon an *auto-verification effect* (Fiedler, Walther, & Nickel, 1999), as no biased encoding, retrieval, or motivated reasoning is required to explain hypothesis confirmation. The influence of sample size, or amount of learning input, can be predicted to favor hypothesis verification even when all information receives the same level of processing, the same chance of being encoded and retrieved, and even when no cognitive and motivational distortion is involved. Hardly anybody would consider the rat in the learning experiment as biased or irrational simply because she discriminates between a setting where she got 16 shocks on 24 trials and another setting where she received 8 shocks on 12 trials. So, no biased process is needed to explain biased outcomes. Many normative principles, such as Bayes theorem, would end up with the same result.

How ecological reality creates belief

Let us now turn to an empirical test of the notion that differential sample size due to positive testing is a sufficient condition for the confirmation of a hypothetical stereotype. In a series of studies, we (Fiedler, Walther, & Nickel, 1999b) examined hypothesis testing in the context of a gender stereotype. Participants in these studies were given the task to search for information about two targets, Heike (female) and Peter (male), in order to test the (double) hypothesis that *female aggression tends to be covert* whereas *male aggression tends to be overt.* In an interactive computer dialog, each trial of the search task involved first selecting a target person (i.e., Peter or Heike) and then one particular target behavior either from the category of overt aggression or from the category of covert aggression. Two extended lists of behaviors from both categories were presented in a pull-down menu on the computer screen (cf. Table 4.1). Following the selection of an item participants received feedback as to whether the selected behavior had been observed in the chosen target or not. The rate of confirming feedback was fixed at 75%. Thus, the computer algorithm warranted an acquiescence bias in that participants' selections were confirmed in 75% of the cases. The next information search loop started immediately after the feedback. This procedure was repeated until the participant had reached a total number of 32 observations (16 about Peter and 16 about Heike, but variable in the number of items referring to overt and covert aggression). The predictions were straightforward according to the logic of auto-verification explained above. We first expected that participants would engage in positive testing; that is, they would draw larger samples about female covert aggression and male overt aggression than about female overt and male overt aggression. Provided this criterion is met, we predicted an auto-verification effect, that is, participants should judge Heike higher in covert aggressiveness and Peter higher in overt aggressiveness on relevant dependent variables. We suggested that this auto-verification effect is a simple result of the fact that participants draw larger samples of hypothesis-matching than non-matching items, which are accompanied then by predominantly (i.e., 75%) confirming feedback. As dependent measures we assessed the proportions of overt versus covert items selected for each target, direct estimates of the observed frequencies of overt and covert aggression in Peter

Table 4.1 Stimulus items representing overt and covert aggression

	Overt aggression		Covert aggression
(1)	Tends to use violence	(1)	Becomes unfair in arguments
(2)	Quickly goes too far with language	(2)	Acts as though others were not there
(3)	Shouts in arguments	(3)	Enjoys disparaging others
(4)	Threatens with violence	(4)	Lies to get an advantage
(5)	Screams when s/he doesn't like something	(5)	Makes a pretense of being friendly with everyone
(6)	Shakes people when angry	(6)	Makes others feel sorry for him/her
(7)	Quickly gets into a temper	(7)	Hangs up when fed up
(8)	Shouts others down	(8)	Simply walks out of an argument
(9)	Doesn't go short of hitting people	(9)	Plays with other's feelings
(10)	Kicks things	(10)	Gossips about people s/he doesn't like
(11)	Was involved in a fistfight	(11)	Cuts others after an argument
(12)	Throws things around the room	(12)	Pretends to be unforgiving
(13)	Gets out of control quickly	(13)	Schemes
(14)	Sometimes smashes dishes	(14)	Sets traps for others
(15)	Defends his/her rights with violence	(15)	Sets people against each other
(16)	Easily gets into a rage	(16)	Manipulates others to fight each other
(17)	Likes to argue with people	(17)	Denigrates others
(18)	May slap someone's face when in rage	(18)	Puts up a show
(19)	Sometimes wants to smash something	(19)	Pointedly ignores others
(20)	Quickly has a fit after insults	(20)	Flatters others

and Heike, and trait ratings of both targets on traits related to overt and covert aggression.

Let us first consider the results pertaining to information search strategies. As already explained, skewed frequencies are a crucial prerequisite for the auto-verification effect to occur. The left side of Table 4.2 shows the proportions of overt items selected about both target persons, Peter and Heike. Apparently, a higher proportion of overt aggression was drawn about Peter, and a higher proportion of covert aggression items was selected about Heike. These findings suggest that participants indeed engaged in positive testing, selecting predominantly hypothesis-matching questions.

Table 4.2 Mean scores for positive testing for proportions of overt behavior in the 75% and 25% confirmation condition

	75% confirmation rate		*25% confirmation rate*	
	Heike	*Peter*	*Heike*	*Peter*
Positive testing proportion overt	0.30	0.59	0.40	0.54

Having established the premise, a sufficiently strong positive testing strategy to guide information search, along with the fixed 75% confirming feedback schedule, the next question of interest is whether frequency estimates would reveal the same "illusory correlations" as described in the last chapter. The pertinent results are summarized in Figure 4.2. Two findings are noteworthy from the CELA perspective. First, frequency estimates were generally quite accurate, though somewhat regressive as usual. In other words, substantial learning had taken place. Second, however, the regression effect (i.e., the underestimation of the invariant 75% aggression rate) was again stronger for those categories for which only small

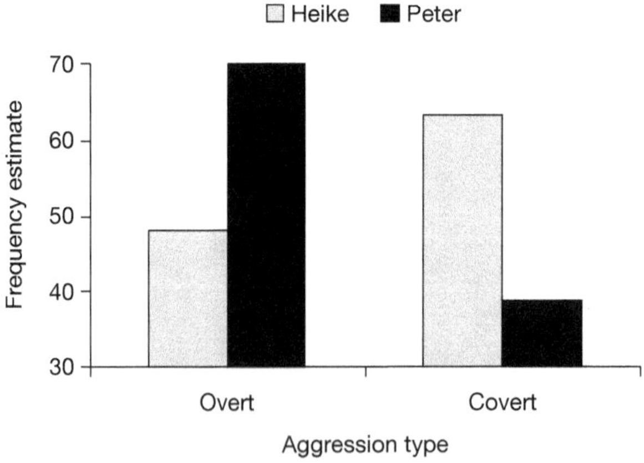

Figure 4.2 Mean estimated frequencies of overt and covert aggression.

samples were available, due to positive testing. The aggression rate was thus judged to be lower for Peter's covert and Heike's overt aggression than for Peter's overt and Heike's covert aggression.

Finally, this illusory difference was also apparent when participants rated the targets on traits related to overt aggression (violence and peacefulness) and on traits related to covert aggression (scheming vs. frankness). Figure 4.3 gives the major results. The trait ratings confirmed the expected auto-verification effect. Heike was judged to be higher in covert aggression, and Peter was judged to be higher in overt aggression. This was the case because participants drew more items about Peter's than about Heike's overt aggression, and the reverse occurred for covert aggression. These larger samples led to better learning and therefore to stronger associations between the targets and the stereotype consistent aggression categories. Evidence to support this interpretation will be presented shortly.

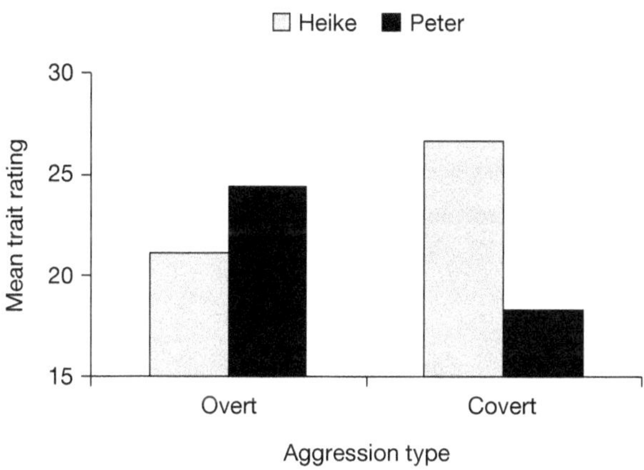

Figure 4.3 Mean trait ratings of overt and covert aggressiveness over both targets.

While these results corroborate the notion of auto-verification, a reasonable objection might be that both positive testing and trait ratings are nothing but a reflection of stereotypical preconceptions held by the judges. Thus, participants might have freely ignored confirmation rates and only relied on superficial stereotypical guessing on all dependent variables. Just because most participants may have expected overt aggression mainly in males and covert aggression mainly in females, they may have looked out for expectancy-congruent cases, and relied on expectancy-based guessing on subsequent judgment tasks. Such skepticism seems justified because a majority of participants indicated in response to a questionnaire that they actually believed in such stereotypical concepts about female covert and male overt aggression. It would indeed be hard to claim that these strong stereotypical preconceptions had had no influence on the trait ratings.

However, regression analyses of the contribution of various factors to predicting the size of the auto-verification effect supported the interpretation that the effect was mainly driven by positive testing, rather than stereotypical expectancies. The one predictor that received the highest weight in predicting both measures of auto-verification—frequency estimates and trait ratings—was a positive testing score defined as the difference between the proportions of overt-aggression items drawn for Peter and Heike. Controlling for the contribution of two other predictors, participants' belief in the aggression–gender stereotype and selective memory for hypothesis-confirming items in a final cued-recall test, the positive-testing score received the highest regression weight (cf. Table 4.3). Together, these findings suggest that differential learning from large versus small samples due to positive testing was the major determinant of auto-verification, but neither stereotype-based guessing nor selective memory.

Table 4.3 Zero-order correlation and regression weights for the predictors of auto-verification

Criterion: Autoverification in stereotype ratings		
	r	*ß*
Predictor		
Positive testing	0.57*	0.47*
Selective memory for confirming items	0.26	0.00
Pre-experimental belief in stereotype	0.44*	0.23

$R = .61, p < .05, F(3,29) = 8.58$
$* = p < .05$

While the findings reported so far at least supported our CELA, the problem remains that sample size and stereotypical preconceptions were confounded, such that larger stimulus samples were gathered for those categories (i.e., male overt and female covert aggression) that were expected on stereotypical grounds. More conclusive empirical evidence for the autonomy of auto-verification from stereotypical preconceptions came from another experiment in which sample size was deliberately detached from prior beliefs. In this study, we manipulated the direction of the hypothesis to be tested. While some participants had to test the common hypothesis, others were instructed to test the reversed—counter-stereotypical—hypothesis that male aggression is predominantly *covert* and female aggression is predominantly *overt*.

In order to detach positive testing from the instruction focus on one particular hypothesis, participants were not asked to select information themselves, but observed how another (computerized) participant drew information about the targets. In this manner, it was possible to have participants witness an information input that involves *negative rather than positive* testing, that is, to include in the stimulus series less positive rather than negative the hypothesis under instructional focus. At the same time, we were able to manipulate whether the hypothesis under focus was stereotypical (male aggression overt, female covert) or counter-stereotypical (male covert, female overt). For example, even when the focus was on the common gender stereotype, a participant could receive 12 items about

Peter's covert aggression and 4 items about his overt aggression, along with 12 items about Heike's overt aggression and 4 items about her covert aggression.

The distinct prediction that can be derived from our environmental learning approach is that sample size should dominate instruction focus and stereotypical expectancies. Thus, subsequent frequency estimates and trait ratings should be higher for male covert and female overt aggression, even though the stereotype was reverse and even when the instruction focus was on testing the hypothesis that male aggression tends to be overt and female aggression covert. The frequency estimates (Figure 4.4) and trait ratings (Figure 4.5) corroborated this predicted pattern. Participants rated Heike higher on overt aggression than Peter, and Peter higher on covert aggression than Heike. These counter-stereotypical judgments convincingly indicated that the impact of sample size was independent of the focus of the hypothesis to be tested, and independent of whether the focal hypothesis was consistent or inconsistent with the stereotype. Larger samples led to better learning and less regressive judgments than smaller samples, even when stereotypical expectancies and stereotype focus counteracted the influence of sample size. Neither the idea nor prejudice participants had in mind but their learning input determined the resulting judgments. This pattern is clearly distinct from a common expectancy effect, which would invariantly predict enhanced or accentuated judgments consistent with the stereotype. It is also incompatible with a demand effect or the assumption that participants want to please the experimenter or comply with the direction of his apparent task instruction.

We hasten to reiterate that these conclusions are by are no means intended to question the potential importance of other factors, such as personal goals and genuine expectancies. The influence of expectancy related to social categories like race, gender, or social status were intensively studied and demonstrated repeatedly. If teachers expect high performance in students, they treat them more warmly, and give them rich opportunities to exhibit high performance (Harris & Rosenthal, 1985), the typical result being a self-fulfilling prophecy. Bailey (1992), for instance,

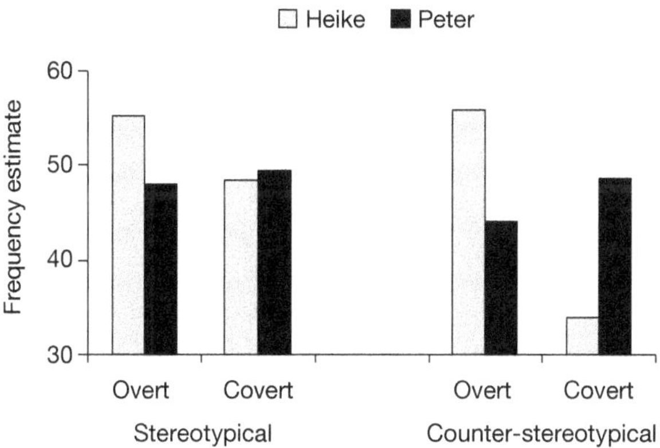

Figure 4.4 Mean estimated frequencies of overt and covert aggression.

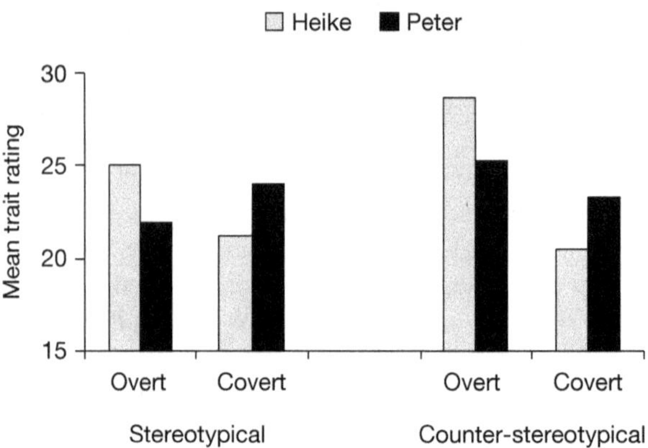

Figure 4.5 Mean trait ratings of overt and covert aggression (Experiment 2).

reported a review, indicating that classroom teachers in principle give more attention and more support to male than to female students. Similar findings have been obtained with respect to other stereotypes showing, for instance, that black kids are encouraged less than white kids (Ross & Jackson, 1991). Such consequences of genuine expectancy-driven confirmation mediated by selective interaction processes—that is, differential treatment of males and females, black and white kids—is also compatible with CELA, just as learning models allow for effects of prior expectancies, or preparedness (Garcia & Koelling, 1966; Seligman, 1970). However, CELA predicts a broader class of auto-verification effects, occurring even when no biased processing is involved and when the true confirmation rate is constant.

The robustness of auto-verification

Under certain conditions, the auto-verification phenomenon even extends to the case when the confirmation rate is relatively low and the modal feedback disconfirms the hypothesis. At first sight, one might expect a reversal when there is no "acquiescence". When the feedback tells 75% of the time that, for instance, overt aggression was not observed, then a large sample might support the participants' learning that overt aggression was low. However, this is not necessarily the case. Even a low rate of overt aggression might be sufficient to infer a disposition of overt aggressiveness. This is because the threshold for inferring such a disposition need not be as high as 75%. Someone who shows overt aggression only 25% of the time may be sufficiently "qualified" as someone who ranks high in overt aggression, just as a rat in a learning experiment that receives painful shocks in 25% of the trials will not infer safety but latent, hard-to-predict danger. It is this asymmetry of positive information (observed aggression, experienced shock) and negative information (lacking aggression, no shock) that permits auto-verification in the case of less than 100% disconfirmation. One or two instances of dishonest behavior (e.g., when your significant other cheats on you) may be more influential than all the other occasions when your partner has been faithful. Few instances of excellent performance are more diagnostic to evaluate an athlete's talent than many mediocre instances (Reeder & Brewer, 1979), and the single lucky chance in which you win the lottery can make you, and all your buddies, lifelong gamblers regardless of the endless series of losses.

Accordingly, when the confirmation rate was reduced from 75% to 25% in the Fiedler et al. (1999b) investigation, the auto-verification effect was not reversed but only reduced (Figure 4.6, Figure 4.7). That means, participants still judged Heike higher on covert aggressiveness and Peter higher on overt aggressiveness. This effect, however, was not simply due to an (illusory) overestimation of confirming response; participants in the 25% confirmation condition exhibited higher

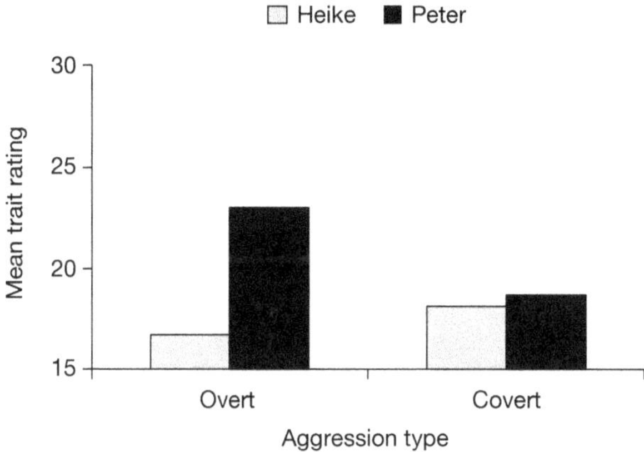

Figure 4.6 Mean trait ratings of overt and covert aggressiveness over both targets in the 25% confirmation condition.

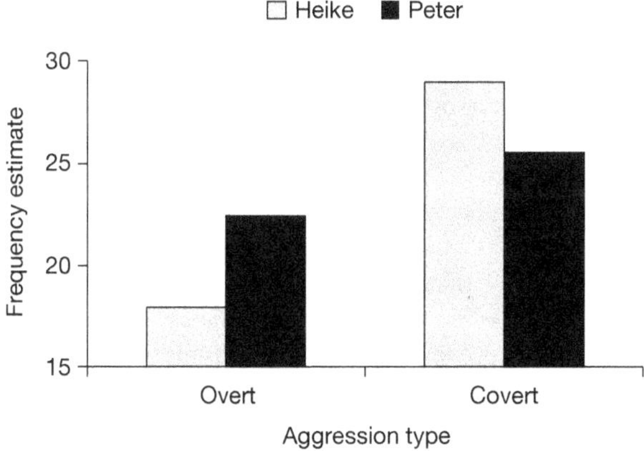

Figure 4.7 Mean estimated frequencies of overt and covert aggression in the 25% condition.

accuracy in the frequency estimates than those in the 75% confirmation condition (see Table 4.4).

These intriguing results, auto-verification under conditions of disconfirmation, are presumably due to the fact that participants "squeeze" more diagnostic information out of a few confirming items than out of a larger number of disconfirming ones. A separate study supported this interpretation in terms of the higher diagnosticity of confirming than disconfirming observations (Lohmann, Fiedler, & Walther, 1998). When participants were required to judge the diagnosticity of observed behaviors (e.g., "Easily gets into a rage") and of missing behaviors ("Does not easily get into a rage"), they attributed generally higher information value to the confirming items. This asymmetry in the diagnosticity of reinforced and non-reinforced trials was particularly observed in cases when the disconfirmation of an attribute had no clear-cut meaningful implications for an opposite attribute. Within our paradigm, for example, the disconfirmation of covert aggressiveness neither implied the target's frankness, nor her overt aggression. Similarly, negation of overt aggression allowed no conclusion about the target's peacefulness.

Table 4.4 Recall accuracy in the 75% and 25% confirmation condition

75% confirmation condition		
Target	Heike	Peter
Overt aggression	0.65	0.77
Covert aggression	0.77	0.76
25% confirmation condition		
Target	Heike	Peter
Overt aggression	0.83	0.83
Covert aggression	0.79	0.80

Whenever attributes are not strictly dichotomous, disconfirmation of the antonym provides no equivalent substitute for the confirmation of the attribute itself. Learning that "Peter does not set traps for others" (absence of covert aggression) is less informative than observing "Peter slapping another's face" (presence of overt aggression). In such not strictly dichotomous cases, positive testing will provide more relevant and diagnostic information than balanced questioning (Hovland & Weiss, 1953; Newman, Wolff, & Hearst, 1980; Trope & Bassok, 1983).

In sum, the latter studies showed that the larger of two samples sometimes even dominates the judgment process when the "environment does not acquiesce very much," that is, when feedback is predominantly disconfirming. Such a seemingly paradoxical outcome can still be explained in terms of environmental learning rules—that allow low "reinforcement rates" to be more informative than several non-reinforced trials.

Can sampling processes provide a remedy against stereotypes?

Nevertheless, provided that disconfirming evidence is sufficiently strong and direct, an obvious implication of learning rules is that it should be possible to unlearn stereotypes by the same rules that underlie their learning. At first glance, this message has a taste of optimism and enlightenment. It seems to be the case that empirical evidence has a real chance to override stereotypical preconceptions. It only seems to be a matter of time and amount of information until stereotypes can be modified and unlearned in much the same way as they have been acquired through environmental learning. However, this prospect may be too optimistic due to a number of non-learning factors. First, the generality of the acquiescence effect may render strong negative feedback quite rare. Moreover, as research on the subtyping phenomenon shows, stereotype-inconsistent observations will often undergo a reinterpretation process by which they are discounted as atypical exemplars (Kunda & Oleson, 1995). For instance, covert aggression exhibited by a male person may not be associated with the category *male* but with the subcategory *softy*. By this mechanism, and a number of other cognitive devices, social individuals can find a way to maintain their stereotypes even in the light of contradictory information. The friendly behavior of a member of a disliked group, for example, can be attributed to external circumstances or the individual can be considered as an atypical group member (Weber & Crocker, 1983). Highly competent female co-workers can be subtyped as belonging to the special category of "career women" which allows one to maintain the gender stereotype (Rothbart & John, 1985). Last but not least, quite independent of such self-deceptive devices for reinterpreting unwanted observations, the social environment will often enough feed us with unequal samples and thereby reinforce existing stereotypes through auto-verification. Thus, figuring out the precise conditions under which stereotypes can be unlearned against the resistance of stereotype-inducing structures in the environment is an ambitious goal for future research.

As we have seen, one universal source of cognitive biases lies in the unequal baserates, or skewedness, of environmental stimulus distributions. Positive testing is one mechanism that produces skewed distributions, but by no means the only one (cf. Chapter 3). Majorities, for example, represent, by definition, larger samples than minorities. The dominant political party normally occupies more space in the newspapers than parties that are not in accordance with the main view. One usually has more information accessible about one's own opinion than about others', leading to higher confidence in one's own position. Also, the so-called egocentric bias (Gilovich, Medvec, & Savitsky, 2000), that is, the tendency to overestimate one's own contributions to various activities relative to the contribution of others, may be partly due to the availability of larger samples of one's own behavior. People also misestimate other people's behavior, for example, the willingness to wear a sign saying "Eat at Joe's" by falsely projecting their own standpoints onto other individuals (Ross, Greene, & House, 1977). Such "false consensus effects" reflect a lack of insight into possible consequences of the fact that samples of self-referent memories are larger than samples of other-referent information. Another sampling effect underlies Jussim et al.'s (1996) demonstration that variations in the focus of information search induced overestimations of people's own ("I am better than the group average") as well as others' ability ("everybody is better than groups' average"; see also Klar & Giladi, 1997). In all these examples, unequal sample size of information may cause serious biases, which to repeat were not contingent on biased processes. In this regard, auto-verification provides a simple and parsimonious alternative explanation for a whole variety of stereotypes and other judgments biases.

Is positive testing irrational?

Even when you are free to select samples of equal size, positive testing may be an appropriate strategy under many conditions (cf. Klayman & Ha, 1987; Oaksford & Chater, 1996). First, under some circumstances, positive testing may be the only way to discover disconfirming instances. This is the case when the correct rule is more restrictive than the hypothesis. For example, when it is true that only a diamond makes her happy, the hypothesis "any gift would make her happy" can only be falsified with positive testing, because a disconfirming strategy will not lead to gifts, and the crucial role of diamonds could never be recognized. Second, as already mentioned, positive testing may be a reasonable strategy when disconfirming feedback is lower in diagnosticity than confirming feedback. For instance, that she wasn't happy with a gift, or with something else, does not mean the opposite, that she was angry or depressive. Third, positive testing is often pragmatically more valuable than other strategies (Einhorn & Hogarth, 1978; Friedrich, 1993). Consider the personnel manager who must select or reject applicants for a secretarial job. It would be hard to check the rejected candidates, who did not meet the criteria, because these persons are usually not available. Fourth, positive testing makes sense when the hypothesis refers to a very small sample. In order to test the hypothesis that all left-handed cab drivers are color blind, it is not very sensible and not very economical to include all the right-handed cab drivers.

These and several other examples illustrate that positive testing is not an inappropriate strategy per se, but may be a reasonable heuristic depending on different situations. Beside this line of argument, there are social goals that may recommend positive testing. To falsify the hypothesis that a person is extremely shy, the question "How would you liven up things on a party?"[1] would be considered relatively rude. Questions derived from positive testing are often perceived as more empathetic, tactful, and warm than falsifying questions (Leyens, Dardenne, & Fiske, 1998).

[1] An item used in the original Snyder and Swann (1978) study.

Further implications of auto-verification

One counter-intuitive manifestation of auto-verification was obtained when confirming feedback was low (say lower than 50%) but the few confirming observations were diagnostic enough to determine the outcome of hypothesis testing. To interpret this finding, we assumed that positive evidence about what was observed can be more informative than negative evidence about what was not observed, or missed. In the empirical research literature, there are several streams of evidence supporting this notion. Merely increasing the frequency of presenting or retrieving a proposition serves to increase the belief that the proposition is true—regardless of whether the evidence for the repeated propositions is strong or weak (Begg, Armour, & Kerr, 1985; Fiedler, Armbruster, Nickel, Walther, & Asbeck, 1996; Gruenfeld & Wyer, 1992; Hasher, Attig, & Alba, 1981; Hertwig, Gigerenzer, & Hoffrage, 1997; Walther, Fiedler, & Nickel, 2002; Wegner, Wenzlafff et al., 1981). Thus, extended discussion, thinking, imagining, or ruminating about criminal offences, airplane crashes, having been abused as a child, contracting a disease, or winning on a gamble can auto-verify the fantasy.

Therefore, the old political notion that "no lie becomes more true through repetition" is psychologically not tenable. In contrary, even denied propositions in a headline (e.g., "Prez has never cooperated with Mafia") may lead to an association between the target and the focal attribute (Wegner et al., 1981). This means that merely raising questions referring to an attribute may be sufficient to increase the corresponding sample, and may thus produce biased judgments, in the absence of affirmative evidence. These demonstrations also highlight the fact that sampling need not result from active information search in the external stimulus world. Analogous effects can be obtained when large versus small samples are drawn from, or construed in, memory, as elaborated in Chapter 5. Consequently, auto-verification is not confined to hypothesis testing in the external environment. It can also result from internal information search in memory, and in general from all situations in which samples of different size serve as a basis for judgments and decisions.

Summary

The present chapter addressed active hypothesis testing. There was ample evidence that people who tested the hypothesis that male aggression is overt and female aggression is covert drew larger samples of observations that matched the given hypothesis. There was also evidence that this one-sided sampling led to the auto-verification of the starting hypothesis. Although the feedback rate was constant for all types of questions, participants arrived at the conclusion that the male target person's aggression was predominantly overt and that the female target's aggression tended to be mainly covert. In contrast to other theories that explain the so-called confirmation bias in social hypothesis testing as a result of selective search for confirming information, as the joint influence of positive testing and acquiescence (Hamilton, 1981; Snyder, 1984; Zuckerman et al., 1995), or as the result of enhanced diagnosticity of the positive testing (Trope & Bassok, 1983; Trope & Thompson, 1997), we delineated an auto-verification effect that is a simple product of skewed sampling and the amount of learning input. This effect of sample size proved to be independent of the participants' prior stereotype expectancies and overrode the focus imposed by the task instruction as well.

5 Information search in the "inner world"

Stereotype origins in constructive memory

In contrast to all previous chapters that focused on information search in the world "out there," the present chapter extends CELA to another ecological space inside the individual, namely, to information search in memory. This expedition to the "inner world" assumes that the basic principles of CELA are equally applicable to hypothesis testing in the external world as well as to the special case of memory sampling. Based on this general assumption the present chapter will address the following empirical and theoretical questions:

- How can hypothesis testing in the "inner world" be described, that is, what basic rules determine sampling processes in memory and what restrictions are imposed on this prominent way of information search?
- How do sampling processes in memory contribute to the explanation of constructive illusions, stereotypical beliefs, and other well-known biases?
- How can the adoption of even false beliefs be explained and what are the consequences of those beliefs for diagnostic judgments?
- Why do experts under some conditions show stronger biases than non-experts?
- How do people think about the future and what guides their decisions of future activities?

Just as information search in the outer world, sampling processes in memory are often one-sided, selective, and incomplete, thus leading to skewed frequencies as a basis of subsequent judgments. In analogy to auto-verification in the outer world, any internal mental activity that increases the amount of information relevant to a hypothesis, such as daydreaming, ruminating, imagining, explaining, basking, and repeating, will often make a hypothesis appear subjectively more valid. Although there are certainly some differences between external and internal environments, especially in terms of subjective control and the variety of stimuli found, the following similarities between both sources of information are particularly noteworthy.

Comparison of information search in memory and in the external world

First, as is the case for information search in the external world, most hypotheses that are tested in memory are determined naturally by the problem environment. Thinking about a person's extraversion implies that the concept of extraversion but not the concept of introversion be activated. Basking in the idea of the next vacations starts a mental film with palm trees on the beach and precludes that the image of the overloaded desk in the office comes to mind. Trying to remember the name of a person you encounter on a conference may interfere with thoughts about other individuals around. Similar effects of competition between different topics of thought can be obtained with other, less intended, procedures such as priming or cueing effects that moderate the accessibility of information in memory (Fiedler & Schenck, 2001; Macrae & Johnston, 1998; Ratcliff & McKoon, 1997; Walther, Dambacher, Dias, & Reich, 1999). Notwithstanding the human mind's capacity for parallel information processing—operations in working memory are often constrained such that one mental focus precludes others—thoughts revolve around one topic at a time, and thereby evade other topics. As a consequence, information search in memory may often focus on a selective sample or a subset of all available information.

Second, following this notion, the outcome of the information search process in both sampling spaces is strongly determined by the distribution of available information. Recent connectionist models indicate that the distribution of information in memory is extremely heterogeneous and multi-dimensional (cf. Smith, 1996). Parallel to stimuli in various parts of the external world, which differ in frequency, proximity, and accessibility, information in memory differs in the degree of elaboration, richness and accessibility, too. Based on the framework proposed by Gill, Swann, and Silvera (1998), *richness* can be defined as the amount of stored information referring to a particular concept, and *elaboration* as the interconnectedness of this knowledge with related concepts. Older and infrequently activated information is less accessible than recently encoded and frequently used knowledge.

The memorized world need not be a perfect reflection of the originally encountered, external world. There are several mechanisms that can cause the memorized ecology to diverge from the original, such as selective encoding, structuring, reorganization, and forgetting. Due to uneven media coverage (Slovic, 1996), particular associations may be more likely to carry over to memory than others. For instance, frequent and vivid reports of criminal acts associated with Turkish immigrants may exaggerate the link. If the group of Turkish immigrants comes to mind, the activation of criminal acts may foster stereotypical judgments, not (or not only) because retrieval processes are biased, but because the memorized ecology is selective in the first place.

In memory, we also encounter ironic processes similar to self-defeating prophecies (Wegner, 1994). Trying to suppress, for instance, the stereotype of a Turkish immigrant can paradoxically *increase* the probability that the Turk comes to mind. This is due to the fact that information in memory cannot be physically avoided as in the case of external information sampling. If I broke the diet on the weekend it is possible to avoid unpleasant feelings on Monday simply by not weighing myself. If I do not want to talk to my mother-in-law I can easily ignore the ringing telephone. However, it is much more difficult, if not impossible, to completely avoid accessible information from memory entering consciousness. On the contrary, the very attempt to avoid memorized information can have the counter-intentional effect of making that information hyper-accessible. This "ironic" effect occurs because the very process of suppression must permanently keep in mind *what* is to be suppressed, at least on a preconscious level (Macrae, Bodenhausen, Milne, & Jetten, 1994; Wegner, 1994). Thus, the very monitoring process about aggressive Turks that is required to avoid thinking about the stereotype of aggressive Turks increases involuntarily the accessibility of the stereotype contents in memory.

Third, if it is true that the external world appears different when observed and experienced from different perspectives, this is even more true for the world in mind, which varies with the psychological state of the individual. For instance, mood congruency refers to the phenomenon that mood-consistent information has an advantage to be retrieved compared to mood-inconsistent information. Other examples are fatigue, depression, cognitive business or thought suppression, to mention but a few from the endless list of variables that modify access to information in memory, due to changes in mental states.

Fourth, in the same way as analyzing sampling processes in the outer world sheds light on general principles of information processing, investigating sampling in memory can enhance our understanding of how memory operates. A clear recollection of an event, for instance, is not always a reliable indicator that an event has actually occurred. For a variety of reasons (e.g., impaired attention, decay, forgetting, repression), it is possible that no recollection is retained even though the stimulus was originally present. Conversely, the presence of a memory trace need not imply that an event actually happened. Due to source confusion, memories of real events may be confounded with states that imagination, dreams, and fantasies have generated (Johnson, Hashtroudi, & Lindsay, 1993).

Fifth, the same basic learning principle, according to which larger samples make predominant tendencies in the ecology more visible than small samples (see Chapters 3 and 4), can be applied to information search in memory. Extended memory search processes that result in a relatively large sample of information relevant to a particular idea will probably increase the subjective meaning or validity of this idea (Begg, Armour, & Kerr, 1985; Gigerenzer, 1984; Hasher, Goldstein, & Toppino, 1977).

Sixth, similar to the preceding chapter, in which no high amount of confirming evidence was necessary for auto-verification to occur, the influence of memory search on hypothesis testing is not strictly confined to recall of information that provides strong confirming evidence. Merely considering the possibility of a proposition ("Is this person a criminal?") can influence subsequent judgments in a congruent direction (i.e., the probability of judging the person as criminal increases). According to Gilbert, Krull, and Malone (1990), such an influence of merely considering a possibility is confined to shallow processing, when people are distracted from critical assessment, but the effect should disappear when participants engage in critical assessment of the proposition's validity. Our learning approach predicts a more robust effect. Even when the proposition is critically evaluated to be wrong (it is denied that someone is mentally ill), merely raising the proposition may affect subsequent judgments. The very act of thinking about the hypothesis entails construing the target person for a moment in the context of the proposed attribute, and the memory and learning process involved in this construal can have an enduring effect.

Before we present several studies that examined this notion empirically, the general process of information search in memory can be illustrated with reference to the graphical representation in Figure 5.1. In this diagram, the elementary case of hypothesis testing is extended to the case in which the agent raises questions matching or mismatching the focal hypothesis, and the target tries to answer these questions by drawing information from memory. Whereas the part of the agent, or hypothesis tester, was examined extensively in previous chapters, in this section we provide evidence that target's memory search will often respond with hypothesis-confirming rather than disconfirming answers. If the target, for instance, is asked about pro-social activities, it is more likely that she will respond consistently than that she will present examples of anti-social behavior. However,

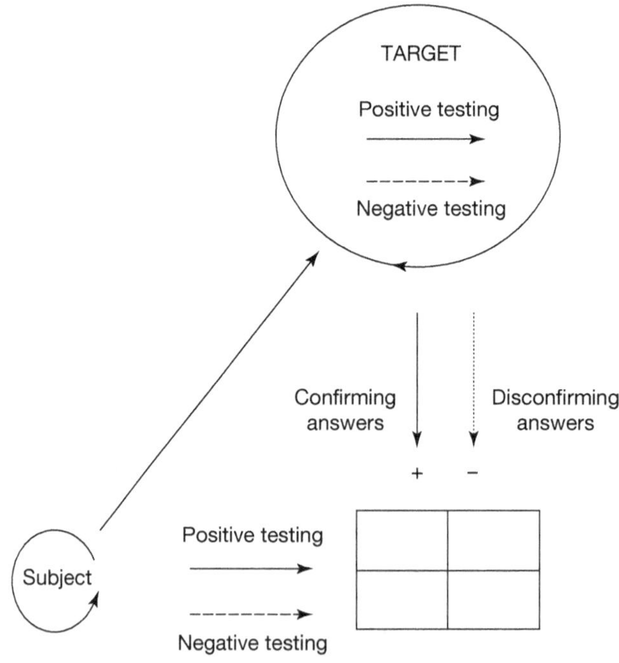

Figure 5.1 Hypothesis testing in memory.

when asked about anti-social behavior, the very same individual will presumably come up with confirming answers. Most people find evidence for different and even opposite behavior in memory, depending on the prompt or focus of hypothesis. Granting corresponding interview questions, almost everyone is able to find evidence for extraverted as well as for introverted behaviors, for intelligent as well as for dump action, for pro-social as well as for anti-social behavioral episodes in memory. Thus, the constructive memory processes dealt with in the present chapter are located within the target, complementing the agent's search processes examined in the last chapter.

Constructive memory

A growing body of experimental research and field studies has shown that suggestive influences (e.g., leading questions, presuppositions, false post-event information) can lead to biased judgments in pre-school children as well as in normal adults (Ceci & Bruck, 1995; Loftus, 1993; Loftus, Feldman, & Dashiell, 1995; Wells & Bradfield, 1998). However, while there is high agreement on the existence of such *constructive memory illusions*, the underlying processes are not entirely clear. One of the most prominent explanations for these phenomena was advanced by Loftus (1979) in her account of eyewitness errors evoked by leading questions. According to this explanation, erroneous eyewitness reports are the result of a mental construction process induced when eyewitnesses are exposed to post-event questions and suggestions about the original episode they have witnessed. The very process of comprehending, and responding to, post-event suggestions is assumed to create a transient representation which is then incorporated into the representation of the original information.

In one pertinent study (Loftus & Palmer, 1974), participants watched a video of a car crash, and then they were asked to estimate the speed of a car that was involved. The estimated speed depended strongly on the wording of the question. The question: "How fast was the car going as they *hit* each other?" led to slower speed ratings than the question: "How fast was the car going as they *smashed* in each other?". Interestingly, the "eyewitnesses" in the "smash" condition also erroneously remembered more broken glass than participants in the "hit" condition. In another series of studies, participants got to read a description of a car crash in which a stop sign was mentioned, whereas the original video contained a yield sign. Subsequent recognition data indicated that several participants falsely believed that a stop sign was part of the original film. These and many similar findings indicate that leading questions or post-event suggestions have a systematic impact on the mental (re)construction of past events.

Applying CELA to memorized information can contribute to the understanding of such constructive memory illusions. In fact, a particularly strong and counter-intuitive variant of constructive memory effects can be derived from the simple associative learning rules that underlie the CELA. Analogous to auto-verification in spite of predominantly disconfirming information (see last chapter), constructive memory illusions can even be induced by disconfirmed suggestions, that is, by suggestions that an individual denies as *not* true, or *not* belonging to the original episode in the first place.

Let us illustrate this point with reference to a typical task situation used in many eyewitness studies. A witness has just seen a video film with a car accident at an intersection where in fact a yield sign could be seen. Later on, the witness is asked whether she saw a stop sign, and correctly disconfirms the proposed information, denying to have seen a stop sign. Nevertheless, when the witness is asked the same question some days later, the very treatment of answering (and correctly denying) the stop-sign question may actually *increase* the likelihood that the witness will now believe having seen a stop sign. Thus, associative rules do not require that the witness believes in the truth of the information suggested in the question or, stated differently, that memory search confirms the hypothesis. Rather, the mere association of a stop sign with the original episode in the transient representation that has to be constructed for a moment in answering the question offers a sufficient explanation. Note that the cognitive process assumed in this explanation does not adhere to logical rules but is driven by more primitive associations that do not conserve logical truth values.

Similarly, if you were asked whether the young Turk, Cueneyt, is a criminal, you might hesitate because you never observed him engaging in criminal acts. Thus, you probably answer the question negatively; there is no evidence of criminality except for the question. Nevertheless, your subsequent judgment about Cueneyt might show a bias towards the criminal category. This is possible because (1) valid information about Cueneyt is scarce so that uncertainty is high enough; (2) one of the few available associations link him to the concept of criminality. When you are then asked to judge Cueneyt, the memory environment created under such conditions fosters an information search process that facilitates references to criminality. We not even need to assume that the target is a member of a stereotyped group (e.g., Turks). The same constructive process might work with a neutral target, "Hans," when the link between the target and aggressiveness is supported by relevant associative structures. Regarding Hans as a criminal for a moment leads to the activation of criminal-related information that is inevitably associated with him during the consideration process. In the absence of any other available information, it is this associated knowledge that guides subsequent judgments.

The remainder of this chapter is mainly devoted to empirical demonstrations of such a strong and counter-intuitive version of constructive memory effects. We demonstrate that when hypotheses are tested through information search in memory, the impact of activated associations will not be greatly restricted by validity concerns, or logical truth value. Even when the hypothesis is denied or disconfirmed, it may still activate associations that serve to verify the hypothesis, psychologically. This will be shown to hold even though alternative accounts in terms of demand effects or a truth bias (i.e., to believe in the suggestion, according to Grice's, 1975 maxim of quality) can be ruled out, as clearly evident in suggestions being (correctly) denied.

That false information can influence subsequent judgments, indeed, is not new. In the aforementioned work of Gilbert and colleagues (Gilbert, Krull, & Malone,

1990), the adoption of false propositions is explained as the result of a two-stage process: In the first step, a proposition is always considered as true by default. That propositions are actually false can only be recognized in a second, critical assessment stage, which requires more cognitive resources than the first step. According to this conception, false propositions will be normally discovered and discarded when they undergo critical assessment; that is, when the second process stage is reached. However, the default truth assumption will survive, and false propositions may be erroneously adopted, when the second stage is precluded, due to cognitive load or distraction. If, however, an individual is asked explicitly whether a proposition is true (e.g., if she saw a stop sign), and if the explicit answer is negative, then the stage of critical assessment—and hence the correct rejection of the false proposition—is enforced. Thus, the refined, two-stage model suggested by Gilbert and colleagues is not able to account for constructive memory effects obtained after denied hypotheses.

Empirical evidence

False recognition: Do you really know what you have seen?

A series of experimental studies (Fiedler, Walther, Armbruster, Fay, & Naumann, 1996) tested the idea that thinking about various never-presented stimuli can lead to the misattribution of these stimuli as really perceived, that is, to a false recognition effect. Participants in these studies answered questions about the interior of a flat presented on a video tape. Questions referred to objects (presented in the film) or non-objects (not presented in film) and were asked in different linguistic format, either as presuppositions (e.g., Was the umbrella stand in the corridor made of brass?) or in open format (Was there an umbrella stand in the corridor?). Later on, the effect of this manipulation on recognition performance was examined. In keeping with previous studies, we hypothesized that presuppositions should be particularly effective in causing constructive illusions (Loftus, 1975, 1979). The advantage of presuppositions in contrast to open questions is presumably due to the fact that presuppositions facilitate constructive processes in memory. In contrast to open questions, which raise the possibility that the non-object might have been present, presuppositions take the object for granted. Accordingly, presuppositions should be a more effective means for including a non-object in the mental representation than an open question. Notwithstanding the higher constructive potential of presuppositions, however, we expected that open questions should be sufficient to produce constructive memory reports.

After participants had answered a series of questions about various objects and non-objects in the film, they were administered a recognition test that included different classes of items: actually presented objects, questioned non-objects, and unquestioned non-objects. For the analysis of memory illusions, we were mainly interested in false recognition of non-objects. We assumed that merely answering a question about a non-object would increase the probability that such a non-object would later be falsely recognized, in comparison with unquestioned (control) non-objects. Unlike other accounts, however, CELA predicts that this should even happen when questions were correctly denied. This is because the association of the question contents with the mental representation of the flat, once built during the process of consideration, cannot be undone and influences subsequent judgments.

The major results from the recognition test are given in Table 5.1. It can be seen that the hit rate of objects correctly classified as belonging to the flat amounts to 77%. At the other extreme, the false alarm rate for incorrect recognition of control non-objects not mentioned in the questioning list was 7%. Most important, however, and consistent with our expectations, the false-recognition rate for non-objects was clearly enhanced, being 35% for presuppositions as compared with 12% for non-objects suggested in open questions.

One aspect that weakens previous accounts of constructive memory effects (Loftus, 1979) is that genuine memory influences cannot be distinguished from guessing and demand effects (cf. McCloskey & Zaragoza, 1985). Thus, our prediction that false recognitions would persist even for denied non-objects is of particular theoretical interest. It rules out demand effects as a cause of false positives in recognition. Had participants fallen prey to demands provided by the experimenter's question for non-existing objects, we would have expected a majority of "yes" answers to the questions. Moreover, the memory intrusions should be largely confined to those items that were already endorsed at the time when the question exerted the demand effect. The right part of Table 5.1 shows that when the outcome of the questioning was controlled, that is, when only denied non-objects were included in the memory analysis, there was still a sizable proportion of memory intrusions. Given the correct rejection of a false presupposition, the recognition rate dropped only slightly, from 35% to 31%. The false recognition rate for non-objects in open questions dropped from 12% to 9% after correct rejection (see Table 5.1).

Taken together, these findings supported the notion that false recognition is neither confined to subjectively true or confirmed information, nor to demand-like artifacts (McCloskey & Zaragoza, 1985). The independence from such restrictions was highlighted in the central finding that false recognition decreased little when

Table 5.1 Mean recognition rates (%) for stimuli of the different conditions

	Recognition	*Recognition/Rejected*
Objects		
Hits	77	—
Non-Objects		
False alarms (control)	07	—
Presuppositions	35	31
Open questions	12	09

only correctly rejected non-objects were considered. The mere process of comprehending and considering a proposition necessary to respond to questions was sufficient to change memory structures, which in turn influenced further judgments. Furthermore, a follow-up study showed that the strength of constructive memory increased when the time interval between questioning and the memory test was extended. In contrast, the time interval between the presentation of the original information and the questioning treatment did not have an influence (cf. Fiedler, Walther, Armbruster, Fay, & Naumann, 1996, Study 2). This corroborates the interpretation that false recognition reflects constructive activities elicited *after* the questioning treatment rather than forgetting of the original information prior to the questioning that might have facilitated guessing effects.

Further support for the notion that merely considering (false) propositions may be sufficient to induce false memories comes from several other lines of research. For instance, the subjective likelihood of an event increases through thinking about the causes of that event (Wells & Gavanski, 1989) or trying to explain the event (Koehler, 1991; Ross, Lepper, Strack, & Steinmetz, 1977). Schul and Burnstein (1985) have long shown that when participants were explicitly told to discount a subset of false information they had received about a stimulus person, they were often unable to do so. This was especially the case when the false information had been encoded in an integrative fashion, linking false propositions to the remaining stimulus information. Perhaps the most impressive demonstration of people's inability to get rid of a falsely induced representation comes from the perseverance paradigm (Ross et al., 1975), in which debriefing of participants is often not sufficient to fully erase the impact of prior experimental deceptions. In these studies the participants first received false feedback, indicating that they had either succeeded or failed on a novel discrimination task, and then were thoroughly debriefed concerning the predetermined and random nature of this outcome manipulation. Nevertheless participants showed substantial perseverance of initial impressions concerning the performance and abilities.

It would not be justified to assume that constructive memory effects occur to the same degree under each and every condition. The next sections will point out specific boundary conditions—particularly relevant to social stereotypes—that specify when hypothetical information will be confirmed or disconfirmed through memory search.

The impact of prior knowledge I: Richness and the degree of elaboration

The studies presented so far did not address the issue of how constructive influences are constrained by the structure of prior knowledge. However, just as the outcome of hypothesis testing in general is contingent on environmental support, the special case of hypothesis testing in memory is contingent on the supporting role of available knowledge structures. The purpose of the present section is to demonstrate how prior knowledge (e.g., schemas, concepts, stereotypes) plays a major role in the cognitive process underlying hypothesis testing in memory, and the resulting constructive judgment effects. One intriguing implication that we pursued in further experiments is that experts who have rich and elaborated knowledge may exhibit stronger constructive biases than non-experts whose knowledge is less elaborated and rich. The richer and more elaborated memorized are the knowledge structures, the more likely and the stronger should be the associative processes that can be solicited when hypothetical attributes are suggested, or primed (Bargh & Pietromonaco, 1982; Higgins & King, 1981; Higgins, Rholes, & Jones, 1977; Srull & Wyer, 1979), and the stronger should be the potential impact on subsequent judgments (Bruner, 1957). As repeatedly emphasized, knowledge activation is not greatly restricted by the subjective truth of a question or a hypothesis. However, although the initial process of knowledge activation is not restricted to valid or true information, the consequences of knowledge activation for subsequent judgments depend on the paths determined by prior knowledge. We examined these epistemic constraints on constructive memory biases in a series of studies in which knowledge structures were operationalized in different ways.

In one study (Walther, 1997) undergraduate students were considered as non-experts in clinical psychology, whereas graduate students who had already received some training in clinical psychology were considered experts. Similar to most studies that examine constructive processes (Loftus, 1979), the study consisted of two phases: a pre-information phase and a (suggestive) questioning phase. In the pre-information phase participants were provided with test data and clinical information implying that a target patient suffered from depression. In the questioning phase, then, they had to listen to a tape-recorded clinical interview. Many interview questions concerned the hypothesis that the target patients could be characterized by mania (i.e., "Would you say that you overestimate your abilities?" "Are you restless?"). The clinical judgment setting and the mania hypothesis were chosen for a number of theoretical and practical considerations: First, it was necessary to find a content domain in which the level of knowledge can vary sufficiently. Mania was chosen because pilot tests had indicated that this disease met the necessary criterion: unlike other clinical concepts such "schizophrenia" or "autism", which appear to be equally familiar to virtually all students, the mania concept is rather unknown to laypeople without clinical training. Second, in order to replicate that constructive biases extend to denied contents, we needed a concept that was not necessarily implied by the major disease, depression. Pre-tests indicated that mania and depression symptoms in the same individual are possible, but not very likely, as clinical experts know (though the mania-depression link is well established in expert knowledge). A clinical judgment task situation was chosen because it provided a prototypical interview and judgment setting. Moreover, constructive biases supposed to be facilitated by expert knowledge may have particularly serious consequences in clinical settings.

While listening to the mania interview, participants were asked to take the role of the target and to answer the questions asked by the interviewer as they believe the target would have. The rationale behind this procedure was threefold. First, we assumed that the mere process of listening, understanding, and responding to the mania questions would be sufficient to activate relevant knowledge and that this effect should be stronger in experts than in non-experts. Second, participants' own responses towards the mania questions were an important source of information because they allow us to estimate the subjective "validity" of the hypothetical suggestions. On theoretical and empirical grounds, we assumed that even questions that elicit disconfirming answers may evoke constructive processes. Because the symptoms of mania are not very likely in a depressive target, we expected a sufficiently high number of denials to demonstrate that constructive biases are not restricted to affirmed information. Third, the primary answers to the mania questions were assessed because they help to rule out alternative explanations for the knowledge-based account in terms of demand effects or other unintended communication effects (Grice, 1975; Orne, 1973). The assumption that participants yielded to demand characteristics would not be tenable if their own answers to the interview questions were predominantly negative.

The final judgments of the target patient on various trait attributes related to depression and mania indicated in fact that experts rated the target higher in mania than non-experts did, although most of the mania questions had been disconfirmed in both groups (see Table 5.2, lower part). Merely considering a target's mania was sufficient to judge the target as manic, even when little evidence could be found to support the hypothesis. These constructive influences were stronger when propositions encountered rich and elaborate knowledge structures. That is, experts exhibited stronger constructive illusions than non-experts. Altogether, these findings confirmed our theoretical predictions.

One might argue that the manipulation of the knowledge structure in the above experiment was rather weak, because it relied on the selection of participants and their pre-existing knowledge. It is also possible that differences other than prior knowledge (e.g., clinical practice, age) were responsible for the results. We thus replicated these findings in another study (Walther, 1997) in which knowledge was

Table 5.2 Mean adjective ratings and responses to the interview. Higher numbers indicate higher mania ratings (standard deviations in parenthesis). The maximum value of denied answers amounts to six

Mania ratings		
Prior knowledge	*Experts*	*Non-experts*
Interview condition		
Interview	62.84 (16.04)	52.04 (16.26)
No interview	42.81 (11.18)	42.01 (13.6)
Responses to the interview ("no" answers)		
Prior knowledge	*Experts*	*Non-experts*
Interview	4.47 (1.55)	4.67 (1.29)

manipulated experimentally, rather than relying on participants with different backgrounds of experience. One group of participants (experts) acquired the mania concept and another group (non-experts) acquired a control concept (assistant manager) in an interactive computer-aided learning procedure in the first phase of the experiment.

At the beginning of this phase, participants were informed that they were required to learn symptoms (characteristics) of a specific mental disorder (job requirement) in an interactive computer session. In the expert condition, participants were to judge some patients' mania on the basis of individual symptom profiles. In this condition students also received background information about mania (e.g., prevalence, distribution in the population) and its relation to depression. In the irrelevant knowledge (non-expert) condition, participants had the task of assessing several applicants' job qualification as an assistant manager. Each profile filled a computer screen and consisted of ten symptoms (characteristics) of which some were diagnostic whereas others were irrelevant to the particular judgment. To make correct judgments, participants had to identify the diagnostic symptoms (characteristics) and had to learn whether a high or a low level on the symptom (characteristic) supported mania (job qualification).

Participants of both groups listened then to the mania questions and answered the questions as they believed the target would have. Again we found that experts judged the target higher in mania than non-experts on subsequent rating scales (see Table 5.3). However, similar to the aforementioned experiment, constructive biases only occurred when existing knowledge was activated through input processing (e.g., listening to and answering questions). Thus, judgments in the assistant manager condition did *not* differ from the other groups on control judgment scales related to the attributes of the assistant manager, although participants in this condition were also provided with relevant knowledge. The lack of differences on these control scales also supported the assumption that demand effects or other communication effects played no major role. If participants had misunderstood the learning procedure as a subtle cue to judge the target afterwards with respect to the learned concept, one would have expected differences on the control scales measuring the characteristics of the assistant manager. The present study also replicated that constructive biases occur even when the judges themselves decided that most questions did not match the target patient.

What we learned from these studies is that expert knowledge per se did not lead to constructive biases. Constructive influences were only obtained when this knowledge was elicited through hypothetical questions. Again, this activation process was not restricted to information that was accepted as valid or true. Even when participants found that questions about the patient's mania have to be denied, the activation of associative links from the patient to mania could not be undone and continued to influence the clinical judgments.

The following study (Walther et al., 2002), however, demonstrated that the constructive consequences of activated knowledge are indeed subject to specific constraints. Another purpose of this study was to extend the evidence for constructive illusions to other associative links than the mania-depression link. "Experts"

Table 5.3 Higher numbers indicate higher mania, depression and control ratings (standard deviations in parenthesis). The maximum value of denied answers amounts to six

Mania ratings		
Knowledge structure	*Experts*	*Non-experts*
Empirical information		
Interview	56.38 (19.30)	33.01 (20.44)
No interview	30.90 (16.62)	32.46 (15.08)
Depression ratings		
Knowledge structure	*Experts*	*Non-experts*
Empirical information		
Interview	71.0 (15.37)	60.94 (23.92)
Non-interview	58.14 (22.82)	61.30 (18.27)
Control ratings		
Knowledge structure	*Experts*	*Non-experts*
Empirical information		
Interview	58.82 (13.60)	62.48 (12.75)
Non-interview	59.02 (12.02)	55.40 (13.41)

in this study acquired a fictitious neurological concept ("Lacroix") and its link to depression. Moreover, this study examined the specificity of constructive biases. Thus, experts in this experiment were not only to judge the target but also the therapist, who raised the questions, on several rating scales including "Lacroix."

Recent studies by Skowronski and colleagues indicated that communicators are associated with the description they give of others (Skowronski, Carlston, Mae, & Crawford, 1998). The authors described this phenomenon, in which communicators are perceived as having traits that they merely describe in others, as spontaneous trait transference. It is therefore possible that a therapist, asking questions about a neurological disease would later himself be described with respect to the trait (i.e., symptoms) he asked.

In contrast, CELA predicts that enhanced "Lacroix" judgments should be restricted to the depressed target because it relied on the specific activated knowledge structure that links the two concepts—depression and "Lacroix". Figure 5.2 indicates, not surprisingly, that all participants judged the target to be depressive, but only the experts who listened to "Lacroix" questions judged the target also as suffering from "Lacroix." That constructive biases could be obtained on the basis of a fictitious disease not only broadened the scope of the empirical findings but was also helpful to rule out other alternative influences stemming from prior world knowledge that could have influenced constructive biases. Moreover, this experiment showed that constructive biases were specific and did not generalize to other individuals, because they relied on the particular knowledge associated with the target. Only the target, not the therapist, got high "Lacroix" ratings (see Figure 5.3). Whereas the activation of stored knowledge is quite similar to priming effects and not confined to valid or confirmed information, the subsequent process of using the activated knowledge for judgmental inferences is apparently constrained by specific links or knowledge structures.

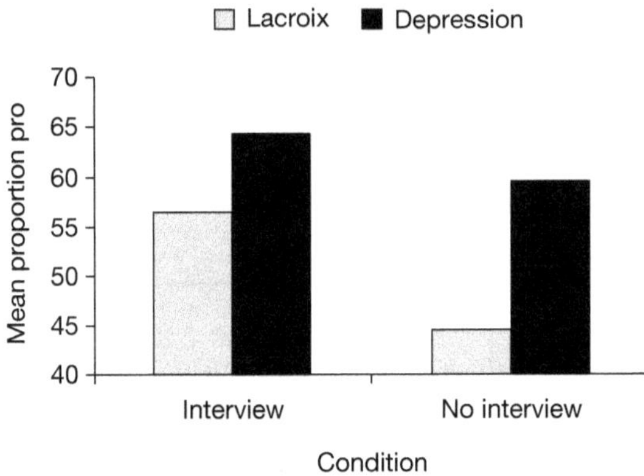

Figure 5.2 Mean "Lacroix-" and depression ratings in the interview and no interview condition.

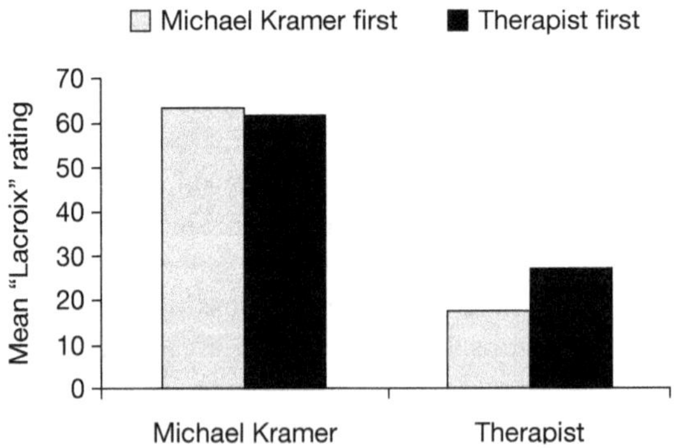

Figure 5.3 Mean "Lacroix-" ratings of the target and the therapist.

The impact of prior knowledge II: The linguistic category model

More evidence for this notion comes from another set of studies (Fiedler et al., 1996). In one of these studies, participants watched a video-taped group discussion on diet food. During the discussion participants were asked to either focus on the talk-master or on an active other male person. Depending on the experimental condition, participants received questions about 12 evaluative positive behaviors (e.g., support, agree, assist) or about 12 evaluative negative behaviors (e.g. insult, provoke, offend). A short time after this questioning treatment, participants were required to judge the target on 12 traits matching the previously answered behavioral questions (e.g., aggressive after offend, or helpful after assist). Although both groups received the same stimulus information in the film, answering the evaluative positive questions led to more benevolent judgments than processing the negative information (see Figure 5.4 for some of the results). Similar to the other studies mentioned above, this constructive effect occurred although most of the behavioral questions were initially rejected as false. Apparently, merely considering evaluative, positive information activated relevant knowledge structures, which in turn influenced subsequent judgments.

However, this study also revealed how the constructive process is constrained by linguistic-semantic knowledge. According to the notion of *implicit verb causality* and the broader framework of the linguistic category model (LCM; Fiedler & Semin, 1988), cognitive inference paths are restricted by the implications of the verbs used in behavior descriptions. One class of verbs, the so-called action verbs (IAVs), elicit a causal schema that supports attributions of the behavior to the sentence subject. For example, the meanings of verbs like *insult*, *provoke*, or *offend* imply attributions of behaviors to the subject person who insults, provokes, or offends others, rather than the object person who is insulted, provoked, or offended. In accordance with this quite general rule (Brown & Fish, 1983; Fiedler & Semin, 1988; Rudolph & Försterling, 1997), only judgments of subject targets

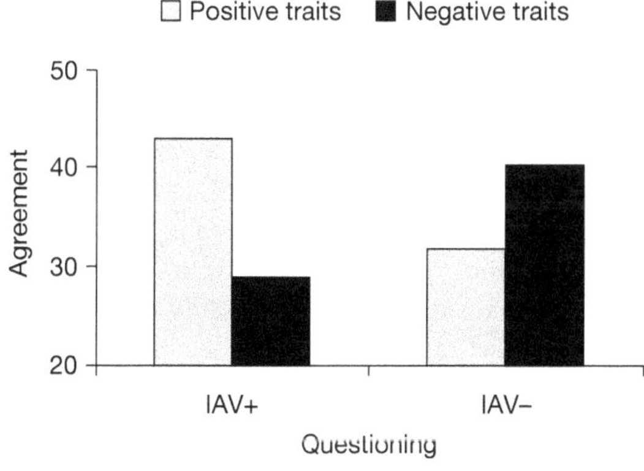

Figure 5.4 Mean ratings of the target on positive and negative traits as a function of positive (IAV+) and negative (IAV–) questions.

who were playing an active role in the film, but not judgments of passive object persons, were influenced by questions that entailed such action verbs. Thus, when judges were asked whether negative action verbs were descriptive of an agent in the film, resulting judgments were more negative (e.g., insult, provoke, offend) than when positive action verbs were used (e.g., help, encourage). Again, this even worked when judges felt they could not find those negative or positive actions in the target's behavior.

In another condition, verbs from a different category were used for questioning, namely, negative (e.g., hate, abhor, disgust) or positive (e.g., love, admire) *state verbs* that imply attributions to the sentence object. Thus, the meaning of hate, abhor and disgust implies that something about the object person being hated, abhorred, or disgusted is the origin of the behavior, rather than something about the subject person who only reacts emotionally, but not intentionally. That constructive effects can follow quite sophisticated constraints is evident in a reversed pattern of results. Questions using state verbs only affected subsequent judgments of persons playing a passive object role in the film and—because external attributions are implied—questions about a target's negative states caused a shift toward more *positive* judgments, because state verb schemas entail an excuse for negative behavior. Conversely, questions referring to positive states induced relatively more *negative* judgments.

Altogether, these results provided reasonable evidence that constructive influences proceed within the confines of specific knowledge structures. Whether the hypotheses raised in questions are met with confirmation or disconfirmation depends on the match between the environment (i.e., the film) and the domain of application of the hypothesis (i.e., the constraints imposed by the verb schema).

The most prominent research evidence for the role of language in stereotype formation and maintenance comes from the so-called *linguistic intergroup bias* (LIB). The LIB (Maass, Salvi, Arcuri, & Semin, 1998; Maass, Ceccerelli, & Rudin, 1996) illustrates how the use of particular word classes in descriptions of ingroup and outgroup behaviors can contribute to the formation and maintenance of outgroup discrimination and ingroup favoritism. Very often, the same behavioral episode can be described at different levels of abstraction, using different linguistic categories. The linguistic category model (Semin & Fiedler, 1988, 1991) distinguishes four levels of increasing abstractness: *descriptive action verbs* (DAVs: telephone, kiss, tickle) at the most concrete level, *interpretive action verbs* (IAVs: help, insult, hurt), *state verbs* (SVs: hate, like, abhor) and, at the abstract end, *adjectives* (ADJs: honest, aggressive, fair). Abstract terms imply more internal attributions of behaviors to disposition traits than concrete terms. The ADJ "aggressive," for example, implies that somebody is essentially hostile and probably dangerous and unlikable, whereas the DAV "raise his hand" used to describe the same physical attack hardly carries any strong person inferences with it.

Maass and colleagues (Maass et al., 1989) found that people encode and communicate favorable ingroup and undesirable outgroup behavior more abstractly (they used more SVs and ADJs) than unfavorable ingroup and desirable outgroup behavior (described with more DAVs and IAVs). Thus, what is desired and expected (Maass et al., 1996; Wigboldus et al., 2000) is described in more abstract terms, and thus given more psychological weight than what is undesired and unexpected. Given these general rules of language use, an information ecology is created in the literature, in newspapers and in public and private conversations that can obviously serve to reinforce and maintain existing stereotypes and prejudices (Karpinski & Von Hippel, 1996; Schmid & Fiedler, 1998).

Memory for reasons for or against a hypothetical judgment

In a series of intriguing studies, Koriat and colleagues (Koriat, Lichtenstein, & Fischhoff, 1980) investigated the possibility that judgments of confidence are biased by attempts to justify one's chosen answer. These attempts include selectively focusing on evidence supporting the chosen answer and disregarding evidence contradicting it. Participants were presented forced-choice trivia questions and required to list reasons for and against each of the alternatives prior to choosing an answer and assessing the probability of being correct. Results strongly suggested that the confidence ratings depended on the amount and strength of the evidence supporting the answer chosen. Interestingly, however, confidence decreased when participants were forced to consider contradicting reasons. The findings of Koriat et al. (1980) provide another demonstration of the manner in which information search in memory can dramatically restrict the information environment available for hypothesis testing.

Inspired by the seminal work of Koriat et al. (1980), we wondered whether the construal of an information ecology through active memory search can be influenced systematically. We were particularly interested in the influence of *temporal perspective*. In a series of studies (Walther & Trope, 2002), we examined participants' spontaneous reactions vis-à-vis future events and assessed the construals people generated in the face of these events. Information searches of future instead of past activities were addressed because we wished to examine the actual process of construction rather than retrograde retrieval processes. Moreover, we assumed that the construction of future events underlies particular restrictions. In accordance with the *temporal construal theory* (TCT) by Liberman and Trope (1998), we assumed that temporal distance influences individuals' responses to future events by systematically changing the way of construal.

More specifically, TCT states that individuals form more abstract representations, or high-level construals, of distant future events but more concrete representations, or low-level construals, of near future events. TCT also predicts that high-level construals are more schematic, coherent, and abstract than low-level construals. Whereas low-level construals are specific, subordinate and context dependent, high-level construals consist of general and superordinate features (Rosch, 1978; Semin & Fiedler, 1988; Vallacher & Wegner, 1987). If distant future construals are guided by abstract schemas, the influence of an abstract concept like desirability should increase with temporal distance. According to TCT, the *desirability* of an event refers to the end state of an action reflecting the *why* aspect of an outcome. This implies that desirability belongs to a high level of construal, whereas *feasibility* constitutes a low level of construal. Feasibility reflects the *how* aspect of an action and refers to the subjective ease with which an action is performed (Trope & Liberman, 2000). TCT predicts that the effect of high-level construals (e.g., desirability) is enhanced with time, whereas the effect of a low-level construals (e.g., feasibility) is diminished over time.

The general assumption thereby is that the *mental representation* of an event, action, or outcome depends on the time perspective. Thus, the imagination of an event that takes place in the distant future (e.g., "going ice-skating with your flame next year") may differ remarkably from the mental scenario that is construed of the very same event that takes place in the near future (e.g., "going ice-skating with your flame tomorrow"). While you may see yourself performing risky pirouettes under the envious eyes of the other skaters in the former case (i.e., focus on desirability), you are presumably more concerned with the issue of your smelly feet, when you take off your shoes, in the latter (i.e., focus on feasibility). Thus the inner decision process ("Should I go ice-skating with my flame?") is presumably based on a fairly different scenario when the event is temporarily distant, than when the activity comes closer and closer.

The aim of the present studies was to examine the differences in the mental construal of future activities. In contrast to mere judgment studies, in which individuals were simply asked to estimate the probability of future outcomes (Weinstein, 1980) or the likeability of future events (Buehler, Griffin, & MacDonald, 1997), we investigated the actual process of construal. We asked people to imagine themselves engaging in everyday life activities (e.g., visiting a friend) occurring in the near (tomorrow) or distant future (a year from now), and to generate arguments in favor of and against these activities. To assess the impact of the time perspective, activities were selected that varied with respect to their level of construal, that is, the activities varied in desirability (high vs. low) as well as in feasibility (high vs. low) (cf. Liberman & Trope, 1989; Trope & Liberman, 2000). The proportion of confirming (i.e., arguments favoring the activity) arguments was chosen as an index for the valence of activities. We believed that the generation of these arguments may also shed some light on the construal process underlying decision making and hypothesis testing in general. On the one hand, an activity may be approached because there are several arguments supporting its performance. On the other, the same outcome may be due to a lack of disconfirming arguments. Participants received a booklet with activities varying in their degree of feasibility and desirability and were to list arguments either for or against these activities. We first computed proportions of confirming arguments separately for the different conditions.

A glance at the mean proportions of pro arguments in Figure 5.5 clearly shows a general preponderance of supportive arguments in almost all conditions (all means were higher than 50). However, it is also apparent that there were large differences in proportions depending on the experimental manipulation. Closer inspection revealed that the proportion of confirming arguments was superior for feasible than for desirable activities in the near future, but higher for desirable than for feasible activities in the distant future condition. This suggests that the same

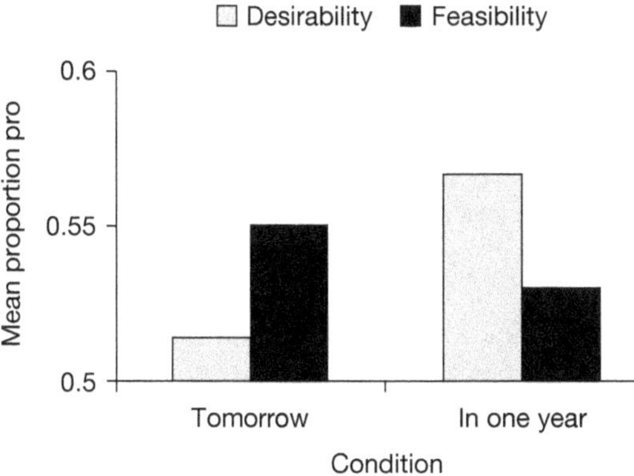

Figure 5.5 Mean proportions of pro arguments for the near and distant future condition.

activities were construed quite differently depending on the time perspective: Whereas arguments for activities that were considered to take place tomorrow were mainly affected by a low level of construal, that is, by considerations of feasibility, pros for activities in the distant future were strongly influenced by a high level of construal, namely their desirability.

In a further study (Walther & Trope, 2002, Study 2), besides the amount of pros and cons, we also assessed the confidence of actually engaging in an activity. The confidence ratings supposedly not only allow an analysis of the mediating role of favoring arguments in predicting confidence (Koriat, Lichtenstein, & Fischhoff, 1980), but also provide an estimation of the attractiveness of the activities in a more direct way. Not surprisingly, the proportion of supportive arguments was strongly related to the confidence to perform the activity. In other words, the relative frequency of arguments mediated further decisions to actually perform the activity.

In sum, this branch of research showed that the construal of information in memory is not a balanced business. In almost all conditions, supporting arguments clearly dominated the responses. Even in the case in which the activities were low in desirability and feasibility, there was still a considerable amount of hypothesis-confirming arguments that came spontaneously to mind within the construal process. However, similar to the aforementioned paradigms (e.g., constructive biases, linguistic category influences) there were also clear-cut constraints imposed on the construction process. Depending on the temporal distance, either desirable or feasible aspects of future activities determined the information contents. Just like the other paradigms reviewed in the present chapter, the manner in which information is sought and construed in memory can substantially alter the information environment in which hypotheses are evaluated and tested.

Summary

The studies reported so far indicated that merely thinking about an attribute or target can result in (stereotypical) judgments even when the incoming information is not believed to be true. Far beyond the explanatory domain of animistic theories, the reported research demonstrated that even counterdictional evidence (i.e., denied questions, rejected propositions) can serve to confirm a hypothesis and influence further judgments. An umbrella stand never perceived in the original film and correctly rejected in the interview still intruded the memory and was falsely recognized in a later memory test. Questions referring to a mental disease (i.e., mania) but hardly confirmed by the target's behavior, and therefore correctly denied by many participants, led to enhanced mania judgments.

Evidence for the idea that invalid information may influence subsequent judgments can also be found in other accounts. Schul and Burnstein (1985), for example, have shown that individuals are often unable to discount a subset of false information. In stereotype research, Macrae and colleagues reported evidence that stereotype-congruent information is not only easy to remember but also particularly hard to *forget* (Macrae, Bodenhausen, Milne, & Ford, 1997). However, none of these accounts addressed the intriguing phenomenon that individuals are biased as a result of intentionally rejected propositions, nor did they experimentally vary knowledge structures.

Another counter-intuitive finding was that experts with differentiated knowledge structures were prone to more constructive influences than non-experts with impoverished knowledge structures. Our results suggest that expert knowledge once activated in the process of comprehending incoming information may lead to constructive biases; that is to say, to judgments not necessarily substantiated by empirical information. Unlike other variables that are widely known to moderate the quality of judgments, the crucial role of prior knowledge has been substantially neglected. Thus, the contribution of our research to applied judgment settings is that we have identified another source of potential failures that are contingent on prior knowledge. However, prior knowledge and schematic structures were not only shown to facilitate constructive processes, but also to constrain the information environment and the hypothesis testing process in characteristic ways.

6 Testing social hypotheses in tri-variate problem space

Further variants of environmental stereotype learning

Returning from the excursion into memory and collective memory (i.e., communication) as an important part of the information environment, we can now go on to refine the paradigm of stereotype learning in a cognitive-ecological framework. Specifically, the present chapter will bring the following extensions and refinements:

- We extend the experimental paradigm from stereotypes as hypothesized bi-variate contingencies to the more complex case of tri-variate contingencies.
- Such a refined paradigm will be shown to provide an integrative account of a larger number of findings from the stereotype literature than the elementary 2×2 frame.
- We will introduce several novel concepts representing stereotype phenomena in the tri-variate space, including pseudo-contingencies, Simpson's paradox, and several variants of competitive learning in the environment.
- Most importantly, we report a number of experiments to fill these new conceptions with concrete empirical contents and psychological meaning.

Recapitulating the premises and the current status of analysis

Before we continue to explore the process of stereotype learning in such a refined framework, a moment of meta-theoretical reflection is in order to recapitulate the distinctive properties of our CELA. The research described in the preceding three chapters provides numerous examples for the central idea that stereotypes need not originate in conflicts, sentiments, and serious cognitive distortions. They may instead result from fully normal, unbiased, inductive learning processes in an uncertain environment. Very basic, parsimonious learning rules can account for stereotype-related biases that appear to be charged with social motives and meaning. For example, we have seen that the devaluation of minorities—one of the most prominent topics of genuine social psychology—can be due to something as profane as sample size, or the number of learning trials. Granting an equal proportion of positive, desirable behaviors in a minority as in a majority, the simple fact that the number of learning trials is typically smaller for minorities than majorities renders the positivity of minorities less apparent, or harder to recognize.

Such a learning approach is rather uncommon and at variance with the traditional approach to stereotyping, which has been characterized as "animistic". As introduced in Chapter 2, this term suggests that research has been mainly concerned with cognitive motivational factors residing within animate subjects, such as expectancies, intentions, goals, wishes, imperfect memory, and distorted cognitive processes. Stereotypes are commonly explained by these animistic forces, the assumption being say, that stereotypes originate in selective forgetting of stereotype-inconsistent information or motivated tendencies to confirm one's prior expectancies through lop-sided information search. For example, to explain prejudice against minorities, it is assumed that negative minority behavior is very salient and therefore more readily memorized than positive minority behavior (Hamilton & Sherman, 1989). Or observations of minority behavior may be interpreted in terms of superficial clichés or scripts, especially when high cognitive load reduces the individual's cognitive capacity (Bodenhausen & Lichtenstein, 1987).

CELA does not contest the relevance of animistic (cognitive and motivational) factors. There is ample evidence, anecdotal and experimental, which demonstrates wishful thinking, selective exposure, biased information processing, and even self-deception as sources of persistent stereotypes. Human beings are extremely creative in maintaining their favorable beliefs, like the belief that risks are higher for others than for oneself (Weinstein, 1980), that one's own group is superior to an outgroup (Tajfel & Turner, 1986), or that superstitious beliefs are well supported by everyday experience. The CELA takes these well-known and uncontested phenomena for granted. However, at the same time, one prominent goal of this approach is to overcome the theoretical confines of the animistic approach, which sometimes runs the danger of being circular, or tautological (Greve, 2001; Wallach & Wallach, 1994). Explaining sexist stereotypes by a corresponding sexist motive or personality trait (e.g., modern sexism), or explaining a bias against minorities by a selective tendency to memorize negative minority behaviors, leaves a feeling of discontent, because the *explanans* is too close to the *explanandum*. The phenomenon to be explained and the construct used for explanation might be nothing but two different measures of the same latent variable (e.g., negative judgments and negative memories reflecting the same latent tendency).

One major goal of a CELA is to offer ways to overcome this problem, or this "developmental task" for social psychological theories. Explaining stereotypes in terms of basic rules of learning that have long been established outside the stereotyping domain evades the danger of being circular. Thus, while cognitive and motivational biases, and other animistic factors, are acknowledged, the meta-theoretical tenet here is that other phenomena might be more interesting in terms of theoretical innovations that go beyond common sense.

The preceding three chapters have dealt with stereotypical biases that arise in *bi-variate* problem space. Stereotypical hypothesis testing was conceived as illusory correlations in a 2×2 table, representing the distribution of a binary attribute (e.g., positive vs. negative behavior) as a function of two groups. The present chapter will raise the paradigm to the *tri-variate* level. In a tri-variate problem space, new learning mechanisms come into play, offering richer and more imaginative ways of construing stereotypical relationships and illusions. Thus, when there is little basis to assume a bi-variate relation between groups and traits, a third variable may help to construe the stereotype. For instance, groups with no apparent trait differences may be characterized by different habits or roles (eating habits, religions, meat vs. vegetable, car brand names) the meaning of which allows for richer trait attributions than the group labels themselves. Let us now illustrate this with reference to a concrete research example.

Stereotyping in a tri-variate problem space

To begin with, an ingenious demonstration of stereotype formation in a tri-variate context comes from experiments conducted by Hoffman & Hurst (1990). Participants observed a number of trait-relevant behaviors associated with two otherwise unknown groups, Orinthians and Ackmians. The traits were either typically male (agentic) or typically female (communal), but there was no correlation between groups and traits; male and female traits were equally frequent for both groups (see Figure 6.1). However, most members of one group were described as having a "city worker" job, whereas most members of the other group were described as having a "child raiser" job. These job ascriptions, or social roles, were also uncorrelated with traits. All three two-variate correlations between the three attributes, groups, roles, and trait meanings, are specified in Figure 6.1. Note

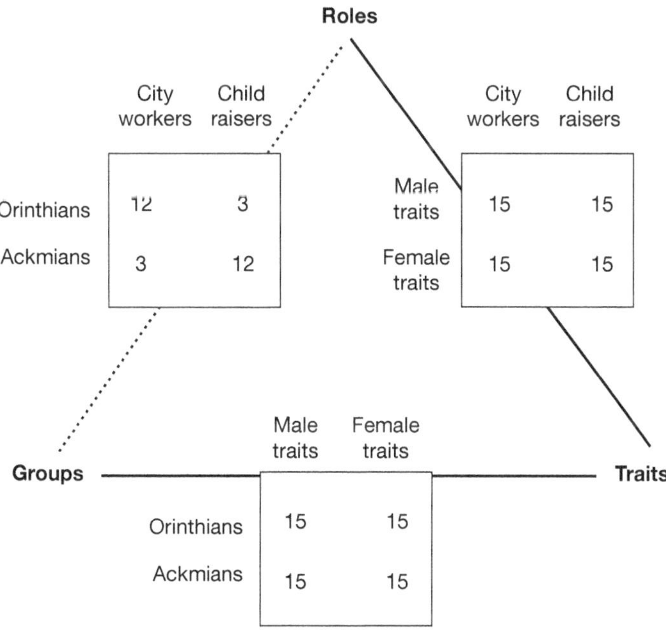

Figure 6.1 The genesis of stereotypes in a tri-variate framework; after Hoffman and Hurst (1990).

that the experimental task asked for judgments of the traits in both groups; the corresponding correlation between groups and traits was actually zero. However, subjective judgments showed a substantial stereotype effect, mediated by the surplus meaning of the social roles prevailing in the two groups. The one group in which city workers were prevalent was seen as more associated with male (agentic) traits than the other group including more child raisers, which tended to be associated with female (communal) traits. Apparently, the social role context that was correlated with groups and semantically confounded with traits provided an associative link between the other two, actually unrelated variables. Note that Hoffman and Hurst's (1990) approach is an experimental analog of Eagly (1987) social-role conception of gender stereotypes.

In more general terms, social roles provide an environmental context for grouping, interpreting, and encoding other variables. The role labels, city workers and child raisers, help to figure out who belongs to different groups, and role labels may also help to extract the common meaning of associated traits. In this way, one group and one trait meaning become associated with the same role category, and another group and trait meaning become linked to another role category. Although groups and traits are statistically unrelated, their common category reference mimics a systematic relationship. Such a constellation directly leads us to a phenomenon named *pseudo-contingency*.

Pseudo-contingencies as a source of stereotypical hypotheses

The concept of pseudo-contingencies is new; it does not appear in the literature on stereotyping but it is of considerable importance for environmental learning. Pseudo-contingencies suggest a powerful way in which the environmental context can mediate stereotypical relations. Two attributes, X and Y, become stereotypically related when they are associated with the same environmental context Z. As a consequence, the actually existing relation between X and Y will be overestimated. Imagine a young child raised in a bi-lingual family. She learns to speak Italian with the father and English with the mother. The father is often in good mood whereas the mother is often depressed. This may raise the (illusory) impression that the Italian language (X) is more positive in evaluative tone (Y) than English—again a quite normal effect from a learning and conditioning point of view. In fact, positive valence (Y) is associated with the father (Z) rather than one language, but due to the association of the father (Z) with the Italian language (X), the father's good mood carries over to the child's experience of the Italian language. Pseudo-contingencies can thus be conceived as second-order associations.

Another example might involve the observation that people having AIDS are often gay, and the (independent) observation that people who have AIDS are often drug addicts. Inferring from these two independent sets of observations a relation between homosexuality and drug consumption would constitute a pseudo-contingency, because the latter two variables may actually be unrelated. Their relation may even be negative. Those AIDS patients who are drug addicts may be more likely those who are *not* gay; most of them may have contracted AIDS for different reasons. A pseudo-contingency may also be at work in the Snyder et al. (1977) example that we have used at the outset. The stereotype that attractive women are high in social skills may (at least partially) reflect the fact that experiences with attractive women and experiences with socially skilled people are both associated with similar pleasant contexts.

A recent study by Fiedler and Freytag (2003) may convey a quantitative impression of the strength of the pseudo-contingency illusion. Observations about one group showed that the values on one personality test X are high in 12 group members, medium in 6, and low in 6. With regard to a second personality attribute Y, participants learned that the same group is high on Y in 12 cases, medium in 6, and low in 6 cases. While these uni-variate frequency distributions suggest that similar levels of X and Y tend to co-occur in the same group, the actually presented correlation between X and Y was negative (–0.43). Again, both X and Y are related to the group, which serves the role of Z, whereas the correlation between X and Y was even negative in this case. This was accomplished by the stimulus distribution in the left part of Figure 6.2. Although it was indeed the case that high manifestations of X often co-occurred with high levels of Y within the same group, in absolute terms, this impression was mainly due to the skewed ecological distribution of both variables X and Y, which tended to take high values in general. If this ecological baserate constraint is taken into account, and if the conditional distribution of one variable is considered at each level of the other variable, the relation turns out to be negative indeed. One will notice that low X values always co-occurred with high Y values and never with low or medium Y values; medium X values always came along with high and never with medium Y values. This strongly negative relation was only slightly corrected by the fact that half of the Y values within the set of high X values were high and the other half were either medium or low (see Figure 6.2).

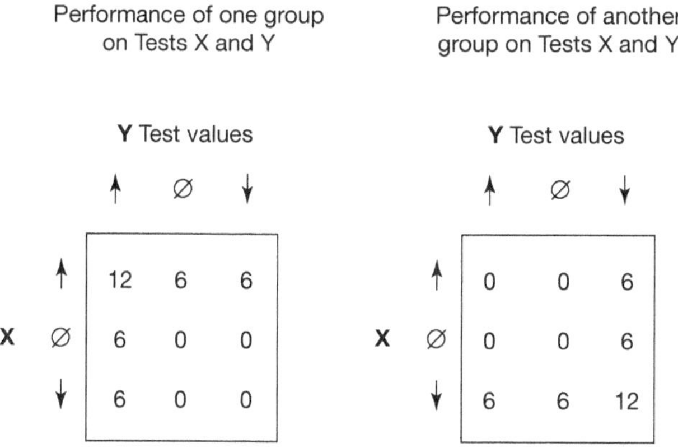

Figure 6.2 Stimulus distributions used in two different conditions of an experiment on pseudo-contingencies, by Fiedler and Freytag (2003). The symbols ↑, Ø, and ↓ represent high, medium and low scores on two tests, X and Y.

Nevertheless, subjective judgments reflected the illusion of a positive correlation between X and Y, yielding a pronounced pseudo-contingency. When observers who had been exposed to the negative correlation (–0.43) shown in Figure 6.2 predicted the values of one variable from given high or low values on the other variable, the average correlation they produced was as positive as +0.82 and +0.88, in two conditions with predominantly high and predominantly low values on X and Y, respectively.

Thus, the impressively strong phenomenon was not confined to the case in which high X and Y values appeared to co-occur. An equal number of observations about another group associated with low test values on X and Y (see right part of Figure 6.2) but otherwise conserving the same negative correlation produced an equally strong bias. The mean pseudo-contingency effect was at least as high for the latter (+0.88) as for the former group (+0.82). That is, when *lack of* X and *lack of* Y appeared to co-occur in a group, because observers did not consider the distributional constraints, there was the same strong illusion of pseudo-contingency between X and Y.

This is not to say that participants did not notice the skewed baserates. In fact, the distribution of their predictions of Y values given high or low X, or of X values given high or low Y, reflected the skewed distributions rather well (i.e., they tended to produce a high baserate of high Y values for the group described on the left of Figure 6.2 and a high baserate of low Y values for the other group described on the right). Although they clearly figured out the prevalence of either high or low values, they failed to correct the learned association between X and Y accordingly.

Pseudo-contingencies afford an almost universal means of constructing stereotypical illusions based on secondary associations. Technically speaking, the illusion arises when relevant information about the correlation of two variables, X and Y, has not been assessed at all. That is, observations do not refer to Y as a function of X, but X and Y have been assessed separately, on different occasions. However, the separate distributions of both variables is skewed, and the most frequent levels of both variables are associated with the same group label. Thus, the conditional probability p(high X / G) of high X values in group G is high as well as the conditional probability p(high Y / G) of high Y values in group G. However, there is no evidence whatsoever about Y conditional on X, or vice versa. In fact, even though both high X and high Y coincide within G, their contingency may be negative, that is, p(high Y / high X) may be lower than p(high Y / low X).

To give one more example, a teacher may have noticed that performance in a physics class tends to be very high and that there are many more boys than girls in the class: p(high performance / class) is high and p(boys / class) is high. However, the teacher did not assess p(performance / boys) or p(performance / girls). Nevertheless, the inference is very likely that high performance reflects the prevalence of boys. Note that the stereotypical expectancy that boys outperform girls in science is not required for such an effect to occur. In the absence of a stereotype, it is sufficient that gender groups and performance levels are frequently paired with the same group context, as evident from the above demonstration with neutral personality tests “X” and “Y”. Generally speaking, whenever observations about two skewed variables are not contingent on each other but gathered separately on different occasions, some dummy group label will suffice to create a potentially very strong pseudo-contingency.

What psychological principle or well-established law might account for this phenomenon? In fact, the repertoire of social psychological theorizing offers at least two explanations of pseudo-contingencies, based on the notions of accentuation and consistency. Both explanations highlight the importance of environmental learning factors. The phenomenon of accentuation, to begin with, goes back to the early contributions of Bruner (Bruner & Goodman, 1947; Bruner & Postman, 1948) and Tajfel (1957, 1959; Tajfel & Wilkes, 1963). When the judgment task calls for the discrimination of stimuli on one attribute dimension, X, judgments are accentuated or polarized if X correlates in a redundant fashion with another variable Z, which is essentially irrelevant for the judgment at hand. Thus, when judges estimate the length of lines (X), the judged difference between long and short lines increases when long lines carry the label “A” and short lines carry the label “B” (Tajfel & Wilkes, 1963), as compared with a control condition where the context labels Z (“A” vs. “B”) are uncorrelated with line length. Using a socially more meaningful task, Eiser (1971) showed, similarly, that the judged difference between attitude statements varying on the dimension permissive versus restrictive (X) increases, when statements expressing opposite attitudes correlate systematically with different fictitious newspaper labels Z (“Messenger” vs. “Gazette”), as compared with a condition in which attitude positions are allocated at random to newspapers.

Note that the labels used to create accentuation are independent of prior expectancies or stereotypes. This basic accentuation effect suggests that the redundancy, or information gain, of a superimposed correlated attribute facilitates distinctions on the focal dimension. Grouping stimulus lines into categories “A” and “B” helps to structure the stimulus field into short versus long lines; grouping attitude statements by newspapers helps judges to extract the underlying dimension. In any case, accentuation means that the perception and encoding of stimuli on one dimension can be facilitated by another, irrelevant but correlated stimulus aspect. In this regard, pseudo-contingencies may occur because context categories serve a grouping function. As observations of high X values are regularly associated with one constant group, and dissociated from another group, they are more efficiently discriminated from low X values that have different group associations. Moreover, high values on Y are discriminated more clearly from low Y values as they are associated with different groups. Pseudo-contingency can thus be considered a double-accentuation effect.

The second explanation can be derived from traditional *consistency* theories (Abelson, Aronson, McGuire, Newcomb, Rosenberg, & Tannenbaum, 1968), such as Heider’s (1958) balance theory. If the two bilateral relations, between the group and high X and between the group and high Y, are positive, there is a tendency to see the remaining bilateral relation, between X and Y, also as positive. There are countless demonstrations of such consistency effects on social learning, social attitudes (Shultz & Lepper, 1996), judgments (Festinger, 1964), and learning (DeSoto, 1960). It is an old gestalt principle, and an obvious fact, that a balanced, orderly structure is easier to comprehend and to remember than an unbalanced, contradictory structure. Pseudo-contingency may thus be understood as a fully normal consistency effect. Environmental categories (groups, cultures, locations, situations) are used to reproduce triadic structures in a consistent fashion, such that two entities that hold the same relation to the environmental category are judged to be similar, or related, and two entities that hold different relations to the environmental category are judged to be dissimilar, unrelated, or even negatively related.

The two explanations depicted so far, accentuation and consistency, are not mutually independent. Almost three decades ago, Eiser and Stroebe (1972) have already shown that both notions are closely related. If a stimulus object belongs to one context category (one Z-level), and this category is closely related to high X-values, consistency implies that the same stimulus be judged high on X too. Also, it is worth noting that modern connectionist models in cognitive psychology (Kruschke, 1992; Shultz & Lepper, 1996; Thagard, 1989) are also governed by consistency rules, and it is no surprise that they can simulate pseudo-contingency effects quite well (Fiedler et al., 1999). For instance, if X is connected to Z and Y is connected to Z in an associative network, the model will establish a positive link from X to Y as well (mediated by Z), unless severe constraints are introduced that inhibit the path from X to Y. From modern connectionist models, it is not far to old associationist models of learning. Accordingly, the pseudo-contingency phenomenon follows from simple principles of learning. If an environmental cue Z is a conditional stimulus associated with one attribute X, another aspect Y that co-occurs frequently with Z will also elicit X—a phenomenon known as secondary conditioning.

Given so many convergent implications from different theories, it is no surprise that when testing hypotheses about X and Y, people not only take direct evidence on the co-occurrence of X and Y into account, but also indirect evidence on the joint association of X and Y to context categories Z (or several categories Z_1, Z_2, Z_3, . . . Z_k). Thus, hypothesis testers should not consider X and Y in isolation, but should take an embedding network into account that can involve many context cues, which may boost the overall consistency and thereby facilitate the confirmation of social hypotheses. This process can be the source of severe stereotyping and prejudice. Many inhabitants of one part of the town may stem from a certain ethnic background, and many inhabitants of the same part may be criminal. The result is an ethnic prejudice even when criminality is not really contingent on ethnic subgroups, or is even lower in the prevalent ethnic subgroup. In a similar vein, professional group labels, geographical locations, or even ill-defined dummy group names such as “workaholics”, “computer-freaks” or “macho”, can be used to create pseudo-contingencies between variables with a skewed distribution.

Simpson's paradox as a source of stereotyping

Interestingly, however, it is not always the case that context variables are taken into account when testing a focal contingency in tri-variate space. Let us now turn to another source of stereotyping that is related, but in a way opposite, to pseudo-contingencies, the so-called *Simpson's paradox* (Schaller, 1992a, 1992b; Schaller & O'Brien, 1992; Waldmann & Hagmayer, 1995). This paradigm can be illustrated by the following problem that we used in an extended series of experiments (Fiedler, Walther, Freytag, & Nickel, 2003). Participants were presented with a series of observations about the success versus failure (Y) of male and female applicants (X) to doctorate programs at two different universities (Z). They were instructed to focus on the relation between X (applicant sex) and Y (outcome) and to consider the hypothesis that female applicants are more likely to be rejected than male applicants. In fact, the overall correlation between sex (X) and success (Y) supported the hypothesis. Altogether, 19 females were rejected and 13 females were accepted, as compared with 13 males rejected and 19 males accepted (see left side of Figure 6.3)—a marked difference in favor of males.

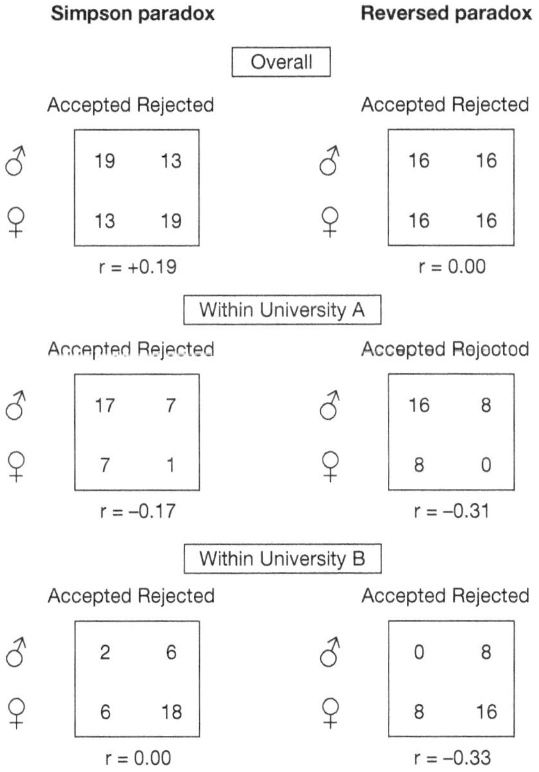

Figure 6.3 Simpson's paradox. The relationships between applicant gender and acceptance rates on aggregate (across University A and B) is different from the relationship within either university.

However, the reference to a "paradox" suggests that things are not that easy. As the context variable, universities (Z), is taken into account, it is apparent that women fare equally well or even better within both University A and University B (middle and bottom part of Figure 6.3). If context variables are utilized automatically, hypothesis testers should be readily influenced by the impact of the context. Accordingly, they should notice that the alleged inferiority of females is only due to the fact that females predominantly apply to University B whereas males tend to apply for A. Since B is the more difficult place with a much higher rejection rate, females appear to be inferior, but are in fact only more ambitious. If the different rejection rate of universities (i.e., the context variable Z) is partialled out, that is, if achievement within both universities is examined separately, it becomes evident that females are actually equal if not superior (cf. Figure 6.3). Thus, Simpson's paradox shows how females can be inferior to males in general, and at the same time equally good or even better if the context is taken into account.

Recall that in pseudo-contingencies, the context attribute Z is utilized spontaneously and has a dominant impact on subjective judgments of the X-Y relation. In contrast, our extended studies with (the above version of) Simpson's paradox suggest that judgments may be quite insensitive to the context. As portrayed in Figure 6.4, there was a strong tendency over several experiments to rate the female rejection rate higher than the male rejection rate. This tendency not only held for overall estimates of all females and males, but also for context-specific estimates within universities. Judges were convinced that more females than males had been rejected within both universities, which was clearly wrong. To be sure, the context variable did not go unnoticed. Participants did recognize that females tended to apply for B and males for A, and they also recognized that more B applicants were rejected than A applicants. However, they failed to recognize that an environmental factor—unequal acceptance thresholds at different universities—provides an alternative account for the *spurious correlation* between gender and academic success. They did not understand that at different levels of analysis, across and

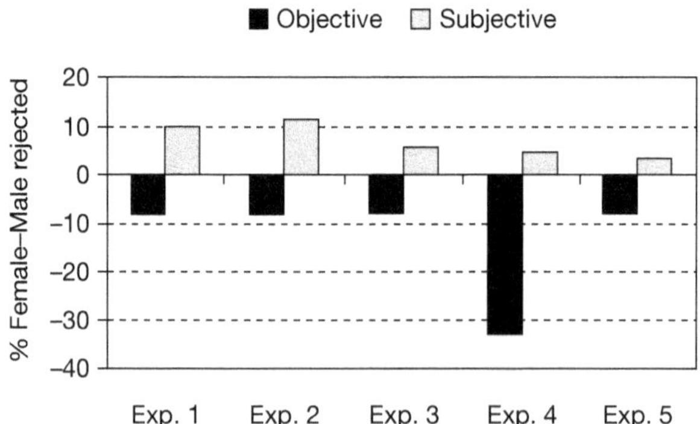

Figure 6.4 Persistent judgment bias in five experiments using Simpson's paradox (Fiedler, Walther, Freytag, & Nickel, 2003). Judges fail to notice that, within specific universities, females are no less successful than males.

within universities, a different or even opposite contingency held between gender and academic success.

This failure to take the context effect of the third variable into account, which seems to be at variance with the spontaneous use of the context in pseudo-contingency effects, was persistently replicated under various task conditions (Fiedler et al., 2003): when participants received an explicit cue regarding the unequal standards of universities; when female failure was attributed externally rather than internally; when the focal hypothesis was reversed asking "why it cannot be the case that females are inferior"; when presentation latencies were increased; and when the stimulus correlations were replaced by a constellation in which the overall correlation was zero and females were even superior within universities. All these manipulations were not sufficient to eliminate the perceived inferiority of females.

It is again tempting to resort to animistic explanations given such a finding. Couldn't the persistent tendency to ignore female success (at least under specific conditions) simply reflect a common gender stereotype? Participants may come with an expectation of a female disadvantage and use this expectation for guessing when making estimates under uncertainty. Indeed, there is some evidence that such animistic factors may actually play a substantial role. Using a similar problem (i.e., alleged female inferiority that can be explained by the fact that females have to work under more difficult conditions), Schaller (1992a) demonstrated that a strong motive to improve and protect female prestige reduced Simpson's paradox significantly. That is, the tendency to attribute the relatively weak performance to reduced ability, rather than unfortunate circumstances, decreased. Note, however, that Schaller did not strictly test whether these motivated people really understood the paradox. He did not assess whether they fully understood that females perform worse, and at the same time understood that they perform better within specific work conditions. What he demonstrated is that global judgments of female targets became more favorable when pro-female motives were raised.

We do not question the potential importance of such motivational factors that may influence the final judgment outcome. However, such influences of motivational factors on global judgments of females versus males are not diagnostic about the cognitive role played by context factors. We do not know whether the pro-female judgments of people with pro-feminist motives are due to more sensitive processing of the full tri-variate structure, or simply to a *guessing bias*, or attitude-sensitive correction of the final judgment. In our own research reported above, some experimental conditions established rather strong motivational forces (female participants, some of them feminist, internal attributions, explicit instructions to falsify the alleged female inferiority), but a full understanding of the tri-variate pattern was never accomplished. Judges failed to acknowledge that qualitatively different relationships can hold at the same time at different levels.

From our environmental learning point of view, the reported findings do not appear that surprising. For instance, when we apply the consistency principle that was already used to explain pseudo-contingencies, the adherence to a sex-based explanation, as opposed to an environmental account in terms of universities, seems pretty plausible. The *attentional focus* of the experimental task is on sex differences; almost all participants find out, correctly, that females are more likely rejected than males. Incidentally, they also notice that females tend to go to University B whereas males tend to apply for A. They also learn that B applicants are more likely rejected than A applicants. So the pattern of all three bivariate relations is in perfect consistency. Females go to B→ B is rejected → and females are rejected. Males go to A → A is accepted → males are accepted.

Given such a consistent structure, and given the gestalt lesson that consistent structures are easy to learn, why should judges change their interpretation? From a consistency point of view, the context variable only supports the primary impression that females are inferior. After all, the context variable, universities (Z), need not be used to discard the relation between sex (X) and achievement (Y) as spurious or superficial. In fact, the context allows for several interpretations. Rather than assuming that universities differ in aspiration level, so that females meet unfortunate conditions, one might as well apply another rationale and assume that the high rejection rate of University B reflects the high proportion of weak females, rather than an enhanced aspiration level. There is no need to explain the impact of X (sex) on Y (achievement) in terms of Z (university aspiration level). It is also possible to explain the impact of Z (university rejection rate) in terms of X (weak females who contaminate University B).

Attentional priority and competitive learning

This analysis examines another major topic highlighted by an environmental learning perspective: Learning is subject to attentional focus and order effects. Whether context factors become dominant or are overridden by other factors depends on the sequence in which different factors are introduced. In the pseudo-contingency paradigm, the primary learning process focuses on the context factor (i.e., the relation of the group Z to X and its relation to Y). The crucial relationship between X and Y is assessed later. Given this sequence, noticing the bridging function of Z for the learning of the X-Y relation seems almost inevitable. In contrast, when the X-Y relation to be judged is learned in the first place, as in Simpson's paradox, the role of the context variable Z may be blocked or overridden.

In the learning literature, this impact of the learning sequence is well known as a so-called blocking effect (Kamin, 1968). When participants (or animals) first learn that one conditional stimulus, X, elicits an unconditional stimulus, Y, they fail to learn in a later stage that another conditional stimulus, Z, also elicits Y when presented in a compound together with X. It is as if the X hypothesis already accounts for the effect, Y, so that the Z hypothesis is blocked, or *discounted*, to use an attributional term (Kelley, 1973). If, conversely, the impact of Z is learned first, X may be blocked instead.

Consistent with such a role ascribed to attentional focus, the only task condition that eventually led participants to discount the spurious correlation between sex and academic success in the above experiments on Simpson's paradox (Fiedler,

Walther, Freytag, & Stryczek, 2002) was one in which we exchanged the temporal structure of the stimulus display. In all other experimental conditions, the instruction focus was to look for differences between male or female applicants and the stimulus display first revealed whether an applicant was male or female, before the participant learned at which university the application was directed and whether the application was successful or not. When the focus was changed by removing the instruction focus on gender differences and by presenting the university label first, before the applicant name and gender was revealed, participants for the first time began to discount the role of gender differences and to explain application success in terms of the unequal aspiration levels of the universities to which males and females tended to apply.

The same role of temporal cues in disambiguating Simpson's paradox was demonstrated in another recent experiment on tri-variate learning (Fiedler et al., 2002). From a series of moving cartoons on the computer screen, participants had to figure out which mating strategy was more successful, direct or indirect communication. Each trial involved a female figure entering the scene from the right and a male figure appearing from the left. The boy attempted to date the girl either in a direct fashion (e.g., "You are the cutest girl I have ever seen") or in an indirect way (e.g., "Could you tell me the way to the railway station?"). Her response was either positive (approaching him with a nice reply) or negative (turning away with a nasty reply). Across all 32 trials, one strategy (say, direct attempts) was more successful (10 successful attempts vs. 6 failures) than the other (indirect: 6 vs. 10). However, there were two types of girls, cool girls and emotional girls, as indicated by turquoise or pink head color, respectively. Within both types of girls, the contingency disappeared. When approaching cool girls, both direct (9 vs. 3) and indirect attempts (3 vs. 1) were equally successful. Given emotional girls, however, both direct (1 vs. 3) and indirect strategies (3 vs. 9) failed most of the time. Thus, when types of girls were taken into account, the advantage of direct mating disappeared.

This tri-variate relation can be disambiguated in two ways, corresponding to a moderator or a mediator model (Baron & Kenney, 1986). The *moderator* model suggests that the whole spurious correlation can be explained by the cool girls being more accepting than the emotional girls. Direct strategies only appear to have an advantage because direct strategies are more often directed at cool girls. The *mediator* model, in contrast, assumes that cool girls' acceptance rate merely reflects the fact that they are often approached in a direct fashion. Here the attribute "cool" only mediates the original causal influence of direct strategies. The findings showed, nicely, that judgments of the differential impact of direct versus indirect strategies depended on a subtle manipulation of temporal primacy. If the color of head indicating either a cool versus an emotional girl was already apparent when she entered the scene, before the boy uttered a direct or indirect statement, then type of girl was treated as a moderator and the perceived difference between direct and indirect attempts was reduced. In contrast, if the girl first appeared without a head color and the head only turned turquoise or pink in response to a direct or indirect utterance, like a mediating emotional response to the mating attempt, then a mediator model was activated and the judged causal impact of strategies was enhanced. Once more, judgments of two causal factors (strategies and types of girls) that vary simultaneously with an effect (acceptance vs. rejection) depended on a focus or temporal primacy manipulation.

The decisive impact of the initial attention focus—a central aspect of an environmental learning approach—also provided the focus of another recent series of attribution experiments (Fiedler, Walther, & Nickel, 1999a), involving also a conflict between two factors, X and Z, competing for the explanation of an effect, Y. In the context of causal attribution, hypothesis testing amounts to finding internal or external conditions that can explain variation in behavior. In this particular investigation, the stimulus series referred to the high or low performance (Y) of five different entertainers (X) in five different disciplines (Z). Concretely, participants were asked to take the perspective of a variety director who was to evaluate the casting performance of five entertainers (Filipo, Leandro, Angelo, Salvatore, and Francesco) on five disciplines (dancing, joking, singing, imitating voices, and magical tricks). The stimulus information was manipulated in such a way that the effect Y (success or failure) was correlated only with entertainers X (lower part of Figure 6.5) or with both entertainers X and disciplines Y (upper part). In the former case, variation in the degree of success was exclusively due to differences between entertainers (producing 5, 4, 3, 2, or 1 positive outcomes), whereas disciplines did not differ in frequency (all giving rise to 3 positive outcomes). In the latter case, however, success covaried with both entertainers and disciplines (5, 4, 3, 2, 1 positive outcomes for both factors); that is, just as entertainers could be ordered by ability, disciplines could be ordered from the easiest to the hardest. Of course, the 25 stimulus items (outcomes of 5 entertainers × 5 disciplines) were presented in random order, rather than in the systematic matrix arrangement in the upper part of Figure 6.5.

In addition to the manipulation of the actually presented covariation of the effect with both causal factors, we manipulated the primary task focus. Participants were either instructed to attend to potential differences between entertainers (X), or to attend to differences between disciplines (Z). Both manipulations, covariation and focus, represent major determinants of attribution. However, while the covariation principle has motivated hundreds of experiments and attained a central status in attribution theories, the focus principle was not given a systematic place in most theoretical models. To be sure, some ecologically minded researchers have repeatedly shown that salience and focus of attention can attract attributions, and although the famous actor–observer discrepancy (Jones & Nisbett, 1972; McArthur, 1981; Watson, 1982) points to focus as a strong source of bias. As observers' perceptual focus is on the actor, they tend to attribute behavior internally to the actor. In contrast, actors themselves often attribute their own behavior externally, because their focus of perception is typically on situational factors. However, none of the major theories of causal attribution (Cheng & Novick, 1990; Hilton & Slugoski, 1986; Jones & McGillis, 1976; Kelley, 1967) assigns a systematic role to focus of attention, in addition to rationalist factors (covariation) and animistic influences (target intention, control, abnormality).

	Dancing	Joking	Singing	Voices	Magical tricks	
Filipo	+	+	+	+	+	5
Leandro	+	+	+	+	–	4
Angelo	+	+	+	–	–	3
Salvatore	+	+	–	–	–	2
Francesco	+	–	–	–	–	1
	5	4	3	2	1	

	Dancing	Joking	Singing	Voices	Magical tricks	
Filipo	+	+	+	+	+	5
Leandro	+	+	–	+	+	4
Angelo	+	–	+	+	–	3
Salvatore	–	+	–	–	+	2
Francesco	–	–	+	–	–	1
	3	3	3	3	3	

Figure 6.5. Stimulus distributions used in experiments by Fiedler, Walther, and Nickel (1999a).

Our environmental learning approach has two noteworthy implications. First, a focus on entertainers should lead to more entertainer attributions of performance differences than a focus on disciplines, when the covariation pattern is held constant. As we have assumed in the above discussion of pseudo-contingencies and the Simpson paradox, whether a context variable is influential or not should depend on the primary focus.

Second, the gestalt notion of consistency, which is so essential for learning in a complex environment, leads us to predict that no *discounting* effect will be obtained when the effect covaries with both factors. Since Kelley's (1973) seminal ANOVA model of attribution, it is commonly assumed that the perceived impact of one causal factor will decrease when another factor covaries with the same effect. Accordingly, differences between entertainers should be discounted in part when performance covaries with disciplines too, as compared with the condition where performance covaries only with entertainers.

However, prior empirical support for discounting mainly stems from experiments in which attribution is operationalized as a verbal reasoning task. After being told that one causal factor is already present, judges actually tend to give lower judgments to another factor. In hardly any attribution experiment the causal hypotheses have to be tested inductively in a sequence of multiple observations from which covariations have to be extracted. If this is required, as in the depicted experiment, a context factor that covaries with the same effect as a focal factor need not lead to discounting. On the contrary, the double covariation should increase the overall consistency and thereby facilitate the assessment of the focal covariation. We therefore predicted a reversal of the normal discounting effect; the judged impact of entertainers should increase when disciplines covary with performance as well.

The gain in consistency is immediately evident from Figure 6.5 above. The pattern in the upper matrix is much more regular and predictable than the pattern below. In the double covariation condition, Francesco, who succeeds only once, does not succeed in any one discipline but exactly in the easiest one, Dancing. Leandro who succeeds in all but one discipline fails not in any arbitrary discipline, but in the most difficult one, Magical Tricks. Thus, the two sources of covariation are perfectly coordinated. Ability of entertainers and difficulty of disciplines can be represented on the same perfectly transitive *joint scale* (Figure 6.6). Filipo, on top, exceeds all other entertainers and all disciplines. Leandro is dominated by Filipo and the most difficult discipline, Magical Tricks, but he dominates all other entertainers and disciplines, etc. There is no way of ordering the single-covariation pattern in the bottom part of Figure 6.5 in such a perfectly consistent way.

Not surprisingly, given the intimate relationship of consistency and accentuation, the reversal of discounting can also be derived from accentuation theory, as formulated by Tajfel (1957, 1959). As the context variable Z, disciplines, correlates systematically with Y, performance, the subjectively perceived differences in performance should be accentuated. If the primary focus is on entertainers, this accentuation of performance differences should also increase the effect strength attributed to entertainers.

Both predictions were clearly borne out by the data summarized in Figure 6.7. On the one hand, attentional focus turned out to be a stronger, and more regular, determinant of attribution than the actually presented covariation. Given a constant covariation between X (entertainers) and Y (success), judges assessed this covariation more effectively, and ascribed traits and abilities in different degrees to entertainers, when the primary focus was on X (entertainers) rather than on disciplines (Z). This focus effect was particularly strong when the effect covaried, in an ambiguous fashion, with both factors at the same time. On the other hand, when comparing judgments of X covariation and X-referent attributions in the single-covariation versus the double covariation condition, the predicted reversal of a discounting effect was obtained. Variation between entertainers was accentuated, rather than discounted, when another correlated factor, disciplines, boosted the overall consistency in the system and thereby highlighted the performance differences between entertainers.

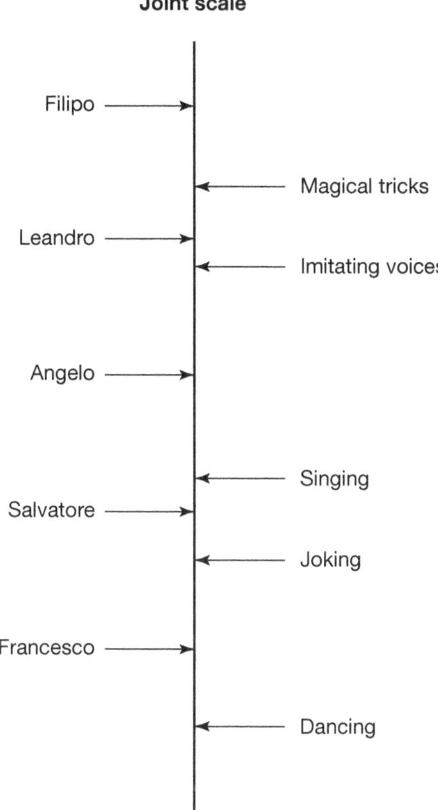

Figure 6.6 Representing the complex trivariate relationship between entertainers, disciplines, and success on a joint scale.

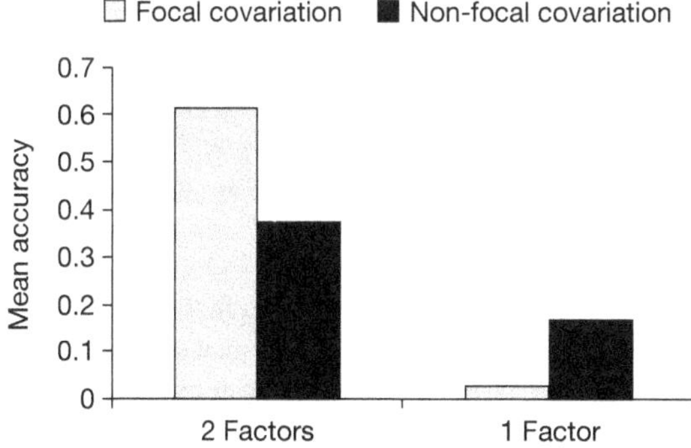

Figure 6.7 The influence of attention focus on the accuracy of judging the covariation between causal factors and an effect, when the effect covaries with only one or with two factors.

In other words, we have demonstrated both (1) that the primary focus determines the locus of attribution and overshadows an equally high covariation with an unfocused factor; and (2) that the redundancy or consistency gained from an unattended, correlated variable can nevertheless support the learning process. Although the direct impact of a context factor may be overridden by a divergent task focus, the context factor may still exert its influence on inductive learning.

What we have interpreted, verbally, as a consistency effect, may also be paraphrased in associative or connectionist terms. In the redundant, double covariation condition, people not only learn directly that the best entertainers, Filipo and Leandro, are associated with high ability, but they also learn that Filipo and Leandro have mastered the most difficult disciplines, Imitating Voices and Magical Tricks, which are associated with high ability. So the direct associations are boosted by a whole network of indirect paths mediated by consistent context effects.

The limited value of experimental strategies for contextual learning

What if attributors (variety directors) can themselves search information about the performance of entertainers in different disciplines, that is, if they engage in active hypothesis testing? In one of the experiments reported in Fiedler et al. (1999a), the 5×5 combinations of entertainers and disciplines were represented as a matrix on the computer screen. On every trial of the computer-assisted experiment, participants could move the cursor to one matrix cell, specifying one entertainer (row) and one discipline (column), and received a feedback about the performance (success or failure) of this factor combination. The remaining parts of stimulus presentation were identical to the other experiments reported above. Those matrix cells for which feedback was already given were marked, but the matrix did not conserve prior outcomes which had to be kept in memory.

The strategies of information search that people applied in this paradigm elucidated the cognitive processes used for testing attributional hypotheses. If covariation patterns were truly independent variables, as suggested in most attribution theories and manifested in the orthogonal manipulations used in attribution research, attributors should resort to experimental strategies. That is, they should hold one factor constant while varying the other factor, to isolate the pure impact of each individual factor. Operationally, such an experimental strategy would be evident in series of trials in which, say, one discipline is held constant, and entertainers are varied systematically, before the search process turns to another discipline.

If, however, the double covariation of an effect with two factors is tested in an interdependent fashion that allows for consistency checks (in accordance with the joint scale model of Figure 6.6), an experimental search strategy is not of advantage. Holding one discipline constant while counting the overall success of one entertainer minimizes the chance of consistency checks involving other entertainers and disciplines. For this purpose, effective information search strategies should switch repeatedly, considering the consistent or inconsistent relation in pairs of entertainers vis-à-vis pairs of disciplines. In a probabilistic environment in which it is important to distinguish systematic structures from noise, an information acquisition process ought to be sensitive to such consistency checks.

Indeed, the empirical results supported this consideration. A score was calculated for each participant measuring the degree to which he/she applied an experimental strategy (i.e., the proportion of trials on which one factor was held constant while the other was varied). Participants with a high value on this score were high in memory for particular cells of the 5 × 5 design. However, in terms of accuracy of covariation judgments, experimental search strategies did not improve, but slightly reduced the attributors' sensitivity to the actually presented covariations. As the use of experimental strategies was generally quite high, it is interesting to note that after self-determined information search attributors where less sensitive to the actually presented covariations than when the same covariation pattern was presented in experimenter-determined random order. Thus, experimental strategies of information search slightly inhibited, rather than facilitated, the cognitive process of covariation assessment, even though the average presentation and learning time was clearly higher in the self-paced active search condition.

Summary

We thus arrive at a more and more interactionist perspective within our cognitive-environmental approach. When strong preconceptions, beliefs, expectations, and other (animistic) sources of a priori hypotheses are controlled for, an initial focus or starting hypothesis has to be formed in a stimulus-driven process. Basic principles of learning and induction provide important guidelines for this process, such as sample size (number of trials), precedence (advantage of initial focus), and consistency (with previously learned materials). Importantly, however, whether small or large samples are available, and which stimulus aspects take priority over others, is not determined by the external environment alone. Rather, the individual plays an active, participating, interacting role as she allocates attention, moves in space, participates in jobs and games, and is more interested in some stimulus aspects than in others. This truly (inter-)active function of the individual in the process of social hypothesis testing will be of even more importance in the next chapter devoted to the vicissitudes of sampling and learning processes in even more complex, probabilistic environments.

7 Explicit and implicit hypothesis testing in a complex environment

In the present chapter, we further extend and refine our framework for studying stereotype learning and hypothesis testing in a social environment of increasing complexity. Whereas Chapter 6 raised the structure of stereotypical hypothesis-testing tasks from bi-variate 2×2 contingencies to tri-variate $2 \times 2 \times 2$ contingencies, the present chapter will maintain this level of dimensionality but at the same time raise the number of levels per dimension. Thus, rather than comparing only the behavioral outcomes (success, positivity) of two targets in two different environments, the experimental task to be introduced now will call for the assessment of the performance of as many as 16 different targets in up to 8 different contexts. As we will see, the resulting task will still be sensible and manageable; that is, the complexity of information processing will not lead to a total breakdown in information processing. In fact, the experimental task situation will turn out to be quite realistic and very common. It is the task of a teacher who has to figure out the performance level of a class of 16 different students in 8 different disciplines, or lessons. Real teachers manage such tasks all the time. Experiments from a simulated school class will corroborate that environmental learning is less restricted by capacity constraints than one might expect from the crucial role devoted to cognitive load and resource limitations in the animistic approach to stereotyping. To provide an overview:

- We will first introduce the task setting and the experimental method underlying the simulated classroom.
- Then we try to demonstrate that studying environmental learning in this rather complex environment opens genuine new insights, as evident in alternative perspectives on three types of stereotypical expectancy effects.
- In the remainder of the chapter, we will also consider several compound biases that result from the joint contribution of different influences examined in Chapters 3, 4, 5, and 6, reflecting environmental constraints, information search, and constructive inferences.

Let us first translate the basic contingency frame to the new task environment. At a more abstract level, teachers are permanently involved in empirical tests of the same kind of elementary hypotheses that we studied in Chapters 3 and 4. One hypothesis that may occupy many teachers (even non-sexist ones) at least implicitly is that boys are better than girls in math and science, as illustrated in the 2 × 2 contingency of Figure 7.1. The rows correspond to complementary hypotheses pertaining to the stereotype being tested, namely, the focal hypothesis H_{focus}: "Boys are good in science" and the rival hypothesis H_{altern}: "Girls are good in science". The columns represent confirming versus disconfirming evidence for these hypotheses. The 2 × 2 table entries describe the distribution of stereotype-related stimulus information, quantified as the relative degree of confirmation for the competing hypotheses. However, as we have repeatedly seen, the input distribution is not completely determined by an objective, independent environment but depends on the manner in which active agents (teachers) and reactive targets (students) interact with each other, and with the environment. For instance, a test of the hypothesis that boys are good in science should be influenced by the fact that teachers often attend to boys and care for boys in science, and by the fact that boys may be in the teacher's attention focus in science and therefore do their best to comply with the demand. Thus, an observer's judgment of boys' and girls' performance in science should depend—in addition to objective, latent student abilities—on such factors as teachers' strategies of information search, their inferences based on memorized ecologies, the students' cooperation rate, and the resulting sample sizes of student answers, and their tendency to provide predominantly confirming or disconfirming performance feedback.

In the traditional, animistic approach, the holder of the stereotype and the hypothesis tester are confounded, theoretically. As stereotypes are assumed to originate in the individual's motives and biases, stereotypical influences are expected when the judge can actively distort the stimulus information through selective exposure, biased information search, expectancy-driven encoding, biased forgetting, etc. Judgments of passive, uninvolved observers who merely witnesses a hypothesis test, without vested interests and without themselves holding stereotypical expectancies, would hardly exhibit a hypothesis-confirmation bias.

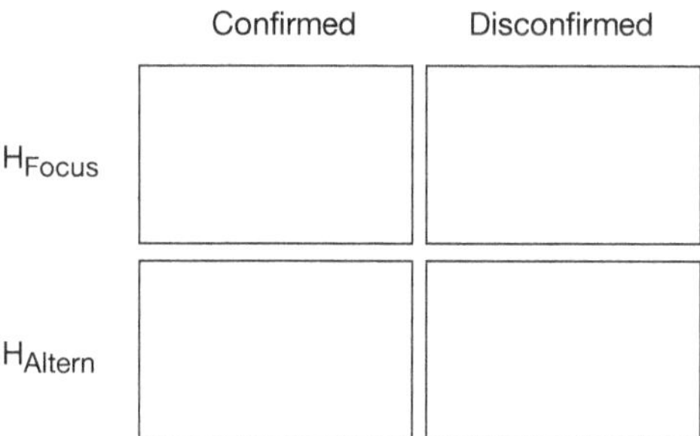

Figure 7.1 Graphical representation of a hypothesis testing task in the simulated school class. The 2 × 2 contingency reflects the amount of confirming and disconfirming evidence for the focal hypothesis that boys are superior in science, as compared with the alternative hypothesis that girls are superior.

One noteworthy result obtained in our environmental-learning approach was that passive observers arrived at similar judgments and fell prey to similar illusions when they were exposed to the same data as hypothesis testers who could actively gather "their own" stimulus samples. In the Fiedler et al. (1999b) experiments, for instance, most participants expected that overt aggression is more common among males than females when in fact the rate of overt aggression was constant. However, when samples of observations about female overt aggression were larger than samples about male behavior (holding 75% confirmation constant), actors as well as observers tended to overestimate *female* overt aggression—contrary to a common stereotype. Thus, from an environmental-learning perspective, the learning samples are crucial. Motives and vested interests are only one of several factors that determine the learning input (e.g., due to attention and serious cooperation). Motivational factors can contribute to the confirmation bias, but they are not strictly necessary.

Regarding the role played by the target, we have also seen that neither selective confirmation (e.g., demand effects mimicking better performance of boys than girls in science) nor a generally high baserate of confirmation (e.g., strong empirical support for generally high performance in science) are necessary for hypothesis verification. Even when the target's rate of behavioral confirmation was constant, and even when the confirming evidence was quite low, environmental learning could lead to artificial hypothesis verification. Let us now see whether similar findings generalize to the simulated classroom.

The simulated school class environment

The experimental setting of the simulated classroom introduces a new quality of semi-naturalistic complexity. We present a series of experiments in which all the mentioned determinants of stereotype learning can be studied within the same task situation: actual contingencies in the database, the actor's focus of attention, constructive inferences, the target's cooperation, and a number of environmental catalysts. To study the interaction of all these factors, we simulated a small world on the computer, consisting of a school class with 16 students (8 boys and 8 girls). Each student was defined by an ability parameter A that determined the proportion of correct responses, and a motivation parameter M that determined how likely the student raised his or her hand when the teacher asked a question. Participants were asked to play the role of a teacher who was to assess all students' performance in as many as eight different lessons (four lessons in language disciplines and four lessons in science disciplines).

In each lesson, the teacher could select questions from a pull-down menu and select one of the students who raised their hand. Feedback was then provided whether the chosen student's answer was correct or wrong. This procedure was repeated for each question, or learning trial. After each lesson (involving some 60 to 80 questions) the teacher was asked to judge all 16 students' ability and motivation; that is, to estimate their percentage of correct responses and the proportion of teacher questions to which each student had raised his or her hand. Over all lessons (distributed over different experimental sessions), the teacher had to extract up to 128 ability parameters (16 students × 8 lessons = 128 parameters) plus the same number of motivation parameters—a truly complex judgment task. Participants were generally highly motivated; they found the experiment very interesting and were eager to make accurate judgments and to be given feedback about their accuracy afterwards. Although the school class was presented only graphically (with the rectangular computer screen representing the classroom and the boys' and girls' names and desks in different locations), teachers could request pictures of all students and reported to have acquired truly vivid impressions of "their" schoolchildren.

In this interactive learning environment, the role of teacher is not confined to passive observations. Rather, the teachers can be instructed to test particular hypotheses and can be encouraged to make inferences beyond the manifest observations given. Moreover, the roles of the judge and the hypothesis tester can be dissociated, as when a participant observes another teacher selecting questions and eliciting student responses. By manipulating the ability (A) and motivation (M) parameters, it is not only possible to establish multiple contingencies (relative rates of correct responses in different students) but also environmental baserates (generally high or low achievement), and differences between lessons in language and science that are consistent or inconsistent with gender stereotypes. Moreover, variation of individual students' motivation parameters affords a natural way of manipulating sample size; given two equally smart students (constant A), a larger sample should be available about the one student who raises her hand more often (high M). As suggested by the results reported in Chapters 3 and 4, this should have a systematic effect on judgments of ability. In any case, the simulated school class allows for the dynamic interaction of different determinants of stereotype learning, while conserving a relatively high degree of experimental control over the target persons (students), the environment, and the actor (e.g., by instructions to the teacher). The paradigm allows us in particular to pit the impact of animistic factors (e.g., gender-related expectancies) against environmental-learning factors (e.g., sample size as a function of the teachers' hypothesis focus).

Judgment biases in the classroom: three types of stereotypical expectancies

Three prominent types of stereotypical expectancies are commonly emphasized in the literature on teacher judgment biases:

(1) Overgeneralization of global differences between more and less intelligent students; students who have shown high (low) performance in one context are classified as high (low) in ability and are therefore expected to show high (low) performance in other contexts as well.

(2) Expectancies derived from gender stereotypes; boys and girls are expected to represent gender-specific assets and deficits in different disciplines. Boys' assets are commonly expected in science, whereas girls' assets are expected in language. Such expectancy influences are particularly prominent in the

stereotype-threat paradigm (Aronson, Quinn, & Spencer, 1998; Steele & Aronson, 1995), which highlights the impairment or "choking" of stereotyped people when negative expectancies are activated.

(3) Scripted knowledge about behavioral episodes; script-like sequences of behavior allow teachers to make inferences beyond their actual observations. For instance, teachers may infer knowledge and ability from a high rate of cooperation, because a typical behavioral script involves the sequence: *Student raises hand → teacher notices → student gives answer → answer is correct.* Having observed this sequence often enough, an inferential shortcut may lead the teacher to infer correct answers when in fact the student has merely raised his or her hand.

Traditionally, all three types of expectancy effects have been explained in terms of animistic concepts. All three effects are supposed to originate in the teacher's internalized beliefs or motives. Whether or not there is a kernel of truth, these beliefs and motivated tendencies may often diverge from reality. According to the prevailing heuristics and biases account, the three types of expectancy effects should be strongest when depth of processing and accuracy motivation is low (Chaiken, 1987; Gilbert, 1989), when objective stimulus information is scarce, and when a shortage of cognitive resources leads people to apply their expectancies in an inflexible, context-independent fashion. In our example, teacher judgment biases should be most pronounced and undifferentiated when teachers are ill-motivated and when actual information exceeds the teachers' processing capacity.

The empirical evidence from the simulated classroom experiments is meant to demonstrate that the cognitive-environmental approach can add some relevant new evidence to all three types of (teacher) expectancy effects. On the one hand, the experiments to be reviewed next supplement available empirical evidence about the three phenomena and their boundary conditions. On the other hand, the environmental learning perspective will give rise to a different "cover story" of the psychological processes that lead to teacher judgment biases. As we shall see, the origin of biases may not reside in the teacher, increased information processing may not reduce the bias, and expectancies may not be applied in an inflexible manner.

To illustrate how discrepant the predictions can be, imagine a student who is female, who shows little motivation in math, and who is rather weak at other disciplines. Would she profit or suffer from teacher judgment biases when her performance in math is evaluated? From a traditional perspective, all three expectancy effects should be to that girl's disadvantage. By overgeneralization, her low performance in other disciplines should give rise to pessimistic teacher inferences. By gender stereotyping, her performance in a typically male domain, math, should be underestimated. By scripted knowledge, her lack of interest and cooperation should foster inferences of lacking ability, based on scripts linking motivation and ability. Nevertheless, our analysis of teacher judgment biases from an environmental learning perspective will show that at least under specific conditions, teacher judgment biases could be in favor of such a student.

Over-generalizing expectancies about high and low student ability

Granting that teacher evaluations cannot be perfectly accurate but that two students with the same performance will sometimes receive different evaluations, let us start with the question of whether smart or dull students will profit from such inaccuracies. Common sense as well as long-established research on the halo effect (Cooper, 1981; Solomon & Saxe, 1977) tells us that teachers should tend to over-generalize expectancies derived from preliminary experience. Expectancy effects should thus benefit those students who are known to be smart from other disciplines and harm those students who have shown to perform less well in other disciplines.

Even when this intuition is correct and such a halo effect is actually at work, our analysis of teacher judgments from the simulated classroom will show that the environmental learning process is dominated by an opposite force that will often override any halo effect, or congruent expectancy effect. The net outcome will then be a *regressive judgment bias* that underestimates the true difference between smart and poor students. In other words, high-ability students suffer, whereas low-ability students profit from the net inaccuracies.

Table 7.1 shows how the difference between high and low ability is operationalized in the simulated classroom (Fiedler et al., 2002b, Experiment 1). Among all eight boys and among all eight girls, one half is high and the other half is low in ability. The term "high ability" means that a student's performance is high in some disciplines (ability parameter A = 0.8, or 80% correct responses) but not in all disciplines (A = 0.5 in other disciplines). Likewise, "low ability" means that performance is rather low in some (A = 0.2) but not all disciplines (A = 0.5). For the moment, we can ignore the other factors varied within the parameter matrix, such as whether the performance differences of boys and girls are consistent with gender stereotypes (girls better in language and boys better in science, or vice versa) and consistent with the similarity structure of disciplines (constant or variable performance within language and within science). Moreover, the student motivation parameters that determine the probability of students raising their hands in the different disciplines were held constant at M = 0.5 (each student raising his or her hand at a 50% rate in all disciplines). We can thus focus on judgments of high and low ability students.

Participants who played the teacher's part in the experiment taught eight different lessons over four experimental sessions, each session lasting longer than an hour. The sequence of lessons was held constant: German/fables, physics/heat (Session 1), math/set theory, English/grammar (Session 2), math/measurement units, German/orthography (Session 3), English/speech exercises, physics/electricity (Session 4). Thus, the first two sessions and the last two sessions included one lesson out of each major discipline (German, English, math, physics). Instructions informed participants that their task was to discern all 16 students' ability and motivation level. Both concepts were clearly explicated operationally as the relative proportion of correct answers (ability) and the relative proportion raising hands (motivation). Accuracy and fairness were emphasized as task-relevant goals in the general instructions.

Table 7.1 Ability parameters used in simulated classroom experiments

	German		*English*		*Mathematics*		*Physics*	
Gender/	*Fables*	*Orthography*	*Grammar*	*Speech exercises*	*Set theory*	*Measurement unit*	*Heat*	*Electricity*
Male								
1 smart	0.5	0.5	0.5	0.5	0.8	0.8	0.8	0.8
2 smart	0.8	0.8	0.8	0.8	0.5	0.5	0.5	0.5
3 smart	0.5	0.5	0.8	0.8	0.8	0.8	0.5	0.5
4 smart	0.8	0.8	0.5	0.5	0.5	0.5	0.8	0.8
5 poor	0.2	0.2	0.2	0.2	0.5	0.5	0.5	0.5
6 poor	0.5	0.5	0.5	0.5	0.2	0.2	0.2	0.2
7 poor	0.2	0.2	0.5	0.5	0.5	0.5	0.2	0.2
8 poor	0.5	0.5	0.2	0.2	0.2	0.2	0.5	0.5
Female								
9 smart	0.8	0.8	0.8	0.8	0.5	0.5	0.5	0.5
10 smart	0.5	0.5	0.5	0.5	0.8	0.8	0.8	0.8
11 smart	0.8	0.8	0.5	0.5	0.5	0.5	0.8	0.8
12 smart	0.5	0.5	0.8	0.8	0.8	0.8	0.5	0.5
13 poor	0.5	0.5	0.5	0.5	0.2	0.2	0.2	0.2
14 poor	0.2	0.2	0.2	0.2	0.5	0.5	0.5	0.5
15 poor	0.5	0.5	0.2	0.2	0.2	0.2	0.5	0.5
16 poor	0.2	0.2	0.5	0.5	0.5	0.5	0.2	0.2

The simulated classroom proper was based on an interactive computer program. The basic menu offered five submenus:

- experimental instructions
- time schedule of lessons across all sessions
- question lists representing the contents of all lessons
- portray photographs of students
- starting the lesson appearing next on the schedule.

Teachers could switch back and forth between the first four submenus, but once the fifth submenu was started, the lesson had to be conducted till the end (defined by a period of 20 minutes). Each lesson consisted of a sequence of question–answer cycles. Each trial started with a pull-down menu of questions for the particular lesson topic. Table 7.2 gives the question list for physics/units of measurement. After the teacher had selected one question (by moving the cursor to the question and pressing the Enter key), a graphical representation of the school class appeared on the screen with those students who raised their hands marked graphically, as in Figure 7.2. The teacher could select one of the students who raised his or her hand (again by moving the cursor to that student and pressing the Enter key). The trial would be completed by feedback indicating whether the answer was correct or not. The number of trials depended on the teacher's self-determined speed (i.e., the number of questions that could be asked within the given time period). At the end

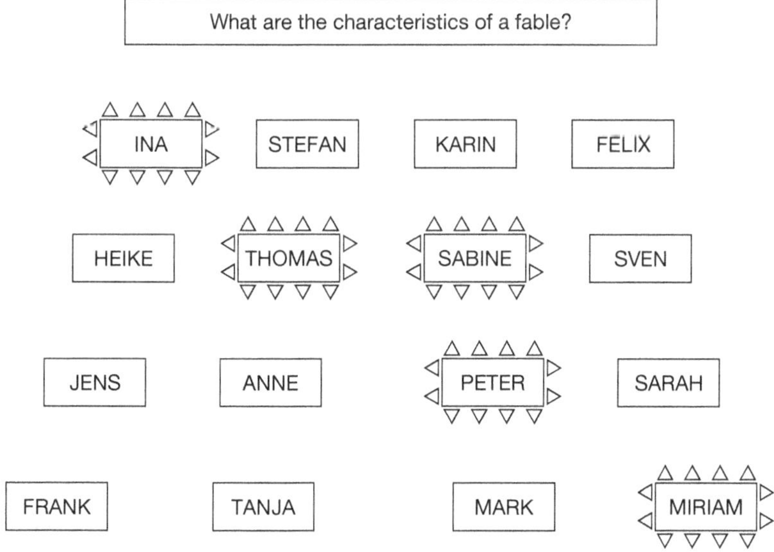

Figure 7.2 The simulated school class environment consisting of 8 boys and 8 girls. Those students who raise their hand in response to the question asked by the teacher are marked graphically.

Table 7.2 Sample pull-down menu for questions in mathematics, units of measurement

Mathematics – Units of Measurement
Identify in "5 kg" the measure and the measurement unit
How many Pfennige are the same as 344 DM 6Pf?
Indicate in DM and Pf an: 81 022 Pf!
How many mm are 4 dm?
How many cm are 6 m?
How many m are 7 km?
Indicate 27 km 640 m 5 cm in the smallest measurement unit!
Translate 7 t into kg!
Translate 586 g into mg!
Translate 703 t into g!
Indicate 581 kg 704 g in the smallest measurement unit!
Translate 5 min into s!
Translate 3 min 45 s into s!
Translate 1 h 33 min into min!
Translate 4 days into h!
Translate 400 s into min and s!
Translate 432 days in weeks and days!
How many minutes have passed on February 29 since the beginning of the year?
What is the distinct feature of a leap year?
How many leap years are there in 10 years?

of each lesson, the teacher was asked to estimate each student's proportion of correct answers (ability) and each student's rate of raising hand (motivation).

In spite of the apparent overload of the inductive judgment task—assessing 128 ability parameters (16 students times 8 lessons) and as many motivation parameters —the resulting estimates were remarkably accurate, contrary to the common claim that high cognitive load will undermine systematic processing and lead judges to rely on prior expectancies and superficial heuristics. In fact, there was only a small tendency to produce halo effects based on the simplified, overgeneralized categorization of students into high versus low ability. As evident from Figure 7.3, higher judgments of smart students were almost totally confined to those informative lessons where their smartness was actually manifested (i.e., where the ability parameter $A = 0.8$ rather than 0.5). Similarly, the lower judgments of weak students were mostly confined to those informative lessons where their deficit was actually manifested ($A = 0.2$ rather than 0.5).

Nevertheless, the two pairs of bars in Figure 7.3 reflect a residual advantage in favor of smart students in those uninformative lessons in which both high and low ability students perform at the same level (i.e., at the $A = 0.5$ level). However, this slight bias in favor of smart students is only one part of the whole story. To understand the full story, one should consider the inaccuracy of judgments in deviation scores (i.e., judged ability–actual ability parameter), as shown in Figure 7.4. Here we encounter once more the basic principle of regression that underlies

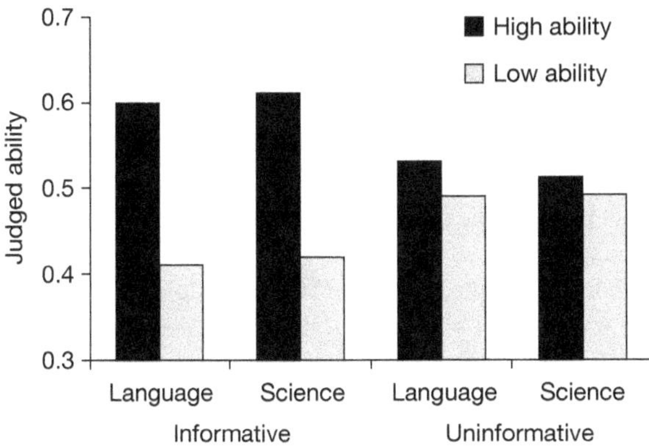

Figure 7.3 Mean ability judgments as a function of student ability (high vs. low), discipline types (language vs. science), and whether ability differences are actually manifested in a lesson (informative vs. uninformative).

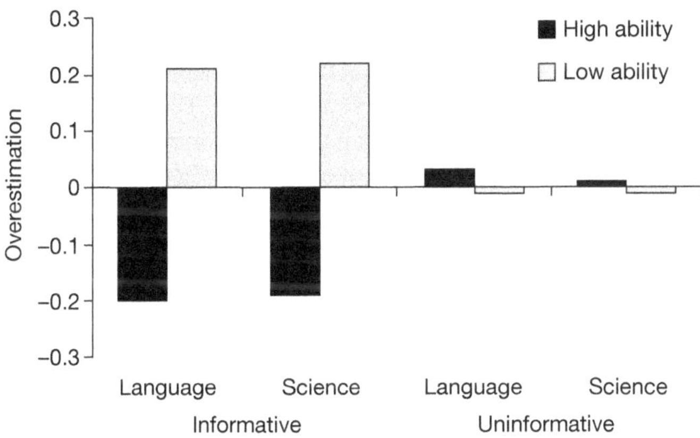

Figure 7.4 Subjective judged ability minus objective ability as a function of student ability (high vs. low), discipline types (language vs. science), and whether ability differences are actually manifested in a lesson (informative vs. uninformative).

all inductive judgment under uncertainty. Whenever judgments are subject to some error component, which is virtually always the case for real problems, judgments tend to be regressive; that is, the true difference between high and low ability (i.e., between A = 0.8 and 0.2) was underestimated. In those informative lessons where the latent differences were actually manifested, the performance of smart students was underestimated markedly, whereas the performance of weak students was clearly overestimated. This bias against high-ability students and in favor of low-ability students, due to the pervasive regression effect, is much stronger than the small advantage of smart students in uninformative lessons.

The regressive nature of judgment can be interpreted in terms of imperfect, incomplete learning. Regression is a direct function of the unreliability or the error component of judgments. As the teacher's learning to discriminate between students of high and low ability proceeded, the error component decreased and judgments became more accurate and less regressive, as apparent from Figure 7.5. From the first to the last session, the underestimation of high performance and the overestimation of low performance decreased. All these preliminary findings reflect fully normal learning effects.

At the same time, the reduction of the regression effect through extended learning entails a source of judgment bias in its own right. Exactly because discrimination performance increases and regression decreases with the number of learning trials—again a fully normal learning effect—judgments of students should depend on sample size. Some students will give more answers than others, yielding performance samples of different sizes. If sample size is large, that is, if there are many learning trials to figure out a student's actual ability parameter, judgments will be more accurate and less regressive than if sample size is small. Thus, discrimination will improve with increasing sample size. This entails a systematic source of bias, or unfairness. If two equally smart students have the same high ability parameter (e.g., A = 0.8) but there are twice as many observations for one student than the other, the resulting evaluations will differ systematically. Judgments will more likely reflect the actually high performance level of the student with the large sample than the equally smart student with the small sample, due to unequal regression. Conversely, the same low performance (A = 0.2) of two equally weak students will be recognized more sensitively when the sample is large than when the sample is small.

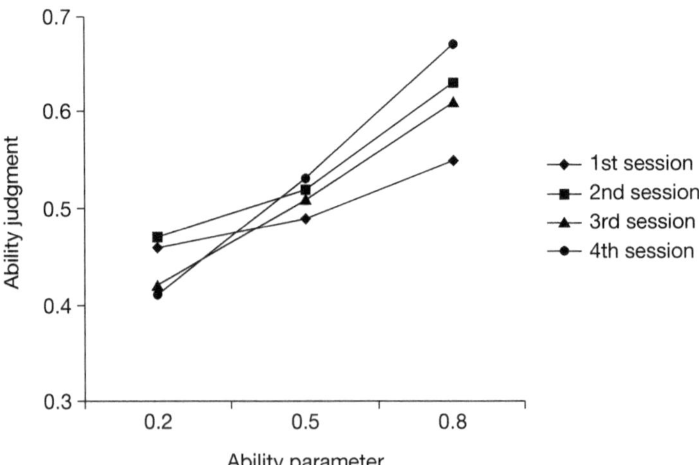

Figure 7.5 With extended learning about the students ability level, from Session 1 to 4, ability judgments become less regressive.

This prediction was clearly supported by the teacher judgments in the simulated classroom. Figure 7.6 gives the mean judgments that high and low ability students received in informative and uninformative lessons from teachers who had drawn a large sample and by teachers who had drawn a small sample from those students. The distinction of large and small was defined as whether the sample size was above or below a teacher's median sample size (across all students in a given lesson). Although judgments were more or less regressive in all conditions, there was a systematic bias due to differential regression. When samples were large rather than small, evaluations of high-ability students were enhanced but evaluations of low-ability students became even worse. This differential influence of sample size on judgments of high- and low-ability students was confined to those informative lessons in which the ability differences were actually manifested, fully in line with an environmental-learning account.

It may be recognized that such a teacher judgment bias is formally equivalent to the illusory correlation effects reviewed in Chapter 3. Just as the prevalence of positive behavior is more easily detected in a majority than in a minority, due to differential sample size or numbers of learning trials, smartness is more readily detected in a student on whom a large sample is available than in a student with a small sample. However, the teacher judgment bias is of a more general kind than the aforementioned illusory correlation effect. In the simulated classroom, we can observe multiple illusory correlations at the same time, one for each pair of students with the same ability level but with different sample sizes. Moreover, in the more complex, semi-realistic environment of the simulated classroom, the reasons for unequal sample sizes are manifold. Some of these reasons may reflect animistic motives or tendencies within the teacher. For instance, teachers' attention may be biased toward those students whom they like or whom they are most interested in. However, other reasons originate in the external environment. Some students may

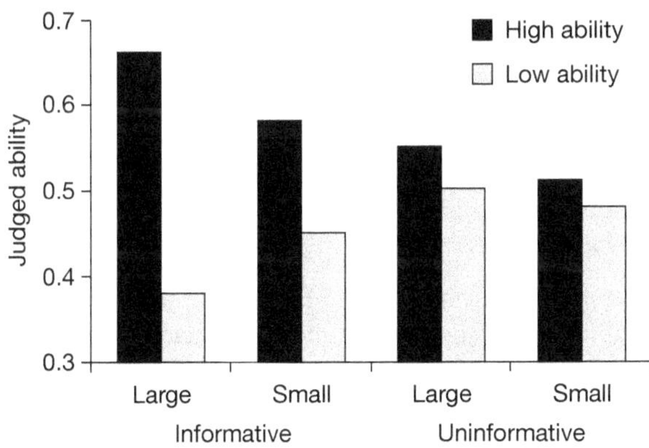

Figure 7.6 Mean ability judgments as a function of actual performance (high vs. low ability), informativeness (whether a student's high or low ability is actually manifested in a specific lesson), and sample size (large vs. small number of questions asked by the teacher).

be more visible or salient, some may be absent very often, and students may differ greatly in motivation so that some raise their hands more often than others. Regardless of whether the teacher is biased or the stimulus environment itself produces unequal sample sizes, the effect will by and large be the same.

Returning to the starting question of who profits more from inaccurate teacher judgments, smart or weak students, the common answer of the heuristics and biases approach has to be corrected or supplemented in several respects. One would have commonly expected that, given their cognitive overload, teachers try to reduce the complexity of the multiple judgment problem by relying on simplifying expectancies. Accordingly, they should have categorized students by ability and overgeneralized this prior classification across lessons, whether informative or not. Students classified as high ability should profit from over-generalized expectancies, whereas students classified as low ability should suffer from it. Because this bias is supposed to reflect a simplifying heuristic process, the advantage of smart students and the disadvantage of weak students should increase with uncertainty, that is, when stimulus samples are scarce.

In contrast to this "heuristic story", the environmental learning analysis shows that the superiority of smart students is most apparent when stimulus samples are rich. Moreover, there is little evidence for a halo effect. Expectancies resulting from high- and low-ability students' performance in prior disciplines are hardly carried over to new disciplines unless their high or low ability is actually manifested in the current lesson. But when high and low ability is really exhibited, the resulting judgments show the same regressive tendency that characterizes all inductive learning. The net result is a judgment bias that tends to harm good students and benefit bad students, contrary to the common-sense notion of expectancy and prejudice, and contrary to the notion of self-fulfilling prophecies. Our learning analysis strongly suggests that over-generalized expectancies and self-fulfilling prophecies, which are commonly presupposed in the literature on teacher judgments (Brophy, 1983; Cooper, 1979; Jussim, 1989, 1991), are by no means the only judgment biases to be predicted. Before the impact of self-fulfilling prophecies can be manifested, the resistance of an opposite regression effect has to be overcome. It remains an open empirical question how likely this will occur, given the upper limit of reliability that teacher judgments can attain.

Teacher evaluations and gender stereotypes

Let us now turn to the second type of expectancy effects, group-related stereotypes or, in particular, gender stereotypes. Boys are commonly expected to show superior performance in science (math, physics) whereas girls might outperform boys in language disciplines (German, English). Within the heuristics and biases research program, again, the function of stereotypes is to reduce cognitive load and to simplify cognitive processes. Therefore, to the extent that gender differences are utilized, the impact of the actual stimulus input on teacher judgments should decrease and the impact of simplifying gender expectancies should increase. The outcome of this heuristic process should be apparent in an undifferentiated judgment bias that favors boys in science and girls in language disciplines. This bias should be detached from the dynamic stimulus input but simply reflect the static gender stereotype.

Our environmental-learning analysis does not contest that such straightforward expectancy biases are possible, but it would not consider them particularly enlightening, from a theoretical point of view. It is well known that expectancy biases, even the more primitive ones, can influence social judgments. The learning approach also assumes that teachers will be sensitive to gender differences, but the impact of gender on their student evaluations will not be confined to undermining systematic processing and engaging instead in shallow guessing, as depicted above. Rather, the learning approach points to more indirect but theoretically intriguing ways in which the teacher's interaction with environmental factors mediates the influence of gender stereotypes.

In another experiment reported by Fiedler et al. (2002a), teachers were asked to test specific hypotheses concerning the performance of boys and girls in science and language disciplines. In each of four successive lessons (distributed over four sessions), each teacher was asked to test a different hypothesis, referring to physics, math, German, and English. Within both discipline types, science (physics, math) and language (German, English), one hypothesis to be tested was stereotype consistent (e.g., find out whether boys have their assets in physics, whether girls have their assets in English) and one hypothesis was stereotype inconsistent (find out whether boys have their assets in German, whether girls have their assets in math). The order of disciplines/lessons was varied and the allocation of consistent and inconsistent hypotheses to disciplines was counter-balanced.

If teachers were not instructed to test explicit hypotheses, they would presumably use their gender stereotypes as implicit hypotheses, looking out for boys' assets in science and for girls' assets in language. As we have seen in Chapter 4, such a hypothesis-testing focus will typically produce a confirmation bias; that is, the manner in which information is sought and processed will often result in hypothesis verification, even when the observations do not objectively support the hypothesis. Again, the common interpretation within the heuristics and biases program is in terms of an expectancy bias. Some judges will some of the time base their judgments on top-down expectancies rather than bottom-up processing of stimulus data. To the extent that this occurs, average judgments should tend to be consistent with gender stereotypes, independently of the manifest stimulus input.

As we have also seen in Chapter 4, however, the auto-verification of hypotheses need not reflect a stereotype-driven, biased guessing process but can be the result of a normal inductive learning process. Indeed, the influence of environmental learning on hypothesis verification may run counter to stereotypical expectancies and may have completely different psychological implications. The experimental design we have just depicted allows for the isolation of hypothesis-testing effects (following normal rules of inductive learning) and stereotype effects proper, because the design includes stereotype consistent as well as inconsistent hypotheses.

How will the information acquisition process be affected by the hypothesis focus? As described in Chapter 4, a common strategy is *positive testing* (Klayman

& Ha, 1987). When instructed to test boys' assets in physics, teachers should ask more questions in a subsequent physics session to boys than to girls. Similarly when testing a hypothesis about girls' assets in English, teachers should direct more questions to girls than to boys in English. This kind of selective information search may originate in the same stereotype that is commonly interpreted as the source of expectancy biases. However, the positive-testing strategy may also mediate a learning-based judgment bias that is independent of expectancies. Given the same proportion of, say, 80% correct responses of boys and girls in physics, positive testing leads teachers to draw a larger sample about boys than girls. As a consequence, the same high ability level will be learned more effectively for boys than for girls, as we have repeatedly demonstrated in other experiments (Fiedler, 1991; Fiedler & Armbruster, 1994; Fiedler et al., 1999a) reviewed in Chapters 3 and 4.

To set the learning account apart from the stereotype account, we have to look at the outcome of stereotype-inconsistent hypothesis tests. When looking for female assets in math or male assets in German, teachers who engage in positive testing should gather large samples for girls in math and large samples for boys in German. If the effect of sample size overrides the potential effect of expectancy-based guessing, smart girls should then be evaluated better than equally high-performing boys in math, and smart boys should appear superior to equally high-performing girls in German.

Let us first consider the information search data summarized in Figure 7.7. As in previous research, positive testing is widely used as an information search strategy. When testing stereotype-consistent hypotheses, teachers address more science questions to boys and more language questions to girls (see left two pairs of bars in Figure 7.7). However, a perfect reversal is obtained when teachers test stereotype-inconsistent hypotheses. Given the reverse focus, they address more

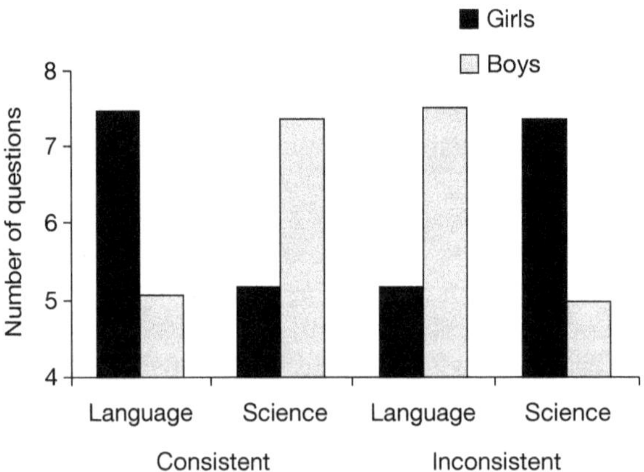

Figure 7.7 Number of questions addressing boys and girls in language and science, when testing hypotheses that are consistent versus inconsistent with the common gender stereotype.

science questions at girls and more language questions at boys. It is not surprising that the lopsided distribution of questions reflects the task constraints. To find out whether girls have their assets in science, the most relevant and diagnostic information can be expected from data jointly related to girls and science (cf. Klayman & Ha, 1987).

The crucial question is whether and how these differential patterns of data acquisition mediate different performance judgments. Before we turn to the relevant results, we have to consider the objective ability parameters used for this experiment. Apparently, for each hypothesis being tested (i.e., within each column of the parameter matrix in Table 7.3), there was an equal number (i.e., 4) of boys and girls with high (A = 0.8) and low (A = 0.2) ability. In other words, the stimulus environment was perfectly neutral, supporting neither the gender stereotype nor the reverse hypothesis. Any tendency to evaluate boys' and girls' achievement differentially should therefore reflect a bias. The question is whether the bias constantly follows the stereotypical expectancies or whether the direction of the bias is determined by differential sample size, due to positive testing.

The relevant empirical results are given in Figures 7.8 and 7.9, pertaining to judgments of boys and girls who perform at the same high level (A = 0.8), as a function of discipline type (science vs. language) and positive testing. Figure 7.8 refers to stereotype-consistent hypotheses only. The majority of teachers who did

Table 7.3 Ability parameters used in experiments on sexist stereotypes. Note that the average ability of male and female students in language (German, English) and science (Mathematics, Physics) is constant

Students	*German*	*English*	*Mathematics*	*Physics*
Male				
1	0.8	0.8	0.5	0.5
2	0.8	0.8	0.5	0.5
3	0.5	0.5	0.8	0.8
4	0.5	0.5	0.8	0.8
5	0.5	0.5	0.2	0.2
6	0.5	0.5	0.2	0.2
7	0.2	0.2	0.5	0.5
8	0.2	0.2	0.5	0.5
Female				
9	0.8	0.8	0.5	0.5
100.8	0.8	0.5	0.5	
110.5	0.5	0.8	0.8	
120.5	0.5	0.8	0.8	
130.5	0.5	0.2	0.2	
140.5	0.5	0.2	0.2	
150.2	0.2	0.5	0.5	
160.2	0.2	0.5	0.5	

engage in pronounced positive testing (left two pairs of bars) clearly show a stereotype-congruent judgment bias. Girls receive higher ratings in language and boys receive higher ratings in science, even though the rated male and female students did not actually differ in their ability parameters. The very fact that this result is confined to judges using positive-test strategies and disappears for (the minority of) judges who do not use positive testing corroborates the crucial role of the acquired stimulus input.

Figure 7.9 speaks to the crucial condition involving stereotype-inconsistent hypotheses. The results clearly support the sample-size principle derived from simple inductive learning laws, rather than the notion of stereotype expectancy effects. Those teachers who do engage in positive testing (see left two pairs of

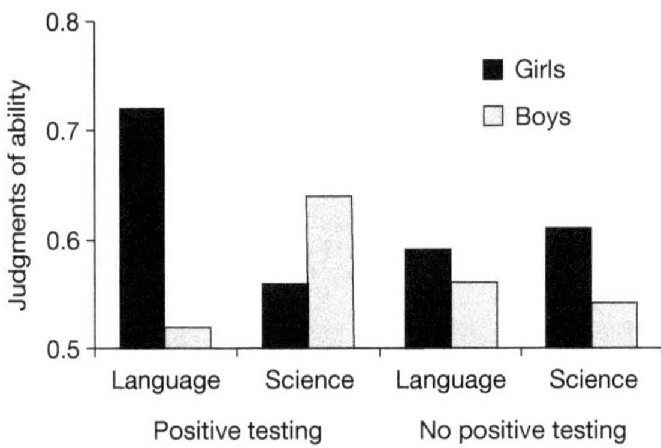

Figure 7.8 Mean ability judgments of boys and girls in language and science disciplines, as a function of information search strategies (positive testing vs. not), given stereotype-consistent hypotheses.

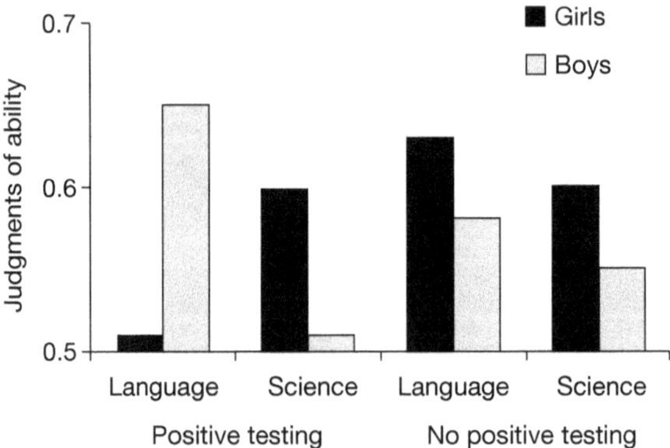

Figure 7.9 Mean ability judgments of boys and girls in language and science disciplines, as a function of information search strategies (positive testing vs. not), given stereotype-inconsistent hypotheses.

bars), gathering large samples on girls in science and on boys in language, actually arrive at more positive ratings of girls in science and of boys in language—contrary to the common gender stereotype. Again, the bias disappears for (the minority of) those teachers who do not engage in positive testing.

Thus, our learning approach leads to a revised picture for the second type of expectancy effects as well. The influence of gender stereotypes on judgments of boys and girls in science and language disciplines need not originate in a heuristic shortcut that circumvents stimulus processing and relies merely on preconceived expectancies. Rather, gender stereotypes, like any other hypothesis, whether consistent or inconsistent with the stereotype, can influence the manner in which the teacher interacts with the learning environment, gathering samples of unequal size as requested by the focus of the judgment task. Judgment biases can emerge as a side effect of this interactive search process, due to the already familiar principle that the same rate of high performance is psychologically more significant and has a stronger influence on subjective judgments when based on a large rather than small sample.

To repeat, there is nothing irrational about positive testing. Normative analyses, based on information theory and Bayesian statistics, tell us that focusing on the very event specified in the hypothesis can be a rational and informative strategy under a wide range of boundary conditions (Klayman & Ha, 1987; Oaksford & Chater, 1994). Moreover, positive testing may often be required simply because alternative event categories are hard to define. To test the hypothesis that girls are good in math, teachers can be sure that looking at girls in math is relevant, but the hypothesis does not strictly exclude that boys are good as well. Also, the hypothesis does not imply strictly that girls should be weaker in other disciplines, nor what relevant other comparison disciplines are. For these and other reasons, positive testing could be the most informative and most diagnostic strategy that teachers can apply. That the resulting samples are unequal and unrepresentative in size is also completely normal; stimulus samples are rarely ever equal. Some event categories are always more frequent, more accessible or visible, more proximal than others. Hypothesis testers are usually interested in certain event categories more than in others if only to take different payoffs into account. The important message to be extracted from such an environmental-learning analysis is that hypothesis confirmation biases are an almost inevitable side effect of all kind of information search. These biases are by no means restricted to stimulus-independent, heuristic shortcuts based on constant stereotypical expectancies.

Scripted knowledge: Episodes linking student motivation and ability

The third type of an expectancy bias relies neither on the overgeneralization of person attributes nor on group stereotypes, but on knowledge about standard behavioral scripts. One common script that can be assumed to affect teacher's performance judgments involves the following sequential episode: *The teacher asks a question → A student raises his or her hand → The teacher notices this and selects one of the students who raise their hand → The selected student provides an answer* → *The answer is correct.* An alternative script may end up with an incorrect answer, but there are good reasons to assume that a student who raises her hand is quite likely to know the correct answer to the teacher's question or is at least not fully ignorant. This assumption is weaker than postulating that motivation (hand raising) and ability (correct answers) are correlated at the interpersonal level, across students. The only assumption here is that at the very moment that a student raises her hand, she is likely to be in the position to provide some substantial answer. She need not exhibit any stable motivation correlated with stable high ability, distinct from other students.

Having acquired such scripted knowledge, the teacher may use the motivational cue *hand raising* as a proxy for inferring *ability* (i.e., a correct answer). In other words, scripted knowledge may be used to infer complete stimulus episodes (i.e., raising hand leading to a correct answer) from incomplete episodes (raising hand). Indeed, such constructive inferences from motivational cues to ability are rather likely to take place, because the stimulus environment renders information about motivation more accessible than the information about ability. After all, given 16 students in a classroom, each individual student's motivation (i.e., raising hand or not) can be observed for each question asked by the teacher. In contrast, individual student's ability can only be observed on every sixteenth trial on average, because only one of the 16 students can answer each teacher question. Given this imbalance of motivation and ability cues, using motivation as a proxy to ability should be quite functional a strategy, provided the statistical contingency, p(correct response / raising hand), is informative.

Just like overgeneralizations and stereotypical inferences, script-based inferences are commonly assumed to reflect preformed, stimulus-insensitive expectancies. Accordingly, teachers are armed with naive theories—such as the theory that raising hand is the first step in a sequence ending in a correct answer—and reliance on these naive theories should increase with decreasing access to valid information and decreasing cognitive capacity and accuracy motivation. In any case, scripted inferences should be based on simplifying rules of thumb, or heuristics that are used in a rigid, stimulus-insensitive fashion.

A slightly different story is suggested by an environmental learning approach. Script-based inferences from motivation to ability need not be used in a rigid and stimulus-insensitive way. They might as well be driven by valid ecological rules, and inferences may change flexibly as the ecology changes. To this extent, utilizing scripted knowledge may augment the overall validity of teacher judgments. To demonstrate this revised picture of scripted inferences, we ran another experiment using the simulated classroom (Fiedler et al., 2002a, Experiment 3). The overall ability level of all 16 students was manipulated in two experimental conditions. Teachers were either exposed to a smart environment in which the ability parameter of all 16 students was constantly set to A = 0.7 (i.e., 70% correct answers), or in a weak environment, the ability level was held constant at A = 0.3. Only the motivation parameters were varied between students and lessons according to the same pattern as in Table 7.1; that is, one half of all boys and girls were high in motivation, but their high motivation (M = 0.8) was only manifested in informative lessons, but not in uninformative lessons (M = 0.5). The other half of all boys and girls was low in motivation but their low parameter (M = 0.2) was confined to informative as opposed to uninformative lessons (M = 0.5).

Given such an environment, with marked variation in motivation but virtually no variation (except for sampling error) in ability, it should be quite likely that teachers use differences in motivation to infer ability when they are forced to judge ability. However, if they do not rely on rigid naive theories (hand-raising as a heuristic cue to ability), but use the motivation cues in an ecologically intelligent fashion, the inference direction should vary with the conditional probability p(correct answer/raising hand) that holds in the given environment. This conditional probability should be high if A = 0.7 but rather low if A = 0.3. Consequently, observing a student raising her hand very often in a smart environment, where raising hand is normally followed by a successful outcome, should support a positive inference. That student should receive more favorable ability judgments than another student who raises her hand less often (inviting less script-based inferences). In contrast, in a weak environment, where the modal outcome of a hand-raising episode is failure, a student who raises his hand very often should be judged more negatively than another student who raises his hand less often. Such a flexible, adaptive use of the motivation cue would be sensitive to valid environmental learning, rather than resting on rigid expectancies alone.

Figure 7.10 reveals that the environmental learning account receives empirical support. Although the actual ability level is held constant, teachers' ability judgments are biased systematically, reflecting inferences from observed differences in motivation. However, these inferences are drawn in a flexible, ecologically adaptive fashion. If the baserate of successful performance episodes is high (A = 0.7), the ability of highly motivated students who raise their hands often is judged

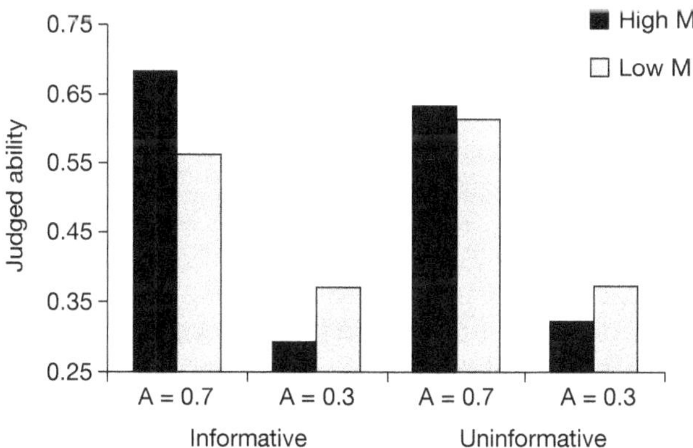

Figure 7.10 Mean ability judgments as a function of ability baserate (A = 0.7 vs. 0.3) and student motivation. Informative lessons are those in which students actually manifest their motivation differences. In uninformative lessons, motivation of all students shifts to M = 0.5.

to be higher than the ability of less motivated students. If the success baserate is low (A = 0.3), in contrast, high motivation supports more unfavorable ability ratings (see left two pairs of bars in Figure 7.10). Note in particular that enriching the sample of manifest observations of correct and incorrect answers with inferences derived from motivation cues *increases the overall accuracy*. That is, judgments of high and low ability students who raise their hands often and invite many inferences from motivation cues come closer to the correct level of A = 0.7 and A = 0.3, respectively, than less active students. This increase in accuracy reflects the fact that scripted inferences are sensitive to actual conditional probability p(correct/raising hands). Script-based inferences which have this adaptive, baserate-sensitive property do not interfere with an accuracy goal but rather support accuracy. Given that the validity of motivation cues is above chance, there is nothing irrational about utilizing motivation cues for inferring ability, if these cues add only a minor part of systematic variance.

That teachers are sensitive to actual stimulus information is not only evident in the opposite inference direction observed for smart and weak environments. Stimulus learning is also evident in the finding that the impact of motivation on ability is confined to those informative lessons where motivation differences are actually manifested. If the same students do not raise their hand very often (or very rarely) in other lessons, the inference from motivation to ability disappears (see right two pairs of bars in Figure 7.10).

Compound biases in semi-realistic environments

Coming back to our challenging starting question, it is now apparent that quite uncommon, distinct predictions can be derived and supported when stereotyping is conceived as a learning process in a complex environment. From a traditional theory perspective, one could hardly think of teacher judgment biases that benefit a female student who shows little motivation in math, and who is rather poor in other disciplines as well. However, all aspects of this seemingly absurd outcome are possible and even likely under clearly specifiable conditions. Girls, like boys, who perform low can profit from the regression effect that characterizes all imperfect assessment in a probabilistic environment. Moreover, this regression effect should be maximal when a girl does not raise her hand very often, due to low motivation. The very fact that she is a girl and that she is evaluated in a male domain, math, will hardly undo these consequences of the number of learning trials on the degree of regression that can be predicted.

The experiments reported so far in this chapter supplement and revise our understanding of all three types of expectancy effects, overgeneralization of personality traits, group stereotypes, and inferences based on scripted knowledge. At the same time, however, these experiments highlight the fact that hypothesis tests in more complex, semi-realistic environments, such as the simulated classroom, involve compounds of different judgment biases that may operate simultaneously. A number of different biases, some of which have been the focus of Chapters 3, 4 and 5, work together in the simulated classroom, in the same or in opposite directions, when teachers evaluate student achievement. We recognize illusory correlations and autoverification effects based on unequal sample size that come to interact with expectancies based on personality traits, group stereotypes and scripts.

Furthermore, the teacher's effective stimulus input is not confined to objectively observed behavior but also includes constructive inferences of the same kind as reviewed in Chapter 5. Thus, the effective stimulus samples that provide the learning input for the teachers' multiple assessment task reflect:

- constraints imposed by the actual ability parameters;
- students' visibility, motivation, and salience;
- teachers' own information search and positive-testing strategies;
- inferred and imagined behaviors;
- guessing based on genuine expectancies;
- compounds of observed and inferred (scripted) information.

Inductive learning is principally open to all these sources of valid and invalid information. Just as in all kind of learning, active elaboration and self-generated inferences are the key to the acquisition of a stable memory code (Craik & Tulving, 1975), the teachers' own internally generated inferences may influence his impressions of the students no less than externally provided observations of actual performance. From a learning and memory point of view, such a generation effect (Dosher & Russo, 1976) would appear to be not very surprising. Integrating actual observations with inferences and constructions is not even irrational, because all information input is error prone and of imperfect validity, whether inferences or actual observations. Assessment of ability from a sample of 10 or 12 student answers to arbitrary questions may be as unreliable and error prone as inferences from motivational cues based on context-sensitive inferences within the teacher. The former cannot be classified as more rational on a priori grounds than the latter.

Upon closer inspection, what appeared to be "actual observations" at first sight are also dependent on knowledge-based inferences simply because no sample of student answers can be equated with the distal concept, ability. As we have no receptors for literally perceiving ability, we have to rely on inferences from a sample of proximal observations. Whether inferences from student answers are more valid than inferences from even more remote cues, such as motivation and collaboration, remains an empirical question. Because validity is a direct function of reliability and because reliability, depends on sample size, a large sample of motivation cues may result in an inference as valid as, or even more valid than, a smaller sample of actual student answers.

How teacher judgments originate in blends of actually observed student episodes and self-generated inferences is illustrated by several other findings from the simulated classroom paradigm. For example, when teachers form judgments of motivation (cooperation rates) and ability (rate of correct answers), they over-estimate the performance of those students at whom they have themselves directed many questions (Fiedler et al., 2002a). That is, they project their own selective attention to particular students onto those students' alleged performance rates. Controlling for students' motivation parameter, and for the number of questions to which they actually raised their hands, teachers will attribute more activity to those students who are the focus of their own activity. This projective tendency is even carried over to ability ratings such that more ability is attributed to those students who are the teacher's favorite focus of attention.

From the perspective of an animistic theory account, an interpretation that quickly suggests itself is that those most focused students who profit from teachers' selective attention are just most attractive or likeable to teachers. According to this account, the confusion of self-generated variation and actual variation in student performance would only reflect the well-known influence of motivated, goal-driven processes. However, it can be shown that teachers' selective attention is not determined by personal and idiosyncratic favoritism alone. For example, when the ability parameter of individual students is varied experimentally, teachers' attention is typically attracted by the more capable students. To the extent that student attributes determine attention allocation, however, teachers' sympathy can be ruled out. While the experimental manipulation of ability leads teachers to address many questions at specific students, they in turn project this attention onto students' alleged cooperation level, as manifested in judgments of the rate of hand raising.

The role of redundancy in a complex environment

In a highly complex, probabilistic, and fallible environment, the properties of which may change over time and can only be assessed under high uncertainty, the consistency or redundancy of two or more cues is a valuable source of information. If two cues or predictors correlate in a reasonable way, consistent with approved world knowledge, this provides useful evidence that the redundant cues reflect systematic variance rather than merely error variance, or noise. In their seminal article on "The Psychology of Prediction", Kahneman and Tversky (1973) referred to this extra value of redundant information as an "illusion of validity". Although normative statistical models would require that redundant predictors be given less weight than independent predictors, human judges seem to be misled by the "illusionary" validity of redundant cues, which induce a sense of consistency. For example, a student's high record of correct answers should be worth more, and should lead to even better teacher judgments, if it comes along with a high cooperation rate, that is, if ability correlates with motivation so that correct answers and hand-raising provide redundant cues. Similar evidence for a redundancy gain can be found in many other areas of social judgment and decision making, such as the shared information bias in group decision making (i.e., the higher weight given to information shared by many group members; Greitemeyer & Schulz-Hardt, in press; Kelly & Karau, 1999; Stasser, 1992; Stasser & Titus, 1985), or the general accentuation effect (Eiser & Stroebe, 1972; Tajfel, 1959).

However, depreciating the extra weight given to redundant information as an "illusion" would appear to ignore the adaptive value that redundant information has in a probabilistic environment. Whenever the predictors to be used for a judgment task are error prone or of limited reliability, the judge faces the double task of not only *using* the predictors in a way that maximizes explained variance but also to critically *monitor* the predictors' reliability and validity; that is, to discriminate between reliable predictors and erroneous predictors. Of course, the intercorrelation between predictors is commonly considered a prominent way of establishing cue reliability—in psychometrics as in the naive theories of everyday judges. Within the domain of teacher judgments, for example, a substantial correlation between persistent cooperation (motivation) and correct answers (ability) can be taken as evidence for the systematic nature of the high performance. Apparently, the observed correct answers were not haphazard (reflecting local knowledge in a single topic), artificial (reflecting helpful suggestions by neighboring students), or unstable (reflecting a sampling error). Rather, when the same students who tend to give correct answers are also those who demonstrate their readiness to give the correct answer by raising their hands, then the teacher's judgment can rest on firmer ground.

Indeed, several findings from the simulated classroom experiments suggest that teachers use by default motivation and ability as correlated aspects of performance. When students do not differ in motivation but only in ability (according to the parameters of Table 7.1), teachers tend to ascribe higher hand-raising rates to those students who gave more correct answers. Conversely, when ability is constant and only motivation varies between students, we have seen that teachers ascribe high ability to those students who raise their hands often. However, notably, they use the redundancy of cues in a flexible, ecologically sensitive fashion. As we have seen above (Fiedler et al., 2002a, Experiment 3), when raising hands is likely to be followed by a wrong rather than a correct answer, teachers may switch to an inverse inference strategy, inferring low ability from high motivation.

Again, it is important to note that such a flexible utilization of redundancy in a complex, multiple-cue environment does not require an animistic explanation, based on beliefs, wishes, and deliberate intentions. That is, teachers may not be aware of the manner in which they utilize redundancy information, just as a reader is not aware of her utilization of orthographic redundancy between successive letters. This independence from conscious, controlled reasoning is evident in a persistent finding obtained in all the simulated classroom experiments reviewed so far. After teachers had rated all students' ability (% of correct answers) and motivation (% of raising hands), they were also asked explicitly to predict the percentage of correct answers that each student would have given had he or she been asked when *not* raising his or her hand. These ratings of prospective ability were highly correlated with, and also of similar magnitude to, ratings of the manifestly observed success rates. Apparently, teachers construe ability as a latent personality trait in students that exists quite independently of their cooperation rate. Thus, they do not seem to notice that motivation is an integral component in their own assessment of the latent ability construct.

The manner in which redundant information is utilized at a lower level than deliberate reasoning, using beliefs and intentions, can be illustrated by another experiment conducted in the simulated classroom (Fiedler, Freytag, Walther,

& Plessner, 2002). This time, teachers were asked to make comparative group judgments of girls' and boys' performance. The motivation level was always higher for the opposite gender group. For a male teacher, the M parameter varied between 0.5 and 0.8 for two subgroups of girls, and between 0.3125 and 0.5 for two subgroups of boys, as shown in Table 7.4. The ability level and distribution was exactly the same for both gender groups. However, there was some variation in ability between the two subgroups of boys and girls, and this ability variance was either positively or negatively correlated with the variation in motivation. In the *redundant condition*, those four boys/girls who showed somewhat higher ability (shaded cells in Table 7.4) were also the ones who showed somewhat higher motivation, and vice versa. In the *counter-redundant condition*, in contrast, the one subgroup of boys/girls that gave more correct responses were those who raised their hand *less* often (see Table 7.4). Note that if anything the overall ability was somewhat higher in the counter-redundant condition (between 0.5 and 0.8) than in the redundant condition (between 0.5 and 0.6875). Note also that the expected value of observing a student giving a correct answer, i.e., the product of motivation (i.e., to raise hand), and ability (i.e., to give a correct answer when raising hand and being asked), was the same in the redundant and the counter-redundant condition, across all students and both lessons. This can be easily ascertained by multiplying the corresponding motivation and ability parameters in the table. The

Table 7.4 Manipulation of redundancy between ability and motivation in simulated school class (shaded cells represent students with higher motivation or ability)

Students	*Motivation in both redundancy conditions*		*Ability in redundant condition*		*Ability in counter-redundant condition*	
Gender outgroup	*German*	*Math*	*German*	*Math*	*German*	*Math*
1	0.80	0.50	0.6875	0.50	0.50	0.80
2	0.80	0.50	0.6875	0.50	0.50	0.80
3	0.80	0.50	0.6875	0.50	0.50	0.80
4	0.80	0.50	0.6875	0.50	0.50	0.80
5	0.50	0.80	0.50	0.6875	0.80	0.50
6	0.50	0.80	0.50	0.6875	0.80	0.50
7	0.50	0.80	0.50	0.6875	0.80	0.50
8	0.50	0.80	0.50	0.6875	0.80	0.50
Gender ingroup						
9	0.50	0.3125	0.6875	0.50	0.50	0.80
10	0.50	0.3125	0.6875	0.50	0.50	0.80
11	0.50	0.3125	0.6875	0.50	0.50	0.80
12	0.50	0.3125	0.6875	0.50	0.50	0.80
13	0.3125	0.50	0.50	0.6875	0.80	0.50
14	0.3125	0.50	0.50	0.6875	0.80	0.50
15	0.3125	0.50	0.50	0.6875	0.80	0.50
16	0.3125	0.50	0.50	0.6875	0.80	0.50

overall mean of the motivation × ability product was 0.4 for all students of the gender outgroup and 0.25 for all students of the gender ingroup.

As Figure 7.11 illustrates, teachers tended to notice the outgroup advantage. However, more interestingly, ability ratings were consistently higher in the redundant than in the counter-redundant condition, for both the gender ingroup and outgroup. When the environment supported the use of motivation as a cue that is correlated with ability, the frequent joint occurrence of both cues, raising hands and correct answers, led to an impression of higher ability—obviously because two meaningfully correlated performance cues validated each other and thereby supported more extreme judgments. If, however, teachers learned that motivation and ability tend to be inversely correlated in that different subgroups of students stand out in terms of motivation and ability, then the group ability ratings for the entire class decreased significantly.

Thus far we have considered several findings to demonstrate that teachers do not restrict their student evaluations to samples of correct versus incorrect answers as the most sensible ability cues. Rather, they are influenced by more mediate cues, such as students' cooperation rate, as well. In other words, the effective sample that drives their evaluation includes observations of complete episodes (*question → hand raising → student answer*) as well as incomplete episodes (*question → hand raising → answer unclear*) that have to be completed by internal inferences. As long as these inferences are sensitive to the actually existing contingencies between hand raising and correct responses, using the motivation cue (hand raising) is no less rational than using correct versus incorrect answers. Both cues, M and A, are not identical to, but only statistically related with the distal construct, ability. Using motivation cues is still on the safe ground of actually observed behavior.

What will teachers do when they leave this safe ground? Will they also be

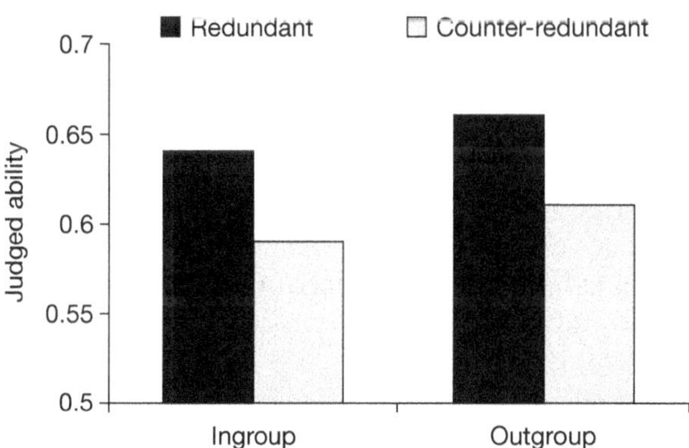

Figure 7.11 Mean ability judgments of students belonging to the teacher's gender ingroup and outgroup, when the correlation between ability and motivation is positive (redundant) or negative (counter-redundant). Note that motivation is always higher for the gender outgroup. The actual ability is identical for both gender groups, and slightly higher in the counter-redundant condition.

influenced by invalid cues that cannot be expected to correlate with ability? One final study of the simulated classroom (Fiedler, Plessner, Freytag, & Walther, 2002) speaks to this question, demonstrating that fully illusory cues, based on inaccurately inferred performance variation, may also be utilized for subsequent judgments. Constructive errors due to erroneous cue inferences seem to be the price to be paid for the judge's readiness to utilize all kinds of available cues in a complex environment.

In this experiment, the motivation parameter was kept constant across all students and lessons at a medium level (M = 0.5). All variation in perceived motivation must therefore be due to sampling error or inference error. The ability parameter varied between students and in a dynamic fashion over three sessions. Smart boys and girls differed in the session in which they showed their performance peak; weak boys and girls also showed their deficit in different sessions. The precise nature of these rather complex changes in the A parameter matrix (see Table 7.5) are not of interest for the present argument and can be ignored. The original goal of the study was to demonstrate that each student's evaluation in Session 3 would be influenced by his or her prior judgment history. Parenthetically, this prediction was confirmed. Although the ability parameter of all smart and weak students was constant in Session 3 (A = 0.625 and A = 0.375, respectively), evaluations were more extreme when the change in A from Sessions 2 to 3 was towards higher extremity (i.e., when smart students showed an increase and poor students showed a decrease from Sessions 2 to 3).

However, more important to the present context was another finding. Although the ability variation between students and over time influenced teachers' judgments, there remained a good deal of inaccuracy, or unaccounted differences in judgments of equivalent students. Interestingly, however, these deviations were not random but could be predicted to a considerable degree by the teachers' prior judgments of the same students in preceding sessions. Those teachers who overestimated students of a particular kind (as defined in Table 7.5) in Session 1, also tended to overestimate the same student type in Sessions 2 and 3. And teachers who initially underestimated the performance of a particular type of student continued to underestimate them later on. These self-consistent trends were quite substantial (i.e., correlations in the range of 0.30 to 0.50, computed within type across judges) across all different student types (see Table 7.5). Moreover, the signed inaccuracies of ability judgments at one time could be predicted from the signed inaccuracies in both ability and motivation judgments at other times. Apparently, then, teachers were using the self-generated variation of their own erroneous judgments in former sessions as cues for judgments in later session.

Note that these findings refer to *deviations* of judgments from the objective correct values. The correlations reflecting consistent under- and overestimations of the same students by different teachers were similarly high regardless of whether we considered the deviations from the latent parameters or the deviations from the actual performance rates in the sample. This means that sampling error cannot account for these findings, which apparently reflect influences of self-generated cues (prior ratings) on subsequent judgments.

Table 7.5 Dynamically changing ability parameters in a simulated classroom experiment

Student	German				Mathematics			
Male	*Type of change*	*Session* 1	*Session* 2	*Session* 3	*Type of change*	*Session* 1	*Session* 2	*Session* 3
1		0.50	0.65	0.80		0.80	0.80	0.65
2		0.80	0.65	0.80		0.80	0.50	0.65
3		0.50	0.65	0.50		0.50	0.80	0.65
4		0.80	0.65	0.50		0.50	0.50	0.65
5		0.20	0.35	0.20		0.20	0.50	0.35
6		0.50	0.35	0.20		0.20	0.20	0.35
7		0.20	0.35	0.50		0.50	0.50	0.35
8		0.50	0.35	0.50		0.50	0.20	0.35
Female								
9		0.50	0.65	0.80		0.80	0.80	0.65
10		0.80	0.65	0.80		0.80	0.50	0.65
11		0.50	0.65	0.50		0.50	0.80	0.65
12		0.80	0.65	0.50		0.50	0.50	0.65
13		0.20	0.35	0.20		0.20	0.50	0.35
14		0.50	0.35	0.20		0.20	0.20	0.35
15		0.20	0.35	0.50		0.50	0.50	0.35
16		0.50	0.35	0.50		0.50	0.20	0.35

Summary

Altogether, these findings and observations from the simulated classroom testify to the manifold sources of ecological variation that can influence stereotype learning in vivo. Regardless of whether these data originate in latent parameters, sampling variation, sound observer inferences, or unjustified memory illusions, they may exert a similar influence on subsequent judgments. Some of the time, it makes sense to classify the data generation process as rational or irrational, valid or illusory. But on other occasions it is hard to separate genuine data from mere inferences, or justified from unjustified inferences. Even when no serious observer bias is involved, there are sufficient sources of environmental variation (in sample size, redundancy, etc.) that have the potential to produce biased judgments without biased processes. In this regard, the present chapter was devoted to illustrating a variety of truly cognitive-environmental interactions. In addition, a special attempt was made to show that such a cognitive-environmentalist approach provides alternative interpretations for three prominent variants of expectancy effects, overgeneralizations, gender stereotypes, and script-based inferences.

8 The vicissitudes of information sampling in a fallible environment

An integrative framework

The superordinate theme of CELA

The notion of relativity

During the twentieth century, Einstein's notion of relativity has become almost common sense, at least part of common high-school education. Even without higher grades in science, most people who did not fully forget their physics training or those who read one of Steve Hawking's bestsellers have acquired some rudimentary understanding of the notion that time, speed, and location do not exist as absolute properties of the world. Scientific progress in physical disciplines has been crucially dependent on the logical and formal understanding of the underlying relativity. There is nothing like the real point in time that is shared by all vantage points in the universe; not even the location or energetic state of a particle can be determined for sure. Rather, we have to accept the basic relativity of the world. Relative to different vantage points (e.g., different relative speed, or in different gravity environments), the rate with which time goes by differs. It is all a matter of perspective, or relative "behavior" of observers vis-à-vis their environment. Note also that the principle of relativity holds both at the macro level and at the micro level of analysis, that is, for the astronomical study of the universe and its genesis, as well as the nuclear physical study of extremely small particles and short-term states.

Although the state of the arts and the formal precision of contemporary psychology may not be comparable to physics, the notion of relativity is similarly applicable to our discipline. Indeed, the application of relativity to psychological phenomena may be even more obvious and universal. In this chapter, as we recapitulate the contents of the present volume, we will find that cognitive-environmental approaches such as CELA must inevitably take a relativistic theory position. The basic tenet of any cognitive-ecological theory approach is that the same environment can look quite different when considered from different perspectives. One has to discard the assumption that there exists a single objective description of reality. Instead, one has to accept the fundamental insight that different realities, created from different vantage points, can exist at the same time, with equal justification. This insight provides us with a common theme for an integrative summary of all preceding chapters.

Organization of the integrative chapter

Accordingly, the present chapter is structured as follows:

- We first elaborate for a moment on aspects of psychological relativity.
- Then we outline an operational framework within which the abstract notion of relativity becomes more concrete. This framework derives from a sampling approach to explain the origins of the environmental data that provide the input to social hypothesis testing. A common insight from CELA is that an analysis of the environmental stimulus input has logical primacy over intrapsychic (cognitive or motivational) processes in the explanation of hypothesis-testing biases.
- We then recapitulate CELA findings as instances of information sampling and its impact on the effective stimulus input, contingent on the observer's relative perspective.
- We also discuss in passing the broader theoretical potential of the sampling approach to psychological relativity, which extends well beyond the applications to social stereotyping reviewed in the present volume.
- We close this chapter with a preview of some intriguing research questions to be answered by future research on psychological relativity.

Thus, rather than merely repeating the essentials of the preceding chapters, we try to delineate a new theoretical framework for understanding the origins of all environmental learning, which depends crucially on the relativity of sampling processes.

A few remarks on relativity in the social-cognitive world

If relativity holds for the physical world, this must be true for the social-cognitive world as well, or even more. In fact, virtually all meaningful social attributes that might become the target of hypothesis testing, or important judgments and decisions, cannot be determined absolutely. They evade objective, unequivocal measurement because they are not amenable to direct observation. Sometimes, one might even ask whether attributes lack any physical or material existence that is independent of their cognitive or collective construction. For an example, consider the evaluative component of attitudes that is so central to prejudice, attraction, and decision making. In different theory contexts, this fundamental component may be termed attractiveness, likeability, sympathy, preference, desirability, valence, evaluative tone, prejudice (inverse scaling), approach (vs. avoidance), or affective attitude. For the moment, let us simply refer to the degree of *positivity* of an attitude target (such as a person, group, consumer product, brand name, or political goal).

Does positivity exist objectively? The answer is both yes and no. Of course, the very existence of positive evaluations is evident in the price that can be obtained for arts and fancy cars, wars suffered for political goals, murders for jealousy, or in the pleasure gained from good music or a sunny day. Nobody would deny the existence of positivity or valence as an eminent construct in psychology, just as it would be cynical just to deny the existence of time in physics. In this regard, we do not subscribe to radical, misleading variants of constructivism. However, just like time in physics, positivity does not have an absolute existence. Here we are not merely concerned with subjective taste, or the fact that different individuals have different utility functions, or give different weight to different attributes in the way they subjectively experience positivity. We are rather concerned, at a deeper level, with the fact that positivity as an objective attribute of environmental entities, independent of subjects' behaviors, does not exist at all. It has to be construed from a particular vantage point, or relative position within the subjective observer. What is highly positive from one point of view, may be less positive, neutral, or even negative from others.

This truism not only holds for opponents having different interests, but also it holds in a much broader sense of relativity. Let us take a soccer fan's positive stereotype of his favorite soccer team as an example for experienced positivity, or attractiveness. As such a stereotype is contingent on the stereotype holder's own perspective and group membership, it highlights the importance of relativity. In the preceding chapters we have encountered (at least) three reasons why the same team could be, and presumably will be, perceived differently attractive from the relative perspectives of the fan's own community (ingroup) versus an opponent fan community (outgroup). First, ingroup fans may define the attraction of a favorite soccer team in terms of different cues than uninvolved observers, or even when using the same cues give differential weights to particular cues. For example, the fans of a typical working-class soccer team might define their conception of attractiveness (of the favorite club with which they identify) in terms of assets like fighting and solidarity, understatement, and equality, as opposed to the allures and mannerisms of superstars. Thus, the very cue system that mediates the perception of positivity is attuned to the cue system that prevails in one region of the environment, but not in others.

Second, the effective stimulus input of ingroup fans is not confined to the currently presented series of stimulus information about their team. Rather, they will presumably enrich the given stimulus data with self-generated inferences and memories of prior experiences and emotions, reinforcements and autobiographical traces from the past (Chapter 5). Thus, even when the ingroup and the outgroup are exposed to the same stimulus series, their effective stimulus input need not be the same, due to enrichment with self-generated information.

Third, the fan ingroup will simply have a larger sample of observations from which to form an impression than the fan outgroup. Even when the positivity rate is the same for the information presented to the ingroup and the outgroup, the ingroup will have more extensive chances to extract positive aspects than the outgroup. We have repeatedly demonstrated the differential impact of large versus small samples on impression formation and evaluative judgments (e.g., in Chapters 3, 4, 5, and 6).

Note that some prominent differences between the ingroup and the outgroup, such as selective perception, unfair appraisal, biased memory etc., are excluded here intentionally. We do not want to claim that these uncontestable sources of ingroup-serving bias in soccer fans do not exist. We rather want to highlight the impact of psychological relativity, or differential perspectives—with or without the operation of motivational biases.

What was illustrated here for the perception or construal of positivity can be generalized to many other target attributes. In the focus of most judgments and decisions are meaningful attributes such as *risk*, *dishonesty*, *danger*, *hostile intention*, *sympathy*, *trust*, potential to be a *good partner*, *health*, or *reliability*, *ability*, *faithfulness*, and so forth. The existence and the quantitative level of these attributes cannot be assessed in an absolute fashion. The same holds in particular for the target concepts that are involved in social stereotypes, such as *personality traits*, *attributes*, *intentions*, *hobbies*, *cultural values*, *criminality*, *norms*, *affective states*, *temperaments*, and *motives*. We cannot literally perceive these attributes because we have no sense organs or receptors to capture physical signals conveying the meaning and quantity of these attributes. Rather than observing these entities directly, we have to infer or construe them actively in an environmental learning process that creates relativity. However, as already mentioned, the impossibility to determine the target objects' true value on positivity, or any other attribute from the above list, is not just due to the lack of a consensual definition. It is also due to the non-accessibility of the distal attributes themselves (cf. Brunswik, 1956).

To illustrate this important point, imagine that positivity could be measured consensually. The true positivity of a soccer team might be simply defined as the relative proportion of successful action produced by the team across all encounters. So we could make the simplifying assumption that there is but one type of outcome, which can take on positive and negative values, and that positivity can be quantified as the relative proportion of positive outcomes. Even then, the true positivity would be a population parameter that cannot be assessed directly, because it is not possible to assess the infinity of all potential outcomes ever produced by the target team. As in statistics, latent population parameters are not amenable to direct measurement. They can only be estimated or inferred from available samples of relevant observations. Crucially, however, sample statistics can differ from population parameters not only because of unsystematic sampling error, but also through systematic sampling biases. These sampling biases reflect the fact that nature rarely provides us with random samples, but normally with strongly perspective-dependent samples. They provide a major source of psychological relativity.

A sampling approach to understanding psychological relativity

Figure 8.1 explicates the central assumption of the sampling approach that will guide the rest of this integrative chapter. Accordingly, latent parameters of the distal environment (such as the "true" degree of positivity) are typically not amenable to direct observation and measurement. Rather, these idealized, distal parameters have to be inferred from statistical estimates based on proximal samples. Samples provide the interface between the objective environment (left side of the

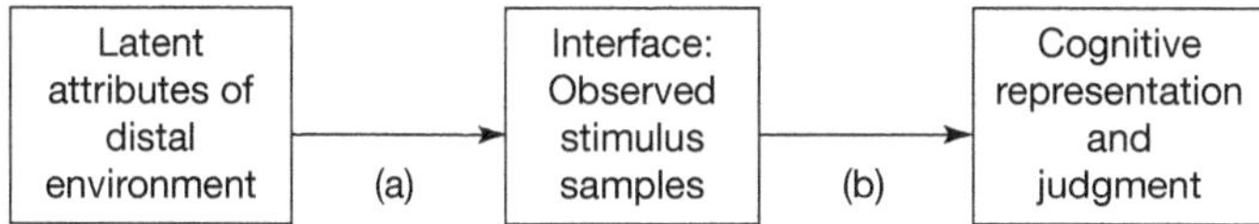

Figure 8.1 Two-stage model of the cognitive representation of the environment: (a) translation of environment into stimulus samples; (b) cognitive assessment of characteristics in the stimulus sample.

diagram) and its cognitive representation or judgmental reproduction (right side), as richly illustrated in Chapter 4. According to this two-stage model, the cognitive representation of the external world can be decomposed into (1) the translation of distal environmental parameters onto proximal stimulus samples; (2) the cognitive assessment of characteristics in the stimulus sample.

The latter stage, pertaining to the cognitive process of inductive assessment in the given stimulus sample, is often remarkably accurate. Even under complex task conditions and high memory load, as in the simulated classroom experiments reported in Chapter 7, judgments are generally rather sensitive to characteristics of the stimulus input, though always somewhat regressive (see also Chapters 3, 4, and 7). However, biases in the hypothesis-testing process—and partly very severe biases—may arise in the first process stage that takes place in the environment, prior to cognitive processes. Because the sampled stimulus information that provides the effective input to subsequent cognitive processes is already biased, or subject to relativity, the basically accurate cognitive assessment process is often fed with misleading data. Although, or just because, inductive assessment is sensitive to the statistical properties of stimulus samples, sampled data will be taken for granted, uncritically, and sampling biases will carry over to subsequent judgments, decisions, and memory representations. Thus, very often, the least controllable problem, or the "Achilles heel", of stereotyping and hypothesis-testing processes does not lie in inaccurate assessment of stimulus data (stage b), but in the meta-cognitive inability, or impossibility, to monitor and control the way in which samples are subject to relativity, and to correct for the biases and constraints that are imposed on stimulus samples in the first place (stage a).

Let us first apply the sampling metaphor to the soccer fan example before we elaborate on the model more systematically. Assume that both ingroup and outgroup fan communities are committed to fair play and motivated to evaluate soccer teams accurately, to the best of their knowledge, even when it is an opponent team. However, this will not prevent the two fan groups from arriving at highly discrepant appraisals of the target soccer team, simply because their respective assessment processes are relative to different samples. As we have seen, ingroup fans will presumably have a larger sample of observations, that is, they will have more opportunities to figure out prominent aspects of their soccer team than outgroup fans. Moreover, the ingroup sample will be enriched with self-generated inferences in addition to the original observations of the soccer team. (We refrain from assuming that these inferences are biased.) Perhaps most importantly, the collection of the ingroup sample will be conditional on search cues that very likely differ from the search cues used by the fan outgroup. The manner in which the ingroup selects relevant observations—in watching TV, reading newspapers, visiting matches, retrieving memories, etc.—is likely to impose quite different constraints on the resulting sample than the conditional search process of the outgroup. For instance, fans belonging to the ingroup may typically prompt their memories (and external information sources) for information shared and discussed with other ingroup members. The resulting stimulus input could be much more positive than the outgroup's input that is mainly determined by information sampled in the media. To the extent that fans are not aware of this selective nature of the samples to which they are exposed, even accurate and fair judgments will inevitably be misguided. How strong an influence such a sampling bias can have on social judgments will be illustrated with experimental evidence in the next section.

For the moment, let us briefly summarize that samples can differ systematically in terms of *size*, *source*, and *conditionality*. Of course, samples may also vary in more "irrational" respects, due to selective exposure to desired outcomes or neglect of unwanted, unexpected, or incomprehensible observations. But the above triad—size, source, and conditionality—is most germane to the notion of relativity, as distinguished from goal-driven biases.

Who is to blame?

Judgments of ingroup and outgroup members, even when intending to be fair and accurate, relative to the input sample, may exhibit huge discrepancies, due to discrepant samples, as we shall see shortly. One might raise the ideological question of who is to blame for this permanent source of bias, human irrationality or the pitfalls of the environment. But as we have already seen in Chapter 7, this question is actually not essential to the sampling approach. It just doesn't matter. Whether biased samples reflect lopsided information search, biased memory, wishful thinking, or inevitable constraints of the environment is unimportant. Regardless of who is to blame and which sampling process led to biased samples, the consequent influence on the effective stimulus input will by and large remain the same. Judges will typically take their own samples for granted and not understand to which degree their sample might have been different, had it been drawn from a different vantage point. The major drawback in the human cognitive equipment is not a lack of accurate assessment procedures, as we have repeatedly emphasized, but, if anything, a *lack of meta-cognitive devices* for understanding, controlling, and correcting the constraints that are imposed on the samples to which they are exposed. However, blaming the cognitive system for this meta-cognitive difficulty would again be premature. Even the most sophisticated mathematical and logical instruments that exist in science would be hardly free from relativity due to sampling effects. That is, for most sampling problems, logically correct debiasing or sample-correction algorithms (e.g., complex Bayesian correction procedures for conditionally dependent samples) are not available.

CELA findings and the sampled information input: An integrative summary

Predictor sampling, illusory correlations, and other illusions of sample size

Let us now recapitulate and integrate the research presented in this volume in terms of the relativity of the information input sampled from different vantage points. In other words, we want to reconsider the process of social hypothesis testing in terms of the environmental data samples that inform the cognitive processes. For this purpose, we have to develop a taxonomy of different sampling effects for which we first need to introduce a terminology. To begin with, we distinguish between two kinds of variables that are involved in hypothesis-testing problems, the independent variable or *predictor*, and the dependent variable or *criterion*. Expanding the 2 × 2 scheme that underlies the soccer fan example (see Figure 8.2), we can see that the positive (vs. negative) outcome is the dependent variable or criterion, whereas the comparison of the target soccer team with other teams is the independent variable or predictor. This logical structure underlies the task to assess the relative positivity as a function of judgment targets. Depending on the specific instruction, the task might call for estimates of the *conditional probability* p(+ / target team X), or the full contingency p(+ / target team X)—p(+ / other teams non-X).

Predictor sampling means to sample observations conditional on the predictor variable, or independent variable. Thus, an observer might look at the focal target team X, or at comparison targets non-X, and register if the sampled behavior happens to be positive or negative. Given the task is to judge positivity as a function of teams, conditionalizing information search on teams (i.e., on the predictor) is logically adequate. If information search is not selective, sample estimates of p(+ / team X) and p(+ / team non-X) will come more or less close to the actual proportions in the population, apart from sampling error. For example, assuming

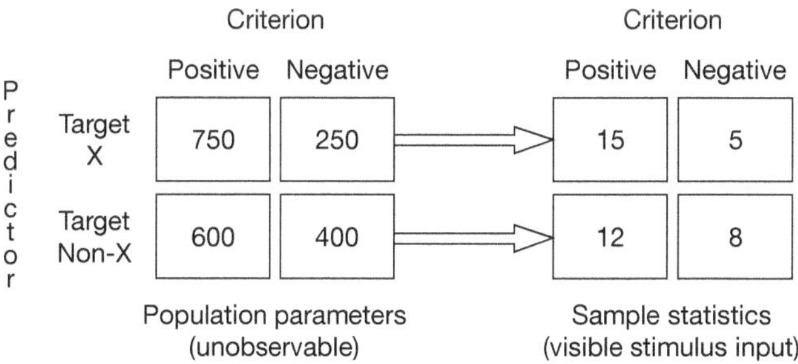

Figure 8.2 Graphical illustration of predictor sampling. A high probability of positive outcomes associated with a focal predictor level, p(positive / Target X) = 75%, is conserved in any sample of cases drawn from each predictor level. Inaccuracy will only reflect random sampling error.

that the "true" positivity parameter of soccer team X (in the idealized universe of all outcomes) is 75% (as expressed by very high total frequencies on the left side of Figure 8.2), predictor sampling will very likely reveal the high proportion of positive outcomes produced by team X, even when sample size is as low as 20 observations (right side of Figure 8.2).

Most of the research reviewed in preceding chapters has been concerned with predictor sampling processes. We have seen that even though predictor sampling is only subject to unsystematic sampling error, differences in sample size can nevertheless result in substantial biases. Thus, in Chapter 3, we have been concerned with studies of illusory correlations showing that the same degree of prevailing positivity is more likely to be apparent from a large sample of a majority group than from a small sample of a minority group. Assuming that from the relative perspective of the self or the ingroup we are fed with larger samples of information about the self and the ingroup than about others and outgroups, we recognized that the self-serving biases or ingroup-serving biases can also be understood as normal illusions of sample size. Similarly, in Chapter 4 it was shown that positive testing leads to larger samples about male overt aggression and female covert aggression than about male covert and female overt aggression. These differences in sample size were sufficient to verify the (false) belief that male aggression tends to be overt while female aggression tends to be covert, although the actual parameters (i.e., confirmation rates of aggression) were the same. Likewise, in Chapter 7, we saw that two students with the same ability parameter will receive different achievement evaluations if a larger sample of observations is available for one than for the other.

Common to all these demonstrations is that assessments of the same quantity can vary as a function of sample size or, in ecological terms, as a function of the density of observations available from a given vantage point. The density of information afforded by the environment is higher for majorities than for minorities, higher for focal than for alternative hypotheses, or higher for students who raise their hands very often than for students who rarely participate. As a consequence of this enhanced density, the judgments resulting from large samples are more extreme than judgments resulting from small samples reflecting the same latent quantity. Large samples result in less regressive judgments that deviate more from the center of the distribution than small samples. This is not even irrational. That predictions under uncertainty are regressive is normatively appropriate and necessary (according to least squares, Bayesian inference and other normative models; cf. Gigerenzer & Fiedler, 2003; Kahneman & Tversky, 1973).

Criterion sampling, baserate fallacies, and quota-sample illusions

Let us now turn to criterion sampling which results in more radical relativity illusions and biases than predictor sampling. Criterion sampling means, with respect to our example, to search information conditional on positive versus negative outcomes, and then to see with which soccer team those outcomes are associated. There are several reasons why such a search algorithm—from criterion to predictor—can obscure the population parameter more dramatically than predictor sampling. First, information about soccer teams that happens to be conveyed in the media or in personal communication is unlikely to reflect a random sample. Outstanding performance and extreme behaviors are more likely to be included in a sample than average or ordinary behaviors. Moreover, this bias of the information ecology will be further enhanced by people's selective exposure and selective memory. Soccer fans are much more likely to encode and retrieve outstanding performance and extreme behaviors than normal, ordinary items. Thus, criterion sampling may be characterized by more items drawn from extreme criterion categories than from the middle categories. As a consequence, the stimulus input is often characterized by dramatic oversampling of extreme outcomes. Any subsequent judgments that rely uncritically on sample estimates will exhibit a corresponding overestimation bias for critical events that attract the information search process.

Figure 8.3 illustrates this phenomenon. Let us assume that the idealized "true" population parameter for outstanding performance is 5% for our own soccer team, as expressed in the upper part in a long-term record of 50 out of 1000 observations of outstanding performance. (Of course, such a long-term record is but an approximation of the "true" parameter.) Now let us assume that media coverage and selective memory result in 180 conserved events, including all 90 outstanding events, which are hardly ever overlooked or omitted, plus an additional set of 90 ordinary, more pallid events. Random draws of 90 cases from each of the two

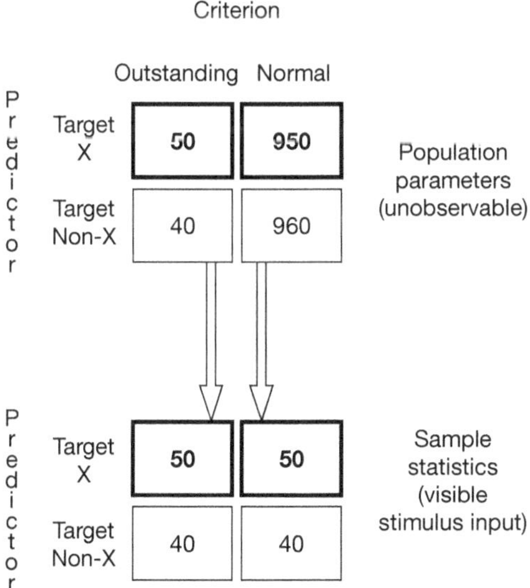

Figure 8.3 Graphical illustration of criterion sampling. Sampling an equal number of cases from both criterion levels, the sample estimate of the conditional probability in question, p(positive / Target X) = 75%, is grossly inflated.

columns of the 2 × 2 table in Figure 8.3 (for outstanding vs. ordinary criterion levels) will result in a sample that grossly inflates the prevalence of outstanding performance. The outstanding performance rate has now increased to 50%.

Apparently, the bias resulting from criterion sampling is overwhelming. A challenging question is whether judges will nevertheless rely on such an extremely biased sample when quantifying, say, the probability of outstanding performance in the target team. As we shall see shortly, the answer is yes. Even intelligent and formally educated judges will fail to notice, at the meta-cognitive level, when the baserate of outstanding performance is dramatically inflated in a sample, and they will still rely on the stimulus sample when making their judgments. Ironically, these judgments are often rather accurate relative to the sample. The drawback is merely that the sample obscures the criterion baserate, making it extremely unrepresentative of the environment from which it was drawn.

The example suggests that criterion sampling processes offer an alternative account for the well-known phenomenon of so-called baserate fallacies. It has been shown and replicated in hundreds of experiments that subjective likelihood judgments of low baserate events are grossly overestimated (Bar Hillel, 1980; Kahneman & Tversky, 1972). The standard explanation for the baserate fallacy is that human likelihood judgments are insensitive to pallid statistical baserates (Borgida & Brekke, 1981; Kahneman & Tversky, 1972; Nisbett & Borgida, 1975), unless baserates are causally meaningful (Ajzen, 1977), naturally imaginable (Gavanski & Hui, 1992), or illustrated in terms of natural frequency formats (Gigerenzer & Hoffrage, 1995). The present notion of criterion sampling from a low baserate population suggests a fully different account based on the information input that results from conditional sampling.

For a striking demonstration, we briefly introduce one more experimental investigation. Fiedler, Brinkmann, Betsch, and Wild (2000) developed a new paradigm directly tailored to investigate criterion-sampling biases. The experimental task called for probability judgments in the context of diagnostic hypothesis testing. For instance, in one case, judges were asked to test the hypothesis that complications arise in one particular hospital X, which in this task served the role of a negative stereotype target. More specifically, stimulus observations referred to the occurrence of complications (criterion) in two different hospitals (predictor); let us call them the Central and the Urban Hospital. Judges were asked to assess the conditional probability *p(complications / Central)* of complications given treatment in the Central Hospital. Instructions were very clear and transparent about the precise definition of the probability to be assessed. Participants could actively search as many observations from an index card file as they felt necessary.

In different experimental conditions, the index card file representing the total population of all data was organized in different ways, enforcing either predictor sampling or criterion sampling. In the *predictor sampling* condition, the index card file was split into two slots, labeled Central and Urban. Participants could draw index cards representing individual cases from whatever hospital they wanted, and they got feedback about whether complications had occurred or not. As soon as they felt that a sufficiently large sample of observations had been gathered, participants could stop the search process and provide their percentage estimate of the probability in question, namely, p(complications / Central).

In the *criterion-sampling* condition, in contrast, the index card file was organized by the criterion, offering separate slots for cases with and without complications. Participants could select as many cases from any slot as they wanted, and for each item drawn they would receive feedback about whether the patient had been treated in Central or Urban Hospital. Figure 8.4 shows a possible population distribution, that is, the overall frequencies of cases in which complications had occurred or not in the two hospitals. The figure also includes the typical outcome of predictor sampling and criterion sampling processes. Sampling observations by predictor levels (see left panel) clearly reveal, correctly, that the proportion of complications in the Central Hospital is rather low (i.e., 1 out of 26). It matters little whether a small or a large overall sample is drawn and whether the subsamples drawn from both hospitals are equal or not. Apart from the repeatedly mentioned fact that large samples provide stronger and more reliable information than small samples, the basic rarity of complications is generally apparent.

In contrast, criterion sampling can dramatically obscure the complication rate, depending on the composition of the sample drawn. Crucial for the strength of this sampling bias is how many cases are drawn with and without complications. The population parameter for p(complications / Central) will only be conserved in the stimulus sample if information search adheres to the baserates, that is, if judges select no more than about 4% patients with complications. However,

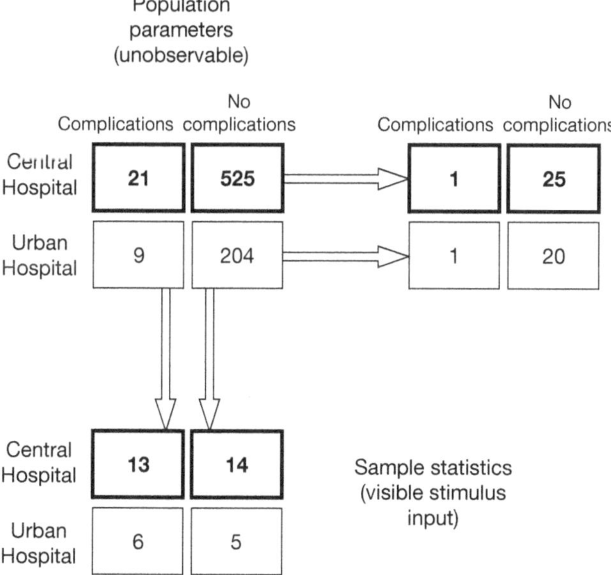

Figure 8.4 Different influence of predictor sampling and criterion sampling on sample-based estimates of the probability of complications in Hospital A (relative to a comparison Hospital B).

such proportional quota sampling is highly unusual. Given the task instruction to assess p(complications / Central), most judges engage to some degree in positive testing (Klayman & Ha, 1987); that is, they oversample cases from the critical criterion category, complications. After all, their job is to assess the (conditional) *complications* rate. As soon as this happens, however, the sample will no longer represent an unbiased picture of the probability to be judged. As a consequence, oversampling of complication cases must result in inflated judgments of p(complications / Central). From Figure 8.4 it is evident that sampling an equal number of cases with and without complications, which is quite a common search strategy, will change the critical probability from 3.85% in the population to 48.15% in the sample! This severe sampling bias will then carry over to sample-based judgments—provided that judges rely on samples, accurately but uncritically, and do not understand at the meta-cognitive level that their own information search has grossly obscured the criterion baserate in the sample.

Figure 8.5. summarizes the results obtained for the complications task and three other diagnostic hypothesis-testing tasks. Judges were asked for estimates of the conditional probability of anorexia given an unresolved sex role conflict; of lung damage given the intake of a pharmacological agent called Dermofit; and of breast cancer given a positive mammogram. Somewhat smaller and less extreme population frequencies than in Figure 8.4 were used to render the index card file manageable. Thus, the index card file for the hospitals' problems included 2 complications versus 27 cases without complications for the focal (Central) hospital and 3 complications versus 68 non-complications for the comparison (Urban) hospital. As derived from the sampling framework, predictor sampling resulted in accurate or moderately accurate estimates for all four problems. Judgments were only slightly regressive, resulting in overestimations of the actually rather low probabilities. In contrast, greatly inflated judgments of the critical criterion events were obtained in the criterion-sampling condition. For example, the mean

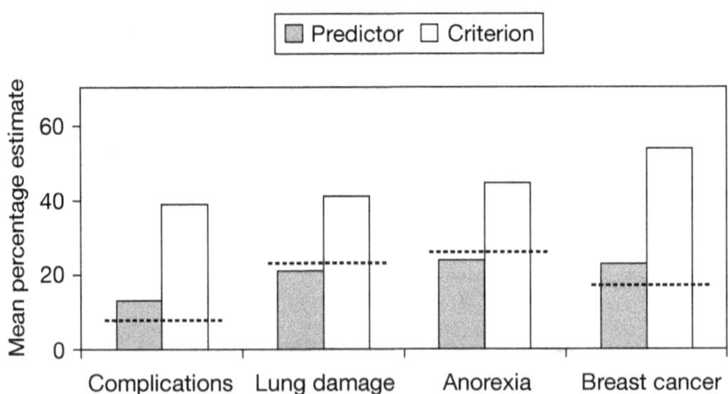

Figure 8.5 Mean percentage estimates of the conditional probability of four criterion events as a function of sampling condition (predictor vs. criterion sampling), after Fiedler et al. (2000, Experiment 3). The correct conditionals are indicated by the dotted lines.

estimate of the likelihood of complications in Central Hospital was as high as 32% due to oversampling of positive cases (i.e., complications), as compared with an actual proportion of 2/29 = 6.9% in the population. Our interpretation is supported by an analysis of the actually sampled data. Indeed, the inflated complication rates in the samples drawn would have justified even more extreme overestimations than were actually obtained in the resulting judgments.

One might argue that forcing participants to criterion sampling is unfair and unrealistic, leaving them little chance to figure out the true probability. This argument is hardly justified, however. First, even participants in the criterion sampling condition had a real chance to find the data they needed for correct judgments. They might have sampled data in a way that conserved the baserates. Second, they could actually see, vividly, the low baserate of the criterion event (e.g., complication cases) in the respective slot of the index card file. The sequential search procedure revealed natural joint frequencies of cases from both hospitals, with and without complications, that could have been multiplied mentally with the criterion baserates. Last but not least, when participants in another experiment could freely choose between predictor and criterion sampling, almost 40% preferred criterion sampling, which then led them into highly inflated judgments. In many realistic contexts, criterion sampling is readily chosen and often preferred to predictor sampling (cf. Klayman & Ha, 1987; Oaksford & Chater, 1994; Wason, 1966).

To be sure, when judgments are analyzed as a function of the sampled data, the local accuracy is indeed quite high. However, judges did not seem to understand the pragmatic constraints imposed by the conditional sampling process. Almost half of them would deliberately search by the criterion, ignoring the tremendous problems that this decision entails. Judges in the criterion condition would not understand that they ought to sample proportionally, in a way that conserves the criterion baserates. Finally, they do not take the sampling bias into account, or utilize the sampled data in a Bayesian fashion. Rather, they take the sample for granted as if it gave an immediate estimate of the probability in question.

Thus, criterion sampling is a powerful source of psychological relativity. When we have to assess the probability of important but rare events (such as car accidents; getting AIDS; severe drug addiction), we often have no choice but to conditionalize sampling on those rare outcomes, rather than sampling by the predictor and waiting until the rare event occurs spontaneously. For instance, to assess the probability p(car accident / at a certain crossing), we have to rely on data about the accidents that actually occurred, rather than lying down at a dangerous crossing and waiting for a suitable number of accidents. Thus, sampling can often be contingent on the relative position of someone who picks up rare events.

Meta-cognitive blindness or ecological dilemma?

However, the emerging impression that a human meta-cognitive deficit alone is responsible for the inability to deal with the relativity of environmental stimulus input would not reflect the full nature of the problem. If people had a better understanding of sampling constraints, such as readers of this chapter may at this moment feel they have, there would still be no safeguard against sampling biases. There would be no generally correct prescription for how to sample data for each and any purpose, using equal or proportional quota, conditionalized on the predictor or the criterion. In Chapter 7 we have seen that teachers' performance ratings are unfair when they collect *unequal* samples, so they ought to draw equal samples. Now we see that drawing *equal* samples can lead to even stronger fallacies when distributions are skewed. Thus, what sampling procedure is appropriate cannot be determined in general but depends on aspects of the environment that are not known beforehand. Even teachers who sample by the predictor and draw equal samples for different students are not on safe ground. When two students have the same latent ability (e.g., 75% correct) but not the same motivation (i.e., one student raises her hand more often than the other), then collecting samples of the same size may impose constraints and biases on subsequent judgments. Thus, a student who rarely raises his hand may do so only on those occasions when the correct solution is easy to find, leading to an inflated sample estimate of the proportion correct. Moreover, drawing equal samples from two students who raise their hands at an unequal rate will obscure the data needed for motivation judgments, or judgments of *spontaneous* or unsolicited performance (requiring ability *and* motivation). When the same number of observations from all students are enforced, regardless of their participation rate, motivation differences are lost in the "sampling jungle". As a matter of rule, whether samples can be trusted or not depends in a complex manner on what judgment is called for, thus invoking the principle of relativity.

Selective-outcome sampling

The impossibility to avoid relativity becomes even more apparent when we consider selective-outcome sampling (cf. Fiedler, Brinkmann, Betsch, & Wild, 2000). This variant of a sampling bias comes closer to the cognitive and motivational selectivity emphasized in traditional stereotype research. It would appear to be more primitive, unfair, and even self-deceptive than predictor or criterion sampling. Selective-outcome sampling means to oversample particular cells of the 2×2 scheme. For instance, a teacher who is collecting his records and notes about two equally smart students when it comes to determining grades at the end of the school year may selectively attend to successful, outstanding episodes with one student, Sonny, while sampling representatively for the other student, Hardy. Such an unfair, lopsided procedure that obviously favors Sonny over Hardy may have different reasons. The teacher may simply like Sonny more than Hardy, that is, his sampling bias may be motivated. However, the opposite may also be true. Exactly because the teacher is more interested in Hardy, rather than Sonny, he may have attentively encoded all of Hardy's performance. In contrast, because of lack of attention to Sonny, the teacher may find it hard to remember what performance Sonny has exhibited, and so he may have to resort to his written notes and tags that are mostly confined to Sonny's outstanding or extreme performance. Thus, it becomes evident why motivational factors may be relevant, to be sure, but not crucial. The teacher's very motive—that he was not interested in Sonny and did not remember Sonny's behavior in the first place—may give an ironic advantage to Sonny when memory is filtered by the teacher's notebook sample. Once more we see that the variety of sampling procedures is rich, and the resulting biases may be detached from such animistic forces as the teacher's personal preferences or motives.

Look what happens when we translate selective-outcome sampling to the hospitals example. A researcher who finds more complications in the Central than the Urban Hospital may simply deceive herself. Blatantly, she may give more attention to complications in Central Hospital and relatively more attention to smooth cases in Urban Hospital. However, again, the same serious bias can be generated in a much more subtle, less blatant way that cannot be attributed to the researcher's unfairness or self-deception. For instance, the two hospitals may use different thresholds for classifying complications. Just because the quality of treatment is particularly high, the Central Hospital may afford to set the threshold for detection complications at a rather low level. Ironically, then, the very safety and high quality in Central Hospital may be responsible for a sampling bias that mimics many complications, as compared with Urban Hospital with lower treatment quality and a stricter complication threshold.

Selective-outcome sampling is at the heart of many findings reported in Chapter 5, showing that constructive memory intrusions can be induced by one-sided questions and externally provided memory prompts. In several of these experiments, too, an attempt was made to demonstrate that such constructive memory effects can come along as cognitive by-products of completely normal, unbiased cognitive processes.

The virtual inevitability to avoid selective-outcome sampling—which favors specific cells in a contingency scheme—is vividly apparent in one area of environmental inquiry that can be considered the prototype of accuracy-driven or validity-driven inquiry, namely scientific research. For several decades we have been sensitized to the problem of a significance bias in journal publication policy. In Figure 8.6, a 2 × 2 contingency is depicted between the outcomes of research findings (significant vs. not significant) and publication decisions (accept vs. reject). Scientific journals present a selective-outcome sample of observations representing the upper left cell. That is, observers of the scientific enterprise are selectively exposed to significant findings that happen to be published. This feature of the scientist's environment has hardly been changed since the problem was identified by influential critiques (Greenwald, 1975). The consequences are obvious. The (relative) validity of established theories is presumably inflated by selective sampling of significant theory confirmations. Once more, this occurs regardless of deliberate intentions or motives to deceive oneself, or to violate sound methodological rules. Impartial editors and honorable expert referees are involved in the process in order to avoid the pitfalls of individual researcher's motives and wishful illusions, but all these efforts do not provide efficient remedies against the sampling biases that result as human individuals come to interact with their information ecology.

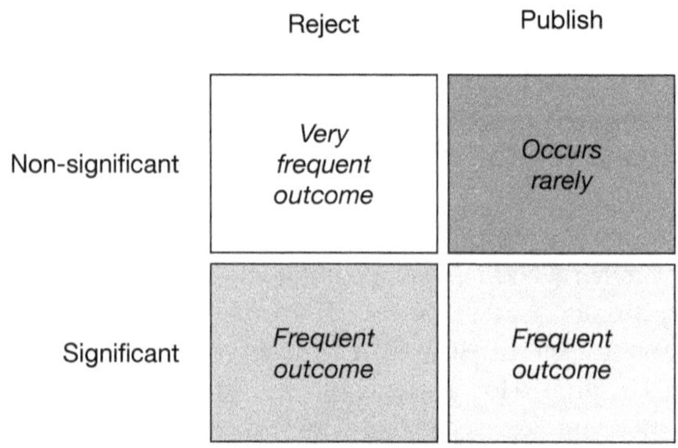

Figure 8.6 Selective-outcome sampling and journal publication policy. Some outcomes of research are more likely to be sampled by scientific journals than others, creating a persistent sampling bias in scientific communication.

One telling example from Einhorn and Hogarth (1978) may round up this picture of truly emergent sampling biases, arising beyond all intention, motivated attention, or carelessness. Personnel managers are exposed to samples that are biased systematically towards the impression that their application selection decisions have been very effective. Thus, they have good reasons for self-attributions of success and effectiveness. However, their professional environment is likely to feed them with a radically selective sample. On the one hand, in these days of high unemployment rates, the number and density of highly qualified applicants is likely to be very high for each and any job announced. Any reasonable selection of applicants, based on nothing but a superficial scanning of paper documents alone, will result in a smart subset of applicants. On the other hand, there are pragmatic sampling constraints that prevent personnel managers from observing rejected candidates, who are gone for ever, rendering it impossible to observe rejected applicants who outperform those who were accepted and employed.

As a take-home message of the CELA, we have to realize that biased samples are ubiquitous—as a natural, almost inevitable by-product of cognitive-environmental interaction. Some events are oversampled whereas others are underrepresented. However, as clarified repeatedly, it would be an extremely unrealistic and impoverished sketch of inductive learning to attribute this problem exclusively to the individual's expectations, selective attention, goals, motives, or lopsided search strategies. In fact, the selective nature of the environment itself produces the biased input, or else the interaction of the individual with the environment.

Sampling in two-factorial and multi-factorial space

The variety of sampling procedures—and sources of relativity—increases further as one considers stimulus sampling in two-factorial or multi-factorial spaces, that is, problem spaces involving two or more independent variables. Let us only discuss a few variants of sampling in more complex problem contexts, without attempting to provide a systematic overview (for a more extensive account, see Fiedler et al., 2000).

One sampling phenomenon in two-factorial space that was explained in Chapter 6 is *Simpson's paradox*. Applying this model, we may assume that the Central Hospital has in fact an enhanced complications rate (see Figure 8.7). But upon closer inspection, it becomes evident that patients administered to both hospitals come from different socio-economical strata. Suspicion arises that the enhanced complications rate in Central Hospital may be an artifact of an enhanced rate of unhealthy patients administered, having impaired immune systems. Thus, re-analyzing the relationship between hospitals and complications separately for healthy versus unhealthy patients (i.e., partialling out degree of patient health) shows that—in spite of the higher overall aggregate complications rate—the split complications rate for Central Hospital is actually either the same (unhealthy patients) or even lower (healthy patients) for Urban Hospital.

	Number complications	Number no complications	Complication rate	
Central	22	110	1/5	Overall
Urban	10	80	1/8	
Central	20	80	1/5	Unhealthy patients
Urban	2	8	1/5	
Central	2	20	1/10	Healthy patients
Urban	10	80	1/9	

Figure 8.7 Simpson's paradox applied to evaluating complication rates in different hospitals. Although the overall complication rate is clearly higher in the Central Hospital (1/5) than in the Urban Hospital (1/8), this only reflects the fact that more unhealthy patients go to Central Hospital, whereas more healthy patients go to Urban Hospital. Within the subsets of healthy and unhealthy patients, respectively, the Central Hospital is at least as low in complications as the Urban Hospital.

In other words, sampling at aggregate level will lead to different conclusions than sampling at specific levels. Even when data are assessed carefully and analyzed thoroughly, selecting one level of sampling will inadvertently provide a premature answer to the two-factorial problem. With regard to relativity, it is important to note that there is no correct way to select the "true" sampling level. At first glance, one might suggest, again prematurely, that informed sampling ought to be conditionalized on healthy versus less healthy patients, separately. That is, the partial correlation might be preferred generally over the aggregate correlation, which is often discredited as a "spurious correlation". However, such a conclusion might not be justified. Still closer inspection may reveal that the hypothesis of including more unhealthy patients in Central Hospital is indeed the consequence, rather than the cause, of getting more complications. That is, separate examinations of patient data, before and after treatment, may show that differences in patient health had not existed before hospital treatment, but in fact reflect an artifact of treatment success versus failure. In this case, the aggregate correlation would be more reflective of the true hospital quality than the partial correlation. Again, we have to admit that there is no safe way to sample two-factorial data in a dynamic environment.

Even experimental psychologists' most preferred research design, *orthogonal sampling,* is not immune from sampling effects. Orthogonal sampling means to enforce an equal (or proportional) number of cases sampled for each combination of two (or more) factors. In cases in which factors are actually correlated, this may convey an inappropriate picture of the environment. For instance, the enhanced complications rate in Central Hospital may not be due to the primary factor hospitals (Central vs. Urban) per se, but may be mediated by a second factor, strong differences in the type of disease mostly encountered in each hospital. That is, the enhanced complication rate in Central Hospital may only stem from those cases which suffer from a hard-to-cure type of disease that is most frequently encountered in this hospital. The resulting crucial causal path *Central Hospital → type of disease → complications* will be obscured by orthogonal sampling. Enforcing an equal proportion of patients with each disease type in both hospitals will eliminate the causal path which is actually mediated by the correlation of hospitals and disease type.

The last sampling effect to be mentioned here may be particularly common in the social world. It was immediately derived from the present sampling approach and has been termed *pseudo-contingency* (Fiedler & Freytag, 2003). As already explained in Chapter 6, pseudo-contingencies arise when separately obtained samples are later on combined in memory. To keep within the hospitals example, sampling of complications data may reveal that quite a few complications occur in Central Hospital, whereas hardly any complications occur in Urban Hospital. On a different occasion, a separate sampling process may show that violations of hygienic rules are quite frequent in Central Hospital, but infrequent in Urban Hospital. When the data resulting from these two separate sampling processes are then brought together in memory, the strong impression arises that hygienic rule violations and complications are correlated. This is a category mistake, however,

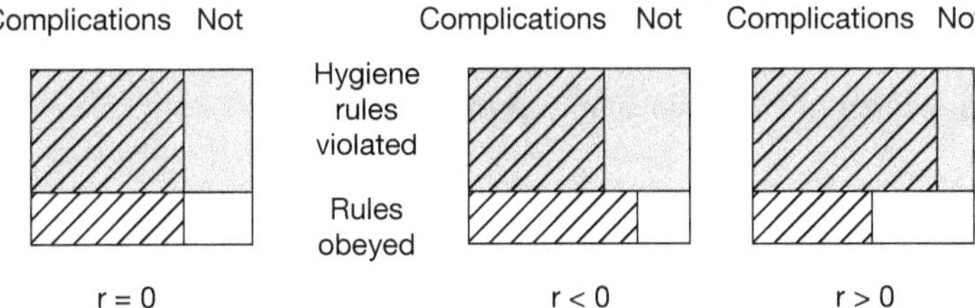

Figure 8.8 Graphical illustration of a pseudo-contingency. The coincidence of a high rate of complications (dashed area) and hygienic violations (gray-shaded area) in a hospital is compatible with all kinds of correlation between complications and hygienic violations: positive (right), negative (middle), and zero (left).

because the contingency of hygienic violations and complications has not been assessed. We only have a pseudo-contingency of two skewed univariate (i.e., marginal) distributions of two trends that coincide in the same hospital. Given both many hygienic rule violations and many complications in Central Hospital does not imply at all that the two variables are correlated. Indeed, the *relative* rate of complications may be higher, equal, or lower in patients exposed to hygienic violations than in patients who did not come into contact with non-hygienic substances (see Figure 8.8).

In general, pseudo-contingencies arise when information about different variables (complications; hygienic rule violations) is sampled on separate occasions and then has to be coordinated post hoc from memory. This is presumably very often the case in everyday sampling and the resulting illusion may be rather strong (cf. Fiedler & Freytag, 2003). Again, we might be quick to blame the individual for the meta-cognitive confusion of two uncoordinated information sources. However, upon reflection, we have to admit that in a complex probabilistic environment, there is no alternative to combining data sampled on different occasions, conditional on different sampling prompts. On some occasions we sample data about risk, on other occasions about hospitality, daytime, gender, climate, location, signals, pleasure, pain, or whatever variable might be of interest for later decision problem. Trying to assess the entire multivariate contingency at the same time is simply impossible for pragmatic reasons, not only because this would exceed cognitive capacity but also because all information is never available at the same time. Therefore, encoding lower level distributions and relying on pseudo-contingencies as a proxy to higher order contingencies may be the best and most adaptive strategy an organism can apply in an uncertain world. After all, attending to both hygienic violations and a high complication rate, and avoiding such a hospital, may be a good strategy to cope with the complex world, even if this insight is only driven by a pseudo-contingency.

The ubiquity of sampling biases revisited

In this chapter, we have so far illuminated the countless ways in which the information input to environmental learning and hypothesis testing can vary as a function of the individual's relative standpoint in the environment. Ecological samples are virtually never random, perspective free, and representative of one unique reality. Instead, borrowing Einstein's notion of relativity, we have argued strongly that stimulus samples are in principle conditional, relative to particular sampling perspectives, and limited to specific angles of reality. Just as there is not one unique time that holds for each place in the universe, most attributes of the social world do not possess a uniquely correct value. As a matter of principle, the assessment of social attributes is relative to the size, source, and conditionality of the samples used for assessment. It is important to understand that this is not merely a problem of imperfect measurement of an objectively given entity but of the basic relativity of the entity itself. The true probability that an individual dies from a traffic accident does not exist objectively but depends on the category from which relevant information is sampled. As the person belongs to many different categories at the same time—age, gender, profession, mileage per year on dangerous streets, whether she rides a motorbike or drives car, living in the country or in the city, whether she drinks alcohol, adventurous temperament, etc.—there are countless ways of defining the reference category that determines her risk. Only when we radically accept this basic indeterminacy, and the relativity of all empirical experience, will we come to understand the crucial role of the information input for the present CELA.

In the present chapter, we have elaborated on various ways in which the effective stimulus input can vary as samples differ in size, source and conditionality. The empirical findings and theoretical ideas presented throughout all previous chapters can be subsumed under this general idea.

To recapitulate, when samples differ in *size*, they make the same latent properties differentially visible. Small samples are more unreliable and error prone, and the same property is more visible in large than in small samples. This basic rule was used in Chapter 3 to account for illusory correlations that discriminate against minorities, because the same prevalence of normal, desirable behavior is learned more completely for large groups (majorities) than for small groups (minorities). In the same vein, the simulated school class experiments reported in Chapter 7 confirmed that high or low student ability is more readily detected when performance samples are large rather than small. These findings also highlight the fact that such influences of differential sample size, or differential reliability, are inevitable because samples cannot be equated. Both the human part and the environmental part in the cognitive-environmental interplay warrant that samples must differ in size. The environment inevitably provides us with more frequent and denser observations about ourselves than about others, about ingroups than outgroups, about familiar than foreign cultures, about famous than hidden persons, about our own professional field than other professions. Just as proximity and distance in time and space varies, inevitably, the size and richness of stimulus samples must vary as well.

Regarding the part played by the individual, the same conclusion must be drawn. Just because we like some people and dislike others, we approach some situations and avoid others, we study one or two subjects and neglect others, or we grow up in one town rather than many others, we selectively expose ourselves to large samples of people, objects, and situations of one type, and small samples of another type. As we have seen in Chapter 3, popular phenomena such as self-serving biases (Zuckerman, 1979) and ingroup-serving biases (Brewer, 1979), unrealistic optimism (Price, 2001; Weinstein, 1980), or outgroup homogeneity (Park & Rothbart, 1982) may reflect to an unknown degree this very basic fact.

In Chapter 4, moreover, we have seen that information search strategies in the course of hypothesis-testing processes will typically yield unequal samples. The very common phenomenon of positive testing—concentrating on the target category focused in a leading hypothesis—yields larger samples about the focal hypothesis than about alternative hypotheses. This can produce illusory verification of the focal hypothesis when in fact alternative hypotheses are equally valid.

Turning to the confusion of *sources* from which information is sampled, we have seen in Chapter 5 that manifest observations are readily contaminated and combined with inferences and imaginations. Such constructive enrichments of externally provided samples with internally generated samples can be hardly avoided, unless human intelligence would sacrifice the use of all prior knowledge to interpret and validate new stimulus data. In the extremely ambitious and broad-minded process of integrating information of different sources, information stemming from assertions, suggestions, questions, omitted propositions, and other subtle speech acts, first-hand observations and second-hand communications, abstract and concrete information, and data having extremely different affective pay-off value, we have to combine samples based on most heterogeneous units, sources, and dimensionality. The phenomena described in Chapter 6, such as Simpson's paradox or pseudo-contingencies, gave us an impression of the extremely demanding problems into which the information integration process runs when such heterogeneous samples have to be combined.

In the present Chapter 8, we have further elaborated on the vicissitudes of sampling processes, and we have particularly demonstrated the importance of the *conditionality* of samples, which bears the strongest resemblance to the notion of relativity. Very often, the structure of a problem calls for judgments of a dependent variable (criterion) conditional on an independent variable (predictor). However, also very often, stimulus sampling has been conditionalized on the criterion rather than the predictor. This is particularly so when problems revolve around rare and important criterion events, such as accidents, diseases, crimes, or existential events, that occur too infrequently to wait for feedback to a predictor sample. Instead, judges (and scientists) have to pick up the very recordings of prior occurrences that exist of those rare events. We have demonstrated the strong biases that can arise from criterion-based samples that typically overrepresent rare criterion events. Moreover, we have pointed out that lack of meta-cognitive monitoring and control facilitates the uncritical reliance on unrepresentative samples. However, we have added quickly that human intelligence could hardly evolve appropriate meta-cognitive devices to control and correct for sampling effects, because the very relativity of the social world renders unclear which samples are valid and which have to be corrected.

The shift in theoretical focus towards an analysis of the input samples resulting from environmental interactions, away from cognitive and motivational processing biases within the individual, led us to the following insight. Ecological stimulus input hardly ever presents us with a natural sample that is representative of the world in general. A completely unconstrained random sample would require us to sample from the whole world, across all places, times, and cultures, to use all available assessment methods at their relative frequencies (whatever that is), to have no access restrictions, to be independent of spatial and temporal distance, and to use no search cue whatsoever. As soon as specific points in time, places, cultures, methods, or search cues are chosen, the sampled data are no longer representative of the world as a whole, but they reflect the relativity of the chosen vantage points.

9 Epilogue

Locating CELA in modern stereotype research

The last chapter is meant as an epilogue intended to locate the present CELA in the landscape of modern stereotype research. In the theoretical introduction in Chapter 2 we had compared our cognitive-environmental learning approach to the *traditional*, animistic approach to stereotyping, which stresses the role of beliefs and desires within the individual. Now, in the last chapter, we want to round up the integrative discussion of different theoretical approaches, comparing CELA with certain dominant paradigms of *modern* stereotype research. The focus thereby is on those prominent new developments that are not so much driven by an animistic meta-theory in terms of beliefs and desires but by the advent of new computer technologies and experimental tools imported from cognitive psychology to investigate priming effects and aspects of implicit memory. In particular, our epilogue revolves around the following points:

- We start the final discussion by briefly summarizing the ways in which CELA points to a whole class of stereotyping processes that are independent of individual's motives.
- We particularly emphasize that the rationality issue, which has dominated the debate of heuristics and biases for such a long time, is of little relevance for CELA.
- Then we discuss the relationship of environmental learning to the growing evidence on priming and accessibility processes that has come to dominate experimental research.
- We shall conclude by pointing out the similarity and proximity of CELA to these modern paradigms, reiterating that if a framework is to integrate the various streams of research, it has to be a cognitive-ecological framework that takes environmental structures into account.
- Last but not least, we argue that ecological learning does not exclude affective, motivated, symbolic, and genuinely social influences but is ideally suited for bridging the gap between merely informational, cold cognition and affectively, personally involving, hot social cognition.

The CELA message in hindsight

In the light of the empirical evidence presented in Chapters 3 to 8, the basic message of CELA has been manifested in a variety of empirical results and theoretical considerations. Ecological stimulus input hardly ever presents us with a natural sample that is representative of the world in general. Accordingly, all subsequent processes are contingent on a reference point, which imposes more radical constraints on environmental learning than intra-individual sources of bias.

Granting such a variable, perspective-contingent input to environmental learning, it should now be evident that CELA does not neglect or exclude the motivational factors (beliefs and desires) that have dominated traditional research. Beliefs and desires—the cornerstones of animistic theories—can certainly be one reason for different learning input, due to selective information search or selective forgetting. However, they constitute but a subset from a much larger set of processes that all lead to biased input samples, and differing perspectives. The soccer fan's bias in favor of his own soccer club, and his discrimination or derogation of rival clubs, may of course result from selective information search and motivated attributions. However, if our soccer fan was not biased at all, his information samples about different clubs would be biased anyway, due to the very relativity of all environmental learning. In this regard, CELA is not really at variance with the traditional approach that we have termed "animistic". It is simply less restrictive.

One important respect in which CELA reduces unnecessary restrictions on theories of social judgment and stereotyping is by circumventing the ideological issue of rationality. The question of whether social judgments are consistent or inconsistent with normative models of the world has dominated a considerable part throughout the last three decades. Accordingly, stereotypes are commonly defined, or at least implicitly assumed to reflect, cognitive representations of groups that typically deviate from a rational and veridical assessment of the target group's attributes. This meta-theoretical premise is evident in many experiments designed to show that the degree of stereotyping increases with the individual's vested interests, own group membership, shallow and heuristic processing, identity threat, and existential fear, and conversely that stereotyping decreases with accuracy motivation, multiple group membership, self-completion, and more exhaustive modes of processing.

Within CELA, one need not deny these well-documented empirical insights, which reflect the importance of affective and motivational processes. However, one need not resort to ideological (and often untenable) assumptions about rationality to account for these intriguing phenomena, which can be understood more parsimoniously as special cases of a much broader class of cognitive-environmental interactions. Given the relativity of all learning input (cf. Chapter 8), and given the fact that many entities have no objective reality at all, the notion of logical or ontological rationality seems to somehow miss the point. Just as there is no objectively correct model of the true superiority of the soccer fan's target club, we have to admit as a matter of principle that no unequivocal normative models exist to quantify the true ability or motivation of a student, the true and ultimate costs and benefits (across all time) of an economical decision, or the true risk of dying in a traffic accident. As I belong to an indefinite number of categories (vocational, residential, motivational, age-related, religious, ethical-moral, environmentalist, driving habits, etc.), the calculation of my risk to die in an accident depends on the arbitrary selection of a subset of all these categories and on imperfect assessment of these categories' contribution to lethal risk. If anything, environmental learning is subject to rules of ecological rationality (Gigerenzer & Todd, 1999), which means to adhere to logical rules when it is of adaptive significance but to violate logical rules, and commit mistakes and biases that match the mistakes and biases that exist in the environment.

Matters of rationality and parsimony aside, the crucial pragmatic question is whether the perspective shift from animistic and rationalistic to cognitive-environmental accounts is useful and fertile in terms of scientific output. So what could be gained through CELA? What insights have been conveyed throughout the preceding chapters that go beyond the state of the arts in the research literature on stereotyping and social hypothesis testing. The following condensed list reflects a variety of innovative findings and theoretical arguments. In particular, CELA has shown:

- that simple rules of learning offer a refined theory of stereotyping;
- that a single property of all probabilistic environments, which is at the heart of any ecological theory, can explain a whole variety of judgments biases;
- that regressiveness is neither equally nor randomly distributed but systematically related to environmental attributes, such as stimulus density and sample size, category structure, and environmental baserates;
- that many prominent findings can be explained alternatively and more parsimoniously;
- that seemingly unrelated phenomena turn out to be intrinsically related;
- that the "heuristics cover story" needs to be revised and refined, giving up the assumption that heuristics are irrational, sloppy, or lazy, and probably giving up the claim that a non-heuristic (i.e., logically correct, calculation-like) processing mode exists at all;
- that associative learning processes may not always support what is plausible or implicated by logical truth values;
- that stereotypes and auto-verification effects arise as an emergent, inevitable side effect of all cognitive-environmental interaction, due to variation in proximity, familiarity, stimulus density, and other structural properties that contribute to psychological relativity—a concept that entails a major program for future research;
- most important perhaps, we have learned that in order to understand stereotypes and related biases, it is at least as central to analyze the stimulus input that impinges on the individual as it is to analyze the cognitive and affective processes within the individual.

Stereotype learning and stereotype accessibility

CELA's affinity to the old behaviorist research program, and basic laws of learning, has been mentioned repeatedly. It is interesting to note that CELA converges with other modern paradigms of experimental stereotype research that also share a neo-behaviorist orientation. In particular, the plethora of recent experiments that have used priming techniques and other implicit memory devices to manipulate the accessibility of stereotypes in memory can be considered a neo-behaviorist, associationist approach to stereotyping that must not be confused with what was called here the old animistic approach. The general assumption underlying this most popular priming and implicit memory research program (cf. Bargh, 1997; Dijksterhuis et al., 1998) is that only a subset of all information that is principally available in memory is activated at any point in time. Due to this gap between effectively accessible and principally available knowledge, a major topic of stereotype research is to describe the priming and association processes that facilitate access to some memory contents (i.e., those that support stereotypes) and inhibit access to others. Typical research examples include subliminal priming (e.g., of words or faces belonging to black people) used to activate racial stereotypes (Bargh et al., 1996; Devine, 1989; Kawakami et al., 2000), implicit measurement of group attitudes (Brauer, Wasel & Niedenthal, 2000; Greenwald, McGhee, & Schwartz, 1998), or unintended activation of thoughts as an ironical consequence of attempted thought suppression (Macrae, Bodenhausen, Milne & Jetten, 1994; Wegner, 1994).

How can the relationship between CELA and this modern research program be characterized? At first sight, the two approaches pursue different answers to the meta-theoretical question of what it means to investigate social stereotypes. One answer is that in order to understand the phenomenon of stereotyping, one has to study the preconditions of activation and access to stereotypes that already exist in memory. The other answer is to investigate the original process of stereotype acquisition in a broader context that includes the individual's memory and the structure of the stimulus ecology. To be sure, both answers sound reasonable; they are not incompatible but complement each other. Both approaches share the common meta-theory that in order to understand social stereotypes, we need to understand the subset or sample of information that provides the effective input to judgments, decisions, and actions at a given point in time, space, and social context. However, while one approach restricts itself to short-term information sampled from memory, the other approach covers both short-term and long-term sampling processes that take place inside and outside human memory. Indeed, employing the current terminology from the priming and accessibility literature, CELA might be characterized as including chronical accessibility of information in internal and external memory systems. In other words, it would not be too far-fetched or inappropriate to consider CELA as a generalized approach to "accessibility" (here termed "psychological relativity").

Having said this, we can nevertheless point out some notable differences in scope and explanatory power, underlining our claim that CELA is less restrictive and covers a broader empirical domain than the purely cognitive notion of priming and memory access. To make this point, one can ask, on the one hand, which approach promises to explain more systematic variance, investigating stereotype access in memory or stereotype acquisition in the environment. On the other hand, different implications for stereotype treatment and change may turn out to be attached to the two approaches.

Let us take, for a concrete example, the stereotype of unemployed people in western nations. Although unemployment is commonly regarded as a serious blow of fate that can happen to everybody, the public image of unemployed people has more and more shifted from a victim of welfare state to a free rider or even a social criminal who exploits unemployment insurances and common goods. Let us consider, in particular, the dependence of such a changing modern stereotype on how unemployment is treated in the mass media as the dominant information ecology.

With respect to this example, CELA would start from an analysis of the distribution of information about unemployed people in the media, the sampling biases that characterize media coverage, the selective exposure of different individuals to different media, and the long-term learning process through which people form their impressions and attitudes—or through which different people exposed to different media form different attitudes. Note, however, that CELA includes both long-term and short-term sampling, both in the external ecology and the internal ecology of human memory. Thus, a child whose father himself has been unemployed for many years, or a child who witnesses the problems of an unemployed family (even when she does not like or belong to that family), will be exposed to a structurally different long-term sample of observations to inform the unemployment stereotype than a child who is merely exposed to second-hand of information. However, just as with such a long-term source of stimulus input, the resulting stereotype may be affected by medium-term (e.g., a political discussion) or short-term versions of cognitive-ecological interaction (e.g., the use of connotative words such as "free rider" or "victim").

How could a priming and accessibility approach be formulated to provide a full explanation of this stereotype and its behavioral consequences? Granting that individuals' knowledge about unemployment is complex enough to include favorable as well as unfavorable concepts and arguments, the assumption would be, for example, that media priming effects determine which of several possible reactions to unemployed people is activated. In other words, the focus here is restricted to short-term oscillations in knowledge activation, superimposed on the long-term acquisition of stable knowledge, to momentary states rather than cumulative knowledge structures. The very notion of a priming effect, as it was imported from cognitive psychology (Meyer & Schvaneveldt, 1971; Neely, 1977), highlights the possibility to exert, for a short moment, an arbitrary influence on the process of memory access through an experimentally controlled prime stimulus. A priming effect was originally defined operationally as an arbitrary facilitation effect that can be elicited in all (or most) people through subtle and often unattended stimuli selected under experimental control. In this regard, priming is arbitrary, momentary, reversible, and controlled experimentally. That is, countless different semantic or epistemic categories can be primed, and priming effects generalize across most people, content areas, or modalities. Priming effects are mostly short-lived and reversible, as highlighted by the fact that the opposite category could be primed as well. Moreover, the experimenter typically uses the same prime stimuli for all participants, demonstrating vividly the basic independence of such priming effects from systematic differences in knowledge and learning history. Virtually anybody who is in full command of language and semantic knowledge can potentially be influenced by the semantic associations of prime words like "free rider" or "victim".

In this regard, priming effects would appear to be opposite, or at least orthogonal, to systematic long-term learning of strong stereotypes and dispositions. To explain a negative stereotype against unemployed people, one would have to assume either that a single priming encounter (e.g., a single exposure to the word "free rider") can account for an enduring stereotype with serious behavioral consequences, which is certainly wrong. If priming effects were that irreversible, priming any concept would block subsequent priming effects for antonymous concepts, and the whole potential of priming influences would soon be exhausted. Alternatively, one would have to assume that the environment exerts a permanent priming of words with negative connotations (e.g., "free rider", "lazy", "unmotivated") while providing only few words with opposite connotations (e.g., "victim", "justice", "dignity"). This assumption would also be rather implausible and, at the same time, would turn the priming notion into an environmental, rather than a cognitive, construct. The explanatory power would reside not in the existence of priming effects but in the assumption that some environmental structures exert permanent lopsided priming effects.

In any case, applying the notion of long-term priming or chronical accessibility (Bargh, 1997) to the explanation of persistent stereotypes raises additional, almost insurmountable problems. On the one hand, the strong assumption that environments constitute permanent priming treatments requires empirical support. Although the conception of chronical accessibility is quite popular, hardly anybody has ever undertaken the necessary comprehensive assessment of information environments (e.g., media, literature, family talk, etc.) to confirm the role of chronical accessibility in stereotype formation and change. On the other hand, when environmental structures are actually playing a systematic role in the genesis and maintenance of stereotypes, the question remains whether passive priming processes can adequately describe the process by which such an environmental influence is brought about. As the preceding chapters have shown, cognitive-ecological interactions can involve many other processes that assign a much more active, participating role to the individual than in a typical priming experiment.

The bottom line of this discussion about the relationship between CELA and priming research must be one that does not propagate a wrong sense of equality. Although it is certainly true that both approaches can contribute to our understanding of stereotypes and their consequences, it would be simply wrong to say that both contribute to a similar degree. Historically and empirically, priming effects are much more well investigated and well established, based on an optimized methodology and high paradigmatical standards. However, in terms of theoretical scope, a cognitive-ecological framework like CELA is simply more inclusive and more capable of providing a comprehensive explanation of the genesis and maintenance of stereotypes than the special case of memory accessibility, which constitutes but one aspect of the entire information environment. The major merits of priming in social cognition would appear to lie not in offering a comprehensive theory of stereotyping, but in highlighting the amazing ways in which tiny treatments can have strong and sometimes irreversible and perpetuating influences. For example, priming can influence the outbreak of an aggression or hostile debate, the decision to help a person in need, the sentencing judgment in a courtroom, or even the outcome of medical diagnosis. The scientific fascination and psychological significance stems here from the richness of subtle, unconscious, sometimes unbelievable influences on seemingly voluntary, reflective behavior. Such demonstrations often have content validity for many realistic judgments and decisions, and they have greatly enriched our theoretical imagination as to what is possible in implicit cognition and how human memory works.

However, as fascinating as priming effects may appear, they remain particularistic, arbitrary, externally driven, and by no means the only way in which ecological information impacts social cognition. To supplement such short-term oscillations in accessibility with systematic long-term learning processes, we believe that a broader approach like CELA is needed. Our conviction is that applying ordinary laws of associative learning to an analysis of stereotype learning in emergent environments can be as interesting and revealing as the analysis of short-term memory access—that has been given so much more attention in the social psychology of the last decades. The theoretical potential of stereotypes conceived as a continuous social learning process is immediately apparent. Learning and relearning processes are clearly involved in many important results of stereotype research, such as the contact hypothesis (reduction of stereotypes through intergroup contact; Pettigrew, 1986), the cross-categorization and subtyping effects (learning of finer category structures; Johnston & Hewstone, 1992; Klauer & Wegener, 1998), the relative impact of stereotype-consistent and inconsistent information (Stangor & McMillan, 1992), and the outgroup homogeneity effect (unequal amount of information learned about ingroups and outgroups; Linville et al., 1989; Park & Rothbart, 1982).

The optimism inherent to CELA

Thus far, we have emphasized that the domain of CELA is broad and unrestrictive, and that ecological learning analyses may be applicable to more phenomena than expected at first. Let us add, quickly, that CELA also has an inherently optimistic quality. It focuses on regular and predictable structures in the environment rather than arbitrary, unpredictable stimulation (e.g., under the control of randomized designs). More importantly, CELA does not need to postulate demons and pathological forces or defective states to account for stereotypes. Just as ordinary learning laws are often sufficient to explain the genesis of intergroup attitudes, the same regular laws of learning suggest the key to stereotype reduction and change. Real historical examples of stereotypes that have been overcome testify to this optimistic assumption. Many positive examples of successful stereotype reduction can be understood in terms of relearning or unlearning processes, in addition to changes in motivation or vested interests. For example, the positive image of Italian restaurant owners in mid-Europe over the last 40 years reflects an extended period of contact and learning experience. There is little reason to assume that personal needs or dependence on Italian business people have changed dramatically. Likewise, the increasing integration of black athletes in mid-European soccer teams has caused a similar relearning process in both team mates and soccer fans, in spite of divergent motives: a more favorable impression in soccer fans—who need the outstanding black athletes as idols and identification figures—but also in white team mates who have to fear the black competitors as rivals.

Don't neglect the environment!

Above and beyond all aforementioned arguments concerning the breadth and theoretical potential of a learning approach to stereotyping, we believe that the major advantage to be gained from CELA is its emphasis on the environment. We are convinced—and we hope to have convinced many readers of this volume—that psychological theories remain premature and incomplete when they fail to take the environment into account. One cannot understand the nature and adaptive value of intrapersonal processes unless the stimulus environment that impinges on the individual is taken into account.

References

Abelson, R. P., Aronson, E., McGuire, W. J., Newcomb, T. M., Rosenberg, M. J., & Tannenbaum P. (Eds.). (1968). *Theories of cognitive consistency: A sourcebook.* Chicago: Rand McNally.

Ajzen, I. (1977). Intuitive theories of events and the effects of base-rate information on predictions. *Journal of Personality and Social Psychology, 35*, 303–314.

Anderson, N. H. (1967). Averaging model analysis of set-size effects in impression formation. *Journal of Experimental Psychology, 75*, 158–165.

Aronson, J., Quinn, D. M., & Spencer, S. J. (1998). Stereotype threat and the academic underperformance of minorities and women. In J. K. Swim & C. Stangor (Eds.), *Prejudice: The target's perspective* (pp. 83–103). San Diego, CA: Academic Press.

Aronson, E., Wilson, T. D., & Akert, R. M. (1998). *Social psychology* (3rd ed.). New York: Longman.

Bailey, S. M. (1992). *Girls in schools: A bibliography of research on girls in US public schools (kindergarten through grade 12).* Wellesley, MA: Wellesley College.

Bargh, J. A. (1997). The automaticity of everyday life. In R. S. Wyer & T. K. Srull (Eds.), *Advances in social cognition* (Vol. 10, pp. 1–61). Mahwah, NJ: Lawrence Erlbaum Associates, Inc.

Bargh, J. A., Chen, M., & Burrows, L. (1996). Automaticity of social behavior: Direct effects of trait construct and stereotype activation on action. *Journal of Personality and Social Psychology, 71*, 230–244.

Bargh, J. A., & Pietromonaco, P. (1982). Automatic information processing and social perception: The influence of trait information presented outside of conscious awareness on impression formation. *Journal of Personality and Social Psychology, 43*, 437–449.

Bar-Hillel, M. (1980). The base-rate fallacy in probability judgments. *Acta Psychologica, 44*, 211–233.

Baron, R. M., & Kenny, D. A. (1986). The moderator–mediator variable distinction in social psychological research: Conceptual, strategic, and statistical considerations. *Journal of Personality and Social Psychology, 51*, 1173–1182.

Begg, I., Armour, V., & Kerr, T. (1985). On believing what we remember. *Canadian Journal of Behavioral Science, 17*, 199–214.

Blau, G., & Katerberg, R. (1982). Agreeing responses set: Statistical nuisance or meaningful personality concept? *Perceptual and Motor Skills, 54*, 851–857.

Bless, H., Clore, G. L., Schwarz, N., Golisano, V., Rabe, C., & Woelk, M. (1996). Mood and the use of scripts: Does happy mood make people really mindless? *Journal of Personality and Social Psychology, 71*, 665–679.

Bodenhausen, G. V. (1990). Stereotypes as judgmental heuristics. Evidence of circadian variations in discrimination. *Psychological Science, 1*, 319–322.

Bodenhausen, G. V., Kramer, G. P., & Suesser, K. (1994). Happiness and stereotypic thinking in social judgment. *Journal of Personality and Social Psychology, 66*, 621–632.

Bodenhausen G. V., & Lichtenstein, M. (1987). Social stereotypes and information-processing strategies: The impact of task complexity. *Journal of Personality and Social Psychology, 48*, 267–282.

Bond, C. F., & Kenny, D. A. (2002). The triangle of interpersonal models. *Journal of Personality and Social Psychology, 83*, 355–366.

Borgida, E., & Brekke, N. (1981). The base-rate fallacy in attribution and prediction. In J. H. Harvey, W. J. Ickes, & R. F. Kidd (Eds.), *New directions in attribution research* (pp. 66–95). Hillsdale, NJ: Lawrence Erlbaum Associates, Inc.

Brandtstädter, J. (1982). Apriorische Elemente in psychologischen Forschungs-programmen (A-priori elements in psychological research programs). *Zeitschrift für Sozialpsychologie, 13*, 267–277.

Brauer, M., Judd, C. M., & Gliner, M. D. (1995). The effects of repeated expressions on attitude polarization during group discussions. *Journal of Personality and Social Psychology, 68*, 1014–1029.

Brauer, M., Wasel, W., & Niedenthal, P. (2000). Implcit and explicit components of prejudice. *Review of General Psychology, 4*, 79–101.

Brehm, S. S., Kassin, S. M., & Fein, S. (1999). *Social psychology* (4th ed.). Boston: Houghton Mifflin Company.

Brewer, M. B. (1988). A dual process model of impression formation. In R. S. Wyer & T. K. Srull (Eds.), *Advances in social cognition* (Vol. 1, pp. 1–36). Hillsdale, NJ: Lawrence Erlbaum Associates, Inc.

Brewer, M. B. (1979). Ingroup bias in the minimal intergroup situation: A cognitive motivational analysis. *Psychological Bulletin, 86*, 307–324.

Brophy, J. (1983). Research on the self-fulfilling prophecy and teacher expectations. *Journal of Educational Psychology, 75*, 631–661.

Brown, R., & Fish, D. (1983). The psychological causality implicit in language. *Cognition, 14*, 233–274.

Bruner, J. S. (1957). On perceptual readiness. *Psychological Review, 64*, 123–152.

Bruner, J. S., & Goodman, C. D. (1947). Value and need as organizing factors in perception. *Journal of Abnormal and Social Psychology, 42*, 33–44.

Bruner, J. S., & Postman, L. (1948). Symbolic value as an organizing factor in perception. *Journal of Social Psychology, 27*, 203–208.

Brunswik, E. (1956). *Perception and the representative design of psychological experiments*. Berkeley: University of California Press.

Buehler, R., Griffin, D., & MacDonald, H. (1997). The role of motivated reasoning in optimistic time predictions. *Personality and Social Psychology Bulletin, 23*, 238–247.

Camerer, C. (1988). Illusory correlations in perceptions and predictions of organizational traits. *Journal of Behavioral Decision Making, 1*, 77–94.

Ceci, S. J., & Bruck, M. (1995). *Jeopardy in the courtroom.* Washington, DC: American Psychological Association.

Chaiken, S. (1987). The heuristic model of persuasion. In M. P. Zanna, J. M. Olson, & P. C. Herman (Eds.), *Social influence: The Ontario Symposium* (Vol. 5, pp. 3–39). Hillsdale, NJ: Lawrence Erlbaum Associates, Inc.

Chaiken, S., Liberman, A., & Eagly, A. H. (1989). Heuristic and systematic information processing within and beyond the persuasion context. In J. S. Uleman & J. A. Bargh (Eds.), *Unintended thought* (pp. 212–252). New York: Guilford.

Chapman, L. J. (1967). Illusory correlation in observational report. *Journal of Verbal Learning and Verbal Behavior, 6*, 151–155.

Cheng, P. W., & Novick, L. R. (1990). A probabilistic contrast model of causal induction. *Journal of Personality and Social Psychology, 58*, 545–567.

Cooper, H. (1979). Pygmalion grows up: A model for teacher expectation, communication, and performance influence. *Review of Educational Research, 49,* 389–410.

Cooper, W. H. (1981). Ubiquituos halo. *Psychological Bulletin, 90,* 218–224.

Corneille, O., & Judd, C. M. (1999). Accentuation and sensitization effects in the categorization of multifaceted stimuli. *Journal of Personality and Social Psychology, 77*, 927–941.

Craik, F. I. M., & Tulving, E. (1975). Depth of processing and the retention of words in episodic memory. *Journal of Experimental Psychology: General, 104*, 268–294.

DeSoto, C. B. (1960). Learning a social structure. *Journal of Abnormal and Social Psychology, 60*, 417–421.

Devine, P. G. (1989). Stereotypes and prejudice: Their automatic and controlled components. *Journal of Personality and Social Psychology, 56*, 5–18.

Dijksterhuis, A., Spears, R., Postmes, T., Stapel, D. A., Koomen, W., van Knippenberg, A., & Scheepers, D. (1998). Seeing one thing and doing another: Contrast effects in automatic behavior. *Journal of Personality and Social Psychology, 75*, 862–871.

Dion, K., Berscheid, E., & Walster, E. (1972). What is beautiful is good. *Journal of Personality and Social Psychology, 24*, 285–290.

Dosher, D. A., & Russo, J. E. (1976). Memory for internally generated stimuli. *Journal of Experimental Psychology. Human Learning and Memory, 2*, 633–640.

Dovidio, J. F., Gaertner, S. L., Validzic, A., Matoka, K., Johnson, B., & Frazier, S. (1997). Extending the benefits of recategorization: Evaluations, self-disclosure, and helping. *Journal of Experimental Social Psychology, 33*, 401–420.

Downing, J. W., Judd, C. M., & Brauer, M. (1992). Effects of repeated expressions on attitude extremity. *Journal of Personality and Social Psychology, 63*, 17–29.

Eagly, A. H. (1987). *Sex differences in social behavior: A social-role interpretation*. Hillsdale, NJ: Lawrence Erlbaum Associates, Inc.

Eagly, A. H., & Steffen, V. J. (1986). Gender and aggressive behavior: A meta-analytic review of the social psychological literature. *Psychological Bulletin, 100*, 309–330.

Einhorn, H. J., & Hogarth, R. M. (1978). Confidence in judgment: Persistence of the illusion of validity. *Psychological Review, 85*, 395–416.

Eiser J. R. (1971). Enhancement of contrast in the absolute judgment of attitude statements. *Journal of Personality and Social Psychology, 71*, 1–10.

Eiser, J. R., & Stroebe, W. (1972). *Categorization and social judgment.* New York: Academic Press.

Fazio, R. H., Jackson, J. R., Dunton, B. C., & Williams, C. J. (1995). Variability in automatic activation as an unobtrusive measure of racial attitudes: A bona fide pipeline? *Journal of Personality and Social Psychology, 69*, 1013–1027.

Festinger, L. (1964). *Conflict, decision, and dissonance*. Stanford, CA: Stanford University Press.

Fiedler, K. (1991). The tricky nature of skewed frequency tables: An information loss account of distinctiveness-based illusory correlations. *Journal of Personality and Social Psychology, 60*, 24–36.

Fiedler, K. (1996). Explaining and simulating judgment biases as an aggregation phenomenon in probabilistic, multiple-cue environments. *Psychological Review, 103*, 193–214.

Fiedler, K. (2000a). Illusory correlations: A simple associative algorithm provides a convergent account of seemingly divergent paradigms. *Review of General Psychology, 4*, 25–58.

Fiedler, K. (2000b). Beware of samples! A cognitive-ecological sampling approach to judgment biases. *Psychological Review, 107*, 659–676.

Fiedler, K. (2000c). On mere considering: The subjective experience of truth. In H. Bless & J. P. Forgas (Eds.), *The message within: The role of subjective experience in social cognition and behavior* (pp. 13–36). Philadelphia: Taylor & Francis.

Fiedler, K., & Armbruster, T. (1994). Two halfs may be more than one whole: Category-split effects on frequency illusions. *Journal of Personality and Social Psychology, 66*, 633–645.

Fiedler, K., Armbruster, T., Nickel, S., Walther, E., & Asbeck, J. (1996). Constructive biases in social judgment: Experiments on the self-verification of question contents. *Journal of Personality and Social Psychology, 71*, 861–873.

Fiedler, K., Brinkmann, B., Betsch, T., & Wild, B. (2000). A sampling approach to biases in conditional probability judgments: Beyond baserate neglect and statistical format. *Journal of Experimental Psychology: General, 129*, 399–418.

Fiedler, K., & Freytag, P. (2003). Pseudo-contingencies. Paper submitted for publication.

Fiedler, K., Freytag, P., Walther, E., & Plessner, P. (2002). *The role of redundancy in complex information processing in the simulated classroom*. Unpublished research, University of Heidelberg.

Fiedler, K., Kemmelmeier, M., & Freytag, P. (1999). Explaining asymmetric intergroup judgments through differential aggregation: Computer simulations and some new evidence. *European Review of Social Psychology, 10*, 1–40.

Fiedler, K., Plessner, P., Freytag, P., & Walther, E. (2002). *Detecting changes in student performance in the simulated classroom environment*. Unpublished research, University of Heidelberg, Germany.

Fiedler, K., Russer, S., & Gramm, K. (1993). Illusory correlations and memory performance. *Journal of Experimental Social Psychology, 29*, 111–136.

Fiedler, K., & Schenk, W. (2001). Spontaneous inferences from pictorially presented traits. *Personality and Social Psychology Bulletin, 27*, 1533–1546.

Fiedler, K., & Semin, G. R. (1988). On the causal information conveyed by different interpersonal verbs: The role of implicit sentence context. *Social Cognition, 6*, 12–39.

Fiedler, K., Walther, E., Armbruster, T., Fay, D., & Naumann, U. (1996). Do you *really* know what you have seen? Intrusion errors and presuppositions effects on constructive memory. *Journal of Experimental Social Psychology, 32*, 484–511.

Fiedler, K., Walther, E., Freytag, P., & Nickel, S. (2003). Inductive reasoning and judgment interference: Experiments on Simpson's paradox. *Personality and Social Psychology Bulletin, 29*, 14–27.

Fiedler, K., Walther, E., Freytag, P., & Plessner, H. (2002a). Judgment biases in a simulated classroom – a cognitive-environmental approach. *Organizational Behavior and Human Decision Processes, 88*, 527–561.

Fiedler, K., Walther, E., Freytag, P., & Stryczek, E. (2002b). Playing mating games in foreign cultures: A conceptual framework and an experimental paradigm for trivariate statistical inference. *Journal of Experimental Social Psychology, 38*, 14–30.

Fiedler, K., Walther, E., & Nickel, S. (1999a). Covariation-based attribution: On the ability to assess multiple covariates of an effect. *Personality and Social Psychology Bulletin, 25*, 607–622.

Fiedler, K., Walther, E., & Nickel, S. (1999b). The autoverification of social hypothesis. Stereotyping and the power of sample size. *Journal of Personality and Social Psychology, 77*, 5–18.

Fishbein, M., & Ajzen, I. (1974). Attitudes towards objects as predictors of single and multiple behavioral criteria. *Psychological Review, 81*, 59–74.

Fiske, S. T., & Neuberg, S. L. (1990). A continuum of impression formation from category-based to individuating processing: Influences of information and motivation on attention and interpretation. In M. P. Zanna (Ed.), *Advances in Experimental Social Psychology*, (Vol. 23, pp. 1–74). Orlando, FL: Academic Press.

Frey, D. (1986). Recent research on selective exposure to information. In L. Berkowitz (Ed.), *Advances in experimental social psychology* (Vol. 19, pp. 41–80). New York: Academic Press.

Friedrich, J. (1993). Primary error detection and minimization (PEDMIN) strategies in social cognition: A reinterpretation of confirmation bias phenomena. *Psychological Review, 100*, 298–319.

Gadenne, V. (1982). Der Bestaetigungsfehler und die Rationalitaet kognitiver Prozesse. *Psychologische Beitraege, 24*, 11–25.

Gaertner, S. L., Rust, M. C., Dovidio, J. F., Backman, B. A., & Anastasio, P. A. (1994). The contact hypothesis: The role of a common ingroup identity on reducing intergroup bias. *Small Group Research, 25*, 224–249.

Garcia, J., & Koelling, R. A. (1966). A relation of cue to consequence in avoidance learning. *Psychonomic Society, 4*, 123–124.

Gavanski, I., & Hui, C. (1992). Natural sample spaces and uncertain belief. *Journal of Personality and Social Psychology, 63*, 766–780.

Gigerenzer, G. (1984). External validity of laboratory experiments: The frequency-validity relationship. *American Journal of Psychology, 97*, 185–195.

Gigerenzer, G., & Fiedler, K. (2003). Minds in environments: The potential of an ecological approach to cognition. Manuscript submitted for publication.

Gigerenzer, G., & Hoffrage, U. (1995). How to improve Bayesian reasoning without instructions: Frequency formats. *Psychological Review, 102*, 684–704.

Gigerenzer, G., & Todd, P. (Eds.). (1999). *Simple heuristics that make us smart*. Oxford: Oxford University Press.

Gilbert, D. T. (1989). Thinking lightly about others: Automatic components in the social inference process. In J. S. Uleman & J. A. Bargh (Eds.), *Unintended thought* (pp. 189–211). New York: Guilford.

Gilbert, D. T., Krull, D. S., & Malone, P. S. (1990). Unbelieving the unbelievable: Some problems in the rejection of false information. *Journal of Personality and Social Psychology, 59*, 601–613.

Gill, M. J., Swann, W. B., & Silvera, D. H. (1998). Attitudes and social cognition: On the genesis of confidence. *Journal of Personality and Social Psychology, 75*, 1101–1114.

Gilovich, T., Medvec, V., & Savitsky, K. (2000). *Journal of Personality and Social Psychology, 2*, 211–222.

Gollwitzer, P. M., & Schaal, B. (1998). Metacognition in action: The importance of implementation intentions. *Personality and Social Psychology Review, 2*, 124–136.

Greene, R. L. (1984). Incidental learning of event frequencies. *Memory & Cognition, 12*, 90–95.

Greenwald, A. G. (1975). Consequences of prejudice against the null hypothesis. *Psychological Bulletin, 82*, 1–20.

Greenwald, A. G., McGhee, D. E., & Schwartz, J. L. K. (1998). Measuring individual differences in implicit cognition: The implicit association test. *Journal of Personality and Social Psychology, 74*, 1464–1480.

Greitemeyer, T., & Schulz-Hardt, S. (in press). Preference-consistent evaluation of information in the hidden profile paradigm: Beyond group-level explanations for the dominance of shared information in group decisions. *Journal of Personality and Social Psychology*.

Greve, W. (2001). Traps and gaps in action explanation: Theoretical problems of a psychology of human action. *Psychological Review, 108*, 435–451.

Grice, H. P. (1975). Logic of conversation. In P. Cole, & J. L. Morgan (Eds.), *Syntax and Semantics* (pp. 41–58). New York: Academic Press.

Gruenfeld, D. H., & Wyer, R. S., Jr. (1992). Semantics and *pragmatics* of social influence: How affirmations and denials affect beliefs in referent propositions. *Journal of Personality and Social Psychology, 62*, 38–49.

Hamilton, D. L. (1981). Illusory correlations as a basis for stereotyping. In D. L. Hamilton (Ed.), *Cognitive processes in stereotyping and interproup behavior.* Hillsdale, NJ: Lawrence Erlbaum Associates, Inc.

Hamilton, D. L., Dugan, P. M., & Trolier, T. K. (1985). The formation of stereotypic beliefs: Further evidence for distinctiveness-based illusory correlations. *Journal of Personality and Social Psychology, 48*, 5–17.

Hamilton, D. L., & Gifford, R. K. (1976). Illusory correlation in interpersonal perception: a cognitive basis of stereotypic judgments. *Journal of Experimental Social Psychology, 12,* 392–407.

Hamilton, D. L., & Rose, R. L. (1980). Illusory correlation and the maintenance of stereotypic beliefs. *Journal of Personality and Social Psychology, 39*, 832–845.

Hamilton, D. L., & Sherman, S. J. (1989). Illusory correlations: Implications for stereotype theory and research. In D. Bar-Tal, C. F. Graumann, A. W. Kruglanski, & W. Stroebe (Eds.), *Stereotype and prejudice: Changing conceptions* (pp. 59–82). New York: Springer.

Hamilton, D. L., & Sherman, J. W. (1994) Stereotypes. In R. S. Wyer & T. K. Srull (Eds.), *Handbook of social cognition* (2nd Ed., Vol. 1, pp 1–68). Hillsdale, NJ: Lawrence Erlbaum Associates, Inc.

Harris, M. J., & Rosenthal, R. (1985). Mediation of interpersonal expectance effects: 31 meta-analyses. *Psychological Bulletin, 97*, 363–386.

Hasher, L., Attig, M. S., & Alba, J. W. (1981). I knew it all along: Or did I? *Journal of Verbal Learning and Verbal Behavior, 20*, 86–96.

Hasher, L., Goldstein, D., & Toppino, T. (1977). Frequency and the conference of referential validity. *Journal of Verbal Learning and Verbal Behavior, 16*, 107–112.

Heider, F. (1958). *The psychology of interpersonal relations*. New York: Wiley.

Helson, H. (1964). *Adaptation-level theory: An experimental and systematic approach to behavior.* New York: Harper & Row.

Hertwig, R., Gigerenzer, G., & Hoffrage, U. (1997). The reiteration effect in hindsight bias. *Psychological Review, 104*, 194–202.

Higgins, E. T., & King, G. A. (1981). Accessibility of social constructs: Information-processing consequences of individual and contextual variability. In N. Cantor, & J. F. Kihlstrom (Eds.), *Personality, cognition and social interaction.* Hillsdale, NJ: Lawrence Erlbaum Associates, Inc.

Higgins, E. T., Rholes, W. S., & Jones, C. R. (1977). Category accessibility and impression formation. *Journal of Experimental Social Psychology, 13*, 141–154.

Hilton, D. J., & Slugoski, B. R. (1986). Knowledge-based causal attribution: The abnormal conditions focus model. *Psychological Review, 93*, 75–88.

Hilton, J. L., & von Hippel, W. (1996). Stereotypes. *Annual Review of Psychology, 47*, 237–271.

Hoffman, C., & Hurst, N. (1990). Gender stereotypes: Perception or rationalization? *Journal of Personality and Social Psychology, 58*, 197–208.

Hovland, C. L., & Weiss, W. (1953) Transmission of information concerning concepts through positive and negative instances. *Journal of Experimental Psychology, 45*, 175–182.

Hu, X., & Batchelder, W. H. (1994). The statistical analysis of general processing tree models with the EM algorithm. *Psychometrika, 59*, 21–47.

Jackson, J. E. (1979). Bias in closed-ended issue questions. *Political Methodology, 6*, 393–424.

Johnson, C., & Mullen, B. (1994). Evidence for the accessibility of paired distinctiveness in distinctiveness-based illusory correlation in stereotyping. *Personality and Social Psychology Bulletin, 20*, 65–70.

Johnson, M. K., Hashtroudi, S., & Lindsay, D. S. (1993). Source monitoring. *Psychological Bulletin, 114*, 3–28.

Johnston, L., & Hewstone, M. (1992). Cognitive models of stereotype change. 3. Subtyping and the perceived typicality of disconfirming group members. *Journal of Experimental Social Psychology, 28*, 360–386.

Jones, E. E., & McGillis, D. (1976). Correspondent inferences and the attribution cube: A comparative appraisal. In J. H. Harvey, W. J. Ickes, & R. F. Kidd (Eds.), *New directions in attribution research* (Vol. 1). Hillsdale, NJ: Lawrence Erlbaum Associates, Inc.

Jones, E. E., & Nisbett, R. E. (1972). The actor and the observer: Divergent perceptions of the causes of behavior. In E. E. Jones, D. E. Kanouse, H. H. Kelley, R. E. Nisbett, S. Valins, & B. W. Weiner (Eds.), *Attribution: Perceiving the causes of behavior*. Morristown, NJ: General Learning Press.

Judd, C. M., & Park, B. (1988). Outgroup-homogeneity: Judgments of variability at the individual and the group levels. *Journal of Personality and Social Psychology, 54*, 778–788.

Jussim, L. (1989). Teacher expectations: Self-fulfilling prophecies, perceptual biases, and accuracy. *Journal of Personality and Social Psychology, 57*, 469–480.

Jussim, L. (1991). Social perception and social reality: A reflection-construction model. *Psychological Review, 98*, 54–73.

Jussim, L. (1992). Prejudice, stereotypes, base rates, and saber-toothed tigers. *Psychological Inquiry, 3*, 169–170.

Jussim, L., Eccles, J., & Madon, S. (1996). Social perception, social stereotypes and teacher expectations: Accuracy and the quest for the powerful self-fulfilling prophecy. In M. P. Zanna (Ed.), *Advances in Experimental Social Psychology* (Vol. 28, pp. 281–388). San Diego, CA: Academic Press.

Kahneman, D., & Tversky, A. (1972). Subjective probability: A judgment of representativeness. *Cognitive Psychology, 3*, 430–453.

Kahneman, D., & Tversky, A. (1973). On the psychology of prediction. *Psychological Review, 80*, 237–251.

Kamin, L. J. (1968). 'Attention-like' processes in classical conditioning. In M. R. Jones

(Ed.), *Miami symposium on the production of behavior: Aversive stimulation* (pp. 9–33). Coral Gables, FL: University of Miami Press.

Kanouse, D. E., & Hanson, L. R., Jr. (1972). Negativity in evaluations. In E. E. Jones, D. E. Kanouse, H. H. Kelley, R. E. Nisbett, S. Valins, & B. W. Weiner (Eds.), *Attribution: Perceiving the causes of behavior*. Morristown, NJ: General Learning Press.

Kaplan, M. F. (1981). Amount of information and polarity of attraction. *Bulletin of the Psychonomic Society, 18*, 23–26.

Karpinski, A., & Von Hippel, W. (1996). The role of the linguistic intergroup bias in expectancy maintenance. *Social Cognition, 14*, 141–163.

Kawakami, K., Dovidio, J. F., Moll, J., Hermsen, S., & Russin, A. (2000). Just say no (to stereotyping): Effects of training in the negation of stereotype associations on stereotype activation. *Journal of Personality and Social Psychology, 78*, 871–888.

Kelley, H. H. (1967). Attribution in social psychology. *Nebraska Symposium on Motivation, 15*, 192–238.

Kelley, H. H. (1973). The process of causal attribution. *American Psychologist, 28*, 107–128.

Kelly, J. R., & Karau, S. J. (1999). Group decision making: The effects of initial preferences and time pressure. *Personality and Social Psychology Bulletin, 25*, 1342–1354.

Klar, Y., & Giladi, E. E. (1997). Are most people happier than their peers, or are they just happy? *Personality and Social Psychology Bulletin, 25*, 585–594.

Klauer, K. C., & Meiser, T. (2000). A source-monitoring analyses of illusory correlations. *Personality and Social Psychology Bulletin, 26*, 1074–1093.

Klauer, K. C., & Wegnener, I. (1998). Unraveling social categorization in the "Who said what?" paradigm. *Journal of Personality and Social Psychology, 75*, 1155–1178.

Klayman, J., & Ha, Y. (1987). Confirmation, disconfirmation, and information in hypothesis testing. *Psychological Review, 94*, 211–228.

Koehler, D. J. (1991). Explanation, imagination, and confidence in judgment. *Psychological Bulletin, 110*, 499–519.

Koriat, A., Lichtenstein, S., & Fischhoff, B. (1980). Reasons for confidence. *Journal of Experimental Psychology: Human Learning and Memory, 6*, 107–118.

Krueger, J., & Rothbart, M. (1990). Contrast and accentuation effects in category learning. *Journal of Personality and Social Psychology, 59*, 651–663.

Kruglanski, A. W., Thompson, E. P., & Spiegel, S. (1999). Separate or equal? Bimodal notions of persuasion and a single-process "unimodel". In S. Chaiken & Y. Trope (Eds.), *Dual-process theories in social psychology* (pp. 293–313). New York: Guilford.

Kruschke, J. K. (1992). ALCOVE. *Psychological Review, 99*, 22–44.

Kukla, A. (1993). The structure of self-fulfilling and self-negating prophecies. *Theory and Psychology, 4*, 5–33.

Kunda, Z. (1990). The case for motivated reasoning. *Psychological Bulletin, 108*, 480–498.

Kunda, Z., & Oleson, K. (1995). Maintaining stereotypes in the face of disconfirmation: *Constructing Grounds for Subtyping Deviants, 68*, 565–579.

Ledley, R. S., & Lusted, L. B. (1959). Reasoning foundations of medical diagnosis. *Science, 130*, 9–21.

Lenski, G. E. & Leggett, J. C. (1960). Caste, class, and deference in the research interview. *American Journal of Sociology, 65*, 463–467.

Lepore, L., & Brown, R. (1997). Category and stereotype activation: Is prejudice inevitable? *Journal of Personality and Social Psychology, 72*, 275–287.

Leyens, J.-P., Dardenne, B., & Fiske S. T. (1998). Why and under what circumstances is a hypothesis-consistent testing strategy preferred in interviews? *British Journal of Social Psychology, 37*, 259–274.

Liberman, N., & Trope, Y. (1998). The role of feasibility and desirability considerations in near and distant future decisions: A test of temporal construal theory. *Journal of Personality and Social Psychology, 75,* 5–18.

Linville, P. W., & Fischer, G. W. (1993). Exemplar and abstraction models of perceived group variability and stereotypicality. *Social Cognition, 11*, 92–125.

Linville, P. W., Fischer, G. W., & Salovey, P. (1989). Perceived distributions of the characteristics of in-group and out-group members: Empirical evidence and a computer simulation. *Journal of Personality and Social Psychology, 57*, 165–188.

Loftus, E. F. & Palmer, J. C. (1974). Reconstruction of automobile destruction: An example of the interaction between language and memory. *Journal of Verbal Learning and Verbal Behavior, 13*, 585–589.

Loftus, E. F. (1975). Leading questions and the eyewitness report. *Cognitive Psychology, 7*, 560–572.

Loftus, E. F. (1979). *Eyewitness testimony*. Cambridge, MA: Harvard University Press.

Loftus, E. F. (1993). The reality of repressed memories. *American Psychologist, 48*, 518–537.

Loftus, E. F., Feldman, J., & Dashiell, R. (1995). The reality of illusory memories. In D. L. Schacter (Ed.), *Memory distortion: How minds, brains and societies reconstruct the past* (pp. 47–68). Cambridge, MA: Harvard University Press.

Lohmann, F., Fiedler, K., Walther, E. (1998). *Diagnostic confirmation and disconfirmation in an hypothesis-testing paradigm*. Unpublished manuscript, University of Heidelberg, Germany.

Lombardi, W. J., Higgins, E. T., & Bargh, J. A. (1987). The role of consciousness in priming effects on categorization: Assimilation versus contrast as a function of awareness of the priming task. *Personality and Social Psychology Bulletin, 13*, 411–429.

Maass, A. (1999). Linguistic intergroup bias: Stereotype perpetuation through language. *Advances in Experimental Social Psychology, 31*, 79–121.

Maass, A. Ceccereelli, R., & Rudin, S. (1996). Linguistic intergroup bias: Evidence for in-group-protective motivation. *Journal of Personality and Social Psychology, 71*, 512–526.

Maass, A., Salvi, D., Arcuri, L., Semin, G. R. (1989). Language use in intergroup contexts: The linguistic intergroup bias. *Journal of Personality and Social Psychology, 57*, 981–993.

Mackie, J. L. (1974). *The cement of the universe: A study of causation*. Oxford, England: Oxford University Press.

Macrae, C. N., Bodenhausen, G. V., Milne, A. B., & Ford, R. L. (1997). On the regulation of recollection: The intentional forgetting of stereotypical memories. *Journal of Personality and Social Psychology, 72*, 709–719.

Macrae, C. N., Bodenhausen, G. V., Milne, A. B., & Jetten, J. (1994). Out of mind but back in sight: Stereotypes on the rebound. *Journal of Personality and Social Psychology, 57*, 808–817.

Macrae, N. C., & Johnston, L. (1998). Help, I need somebody: Automatic action and inaction. *Social Cognition, 16*, 100 117.

Macrae, C. N., Milne, A. B., & Bodenhausen, G. V. (1994). Stereotypes as energy-saving devices: A peek inside the cognitive toolbox. *Journal of Personality and Social Psychology, 66*, 37–47.

Maurer, K. L., Park, B., & Rothbart, M. (1995). Subtyping versus subgrouping processes in stereotype representation. *Journal of Personality and Social Psychology, 69*, 812–824.

McArthur, L. Z. (1981). What grabs you? The role of attention in impression formation and causal attribution. In E. T. Higgings, C. P. Herman, & M. P. Zanna (Eds.), *Social cognition: The Ontario Symposium* (Vol. 1, pp. 201–246). Hillsdale, NJ: Lawrence Erlbaum Associates, Inc.

McArthur, L. Z., & Baron, R. (1983). Toward an ecological theory of social perception. *Psychological Review, 90*, 215–238.

McCauley, C., & Stitt, C. L. (1978). An individual and quantitative measure of stereotypes. *Journal of Personality and Social Psychology, 36*, 929–940.

McCloskey, M., & Zaragoza, M. (1985). Misleading postevent information and memory for events: Arguments and evidence against memory impairment hypotheses. *Journal of Experimental Psychology: General, 114*, 1–16.

Meyer, D. E., & Schvaneveldt, R. W. (1991). Facilitation in recognizing pairs of words: Evidence of a dependence between retrieval operations. *Journal of Experimental Psychology, 90*, 227–234.

Moscovici, S., & Zavalloni, M. (1969). The group as a polarizer of attitudes. *Journal of Personality and Social Psychology, 12*, 125–135.

Mullen, B., & Johnson, C. (1990). Distinctiveness-based illusory correlations and stereotyping: A meta-analytic integration. *British Journal of Social Psychology, 29*, 11–28.

Mummendey, A., & Schreiber, H. J. (1983). Better or just different? Positive social identity by discrimination against, or by differentiation from outgroups. *European Journal of Social Psychology, 13*, 389–397.

Mussweiler, T. (in press). Comparison processes in social judgment: Mechanisms and consequences. *Psychological Review.*

Myers, D. G. (1978). Polarization effects of social comparison. *Journal of Experimental Social Psychology, 14*, 554–563.

Mynatt, C. R., Doherty, M. E., & Tweney, R. D. (1977). Confirmation bias in a simulated research environment: An experimental study of scientific inference. *Quarterly Journal of Experimental Psychology, 29*, 85–95.

Neely, J. H. (1977). Semantic priming and retrieval from lexical memory: Roles of inhibitionless spreading activation and limited capacity attention. *Journal of Experimental Psychology: General, 106*, 226–254.

Neuberg, S. L., & Fiske, S. T. (1987). Motivational influences on impression formation: Outcome dependency, accuracy-driven attention, and individuating processes. *Journal of Personality and Social Psychology, 53*, 431–444.

Newman, J., Wolff, W. T., & Hearst, E. (1980). The feature-positive effect in adult human subjects. *Journal of Experimental Psychology: Human Learning and Memory, 6*, 630–650.

Nisbett, R. E., & Borgida, E. (1975). Attribution and the psychology of prediction. *Journal of Personality and Social Psychology, 32*, 932–943.

Oaksford, M., & Chater, N. (1994). A rational analysis of the selection task as optimal data selection. *Psychological Review, 101*, 608–631.

Oaksford, M., & Chater, N. (1996). Rational explanation of the selection task. *Psychological Review, 103*, 381–391.

Orne, M. T. (1973). Communication by the total experimental situation. Why it is important, how it is evaluated, and its significance for the ecological validity of findings. In P. Pliner, L. Krames, & T. Alloway (Eds.), *Communication and affect: Language and thought.* New York: Academic Press.

Orr, S. P., & Lanzetta, J. T. (1980). Facial expressions of emotion as conditioned stimuli for human autonomic responses. *Journal of Personality and Social Psychology, 38*, 278–282.

Parducci, A. (1965). Category judgment: A range-frequency theory. *Psychological Review, 72*, 407–418.

Park, B., & Hastie, R. (1987). Perception of variability in category development: Instance-versus abstraction-based stereotypes. *Journal of Personality and Social Psychology, 53*, 621–635.

Park, B., Judd, C. N., & Ryan, C. S. (1991). Social categorization and the representation of variability information. *European Review of Social Psychology, 2*, 211–245.

Park, B., & Rothbart, M. (1982). Perception of outgroup homogeneity and levels of social categorization: Memory for the subordinate attributes of ingroup and outgroup members. *Journal of Personality and Social Psychology, 42*, 1051–1068.

Pettigrew, T. F. (1986). The intergroup contact hypothesis reconsidered. In M. Hewstone & R. Brown (Eds.), *Contact and conflict in intergroup encounters* (pp. 169–195). Oxford: Basil Blackwell.

Petty, R. E., & Cacioppo, J. T. (1986). The elaboration likelihood model of persuasion. In L. Berkowitz (Ed.), *Advances in experimental social psychology* (Vol. 19, pp. 123–205). New York: Academic Press.

Plessner, H., Freytag, P., & Fiedler, K. (2000). Expectancy-effects without expectancies: Illusory correlations based on cue-overlap. *European Journal of Social Psychology, 30*, 837–851.

Popper, K. R. (1959). *The logic of scientific discovery*. New York. Basic Books.

Price, P. C. (2001). A group-size effect on personal risk judgments: Implications for unrealistic optimism. *Memory & Cognition, 29*, 578–586.

Pyszczynski, T., & Greenberg, J. (1987). Towards an integration of cognitive and motivational perspectives on social inference: A biased hypothesis-testing model. In L. Berkowitz (Ed.), *Advances in experimental social psychology* (Vol. 20, pp. 297–340). New York: Academic Press.

Ratcliff, R., & McKoon, G. (1997). A counter model for implicit priming in perceptual word identification. *Psychological Review*, 104, 319–343.

Reeder, G. D., & Brewer, M. (1979). A schematic model of dispositional attribution in interpersonal perception. *Psychological Review, 86*, 61–79.

Rescorla, R. A., & Wagner, A. R. (1972). A theory of Pavlovian conditioning: Variations in the effectiveness of reinforcement and nonreinforcement. In A. H. Black & W. F. Prokasy (Eds.), *Classical conditioning II: Current research and theory*. New York: Appleton-Century-Crofts.

Rosch, E. (1978). *Cognition and categorization*. Hillsdale, NJ: Lawrence Erlbaum Associates, Inc.

Rosenthal, R. (1966). *Experimenter effects in behavioral research*. New York: Appleton-Century-Crofts.

Rosenthal, R., & Jacobson, L. (1968). *Pygmalion in the classroom*. New York: Holt, Rinehart & Winston.

Rosenthal, R., & Rubin, D. B. (1978). Interpersonal expectancy effects: The first 345 studies. *Behavioral and Brain Sciences, 3*, 377–386.

Ross, L. (1977). The intuitive psychologist and his shortcomings: Distortions in the attribution process. In L. Berkowitz (Ed.), *Advances in experimental social psychology* (Vol. 10, pp. 174–200). New York: Academic Press.

Ross, L., Greene, D. & House, P. (1977). The false consensus effect: An egocentric bias in social perception and attribution processes. *Journal of Experimental Social Psychology, 3*, 279–301.

Ross, L., Lepper, M. R., & Hubbard, M. (1975). Perseverance in self-perception and social perception: Biased attribution processes in the debriefing paradigm. *Journal of Personality and Social Psychology, 32*, 880–892.

Ross, L., Lepper, M. R., Strack, F., & Steinmetz, J. (1977). Social explanation and social expectation: effects of real and hypothetical explanations on subjective likelihood. *Journal of Personality and Social Psychology, 35*, 817–829.

Ross, S. L., & Jackson, J. M. (1991). Teacher's expectancy for black males' and black females' academic achievement. *Personality and Social Psychology Bulletin, 17*, 78–82.

Rothbart, M., & John, O. (1985). Social categorization and behavioral episodes: A cognitive analysis of the effects of intergroup contact. *Journal of Social Issues, 41*, 81–104.

Rudolph, U., & Försterling, F. (1997). The psychological causality implicit in verbs: A review. *Psychological Bulletin, 121*, 192–218.

Schaller, M. (1992a). In-group favoritism and statistical reasoning in social inference: Implications for formation and maintenance of group stereotypes. *Journal of Personality and Social Psychology, 63*, 61–74.

Schaller, M. (1992b). Sample size, aggregation, and statistical reasoning in social inference. *Journal of Experimental Social Psychology, 28*, 65–85.

Schaller, M. & Maass, A. (1989). Illusory correlations and social categorization: Toward an integration of motivational and cognitive factors in stereotype formation. *Journal of Personality and Social Psychology, 56*, 709–721.

Schaller, M., & O'Brien, M. (1992). "Intuitive analysis of covariance" and group stereotype formation. *Personality and Social Psychology Bulletin, 18*, 776–785.

Schneider, D. J. (1973). Implicit personality theory. A review. *Psychological Bulletin, 79*, 294–324.

Schmid, J., & Fiedler, K. (1998). The backbone of closing speeches: The impact of prosecution versus defense language on judicial attributions. *Journal of Applied Social Psychology, 28*, 1140–1172.

Schneider, D. (1973). Implicit personality theory: A review. *Psychological Bulletin, 79*, 294–309.

Schul, Y., & Burnstein, E. (1985). When discounting fails: Conditions under which individuals use discredited information in making a judgment. *Journal of Personality and Social Psychology, 49*, 894–903.

Schulz-Hardt, S., Frey, D., Lüthgens, C., & Moscovici, S. (2000). Biased information search in group decision making. *Journal of Personality and Social Psychology, 78*, 655–669.

Schwarz, N., & Bless, H. (1992). Constructing reality and its alternatives: An inclusion–exclusion model of assimilation and contrast effects in social judgment. In L. L. Martin & A. Tesser (Eds.), *The construction of social judgment* (pp. 217–245). Hillsdale, NJ: Lawrence Erlbaum Associates, Inc.

Sedlmeier, P. (1999). *Improving statistical reasoning: Theoretical models and practical implications*. Mahwah, NJ: Lawrence Erlbaum Associates, Inc.

Seligman, M. E. P. (1970). On the generality of the laws of learning. *Psychological Review, 77*, 406–418.

Seligman, M. E. P. (1971). Phobias and preparedness. *Behavior Therapy, 2*, 307–320.

Semin, G. R., & Fiedler, K. (1988). The cognitive functions of linguistic categories in describing persons: Social cognition and language. *Journal of Personality and Social Psychology, 54*, 558–568.

Semin, G. R., & Fiedler, K. (1991). The linguistic category model, its bases, application and range. *European Review of Social Psychology, 2*, 1–30.

Shavitt, S., & Sanbonmatsu, D. (1999). Broadening the conditions for illusory correlation formation: Implications for judging minority groups. *Basic and Applied Social Psychology*, 21, 263–279.

Sherif, M., & Hovland, C. I. (1961). *Assimilation and contrast effects in communication and attitude change*. New Haven: Yale University Press.

Shultz, T. R., & Lepper, M. R. (1996). Cognitive dissonance reduction as constraint satisfaction. *Psychological Review, 103*, 219–240.

Shweder, R. A. (1977). Likeness and likelihood in everyday thought: Magical thinking in judgments about personality. *Current Anthropology, 18*, 637–658.

Simpson, E. H. (1951). The interpretation of interaction in contingency tables. *Journal of the Royal Statistical Society, Ser, B, 13*, 238–241.

Skowronski, J. J., Carlston, D. E., Mae, L., & Crawford, M. T. (1998). Spontaneous trait transference: Communicators take on the qualities they describe others. *Journal of Personality and Social Psychology, 74*, 837–848.

Slovic, P. (1996). Informing and educating the public about risk. *Risk Analysis, 6*, 403–415.

Slugoski, B. R., Sarson, D. A., & Krank, M. D. (1992). *The effects of cognitive load on the formation of illusory correlations*. Unpublished research, Pount Allison University.

Smith, D. A., & Graesser, A. C. (1981). Memory for actions in scripted activities as a function of typicality, retention interval, and retrieval task. *Memory & Cognition, 9*, 550–559.

Smith, E. R. (1991). Illusory correlation in a simulated exemplar-based memory. *Journal of Experimental Social Psychology, 27*, 107–123.

Smith, E. R. (1996). What do connectionism and social psychology offer each other? *Journal of Personality and Social Psychology, 5*, 893–912.

Snyder, M. (1984). When belief creates reality. In L. Berkowitz (Ed.), *Advances in experimental social psychology* (Vol. 18, pp. 247–305). New York: Academic Press.

Snyder, M., & Swann, W. B. (1978). Hypothesis-testing strategies in social interaction. *Journal of Personality and Social Psychology, 36*, 1202–1212.

Snyder, M., Tanke, E. D., & Berscheid, E. (1977). Social perception and interpersonal behavior: On the self-fulfilling nature of stereotypes. *Journal of Personality and Social Psychology, 36*, 941–950.

Solomon, S., & Saxe, L. (1977). What is intelligent, as well as attractive, is good. *Personality and Social Psychology Bulletin, 3*, 670–673.

Spears, R., Oakes, P. J., Ellemers, N., & Haslam, S. A. (Eds.). (1997). *The social psychology of stereotyping and group life*. Oxford: Basil Blackwell.

Spears, R., van der Pligt, J., & Eiser, J. R. (1985). Illusory correlation in the perception of group attitudes. *Journal of Personality and Social Psychology, 48*, 863–875.

Srull, T. K., & Wyer, R. S. (1979). The role of category accessibility in the interpretation of information about persons: Some determinants and implications. *Journal of Personality and Social Psychology, 37*, 1660–1672.

Stangor, C., & McMillan, D. (1992). Memory for expectancy-congruent and expectancy-incongruent information: A review of the social and social developmental literatures. *Psychological Bulletin, 111*, 42–61.

Stapel, D. A., Koomen, W., & Ruys, K. I. (2002). The effects of diffuse and distinct affect. *Journal of Personality and Social Psychology, 83*, 60–74.

Stapel, D. A., Koomen, W., & van der Pligt, J. (1996). The referents of trait inferences: The impact of trait concepts versus actor-trait links on subsequent judgments. *Journal of Personality and Social Psychology, 70*, 437–450.

Stasser, G. (1992). Pooling of unshared information during group discussion. In S. Worchel, W. Wood, & A. Simpson (Eds.), *Group process and productivity* (pp. 48–67). Newbury Park, CA: Sage.

Stasser, G., & Titus, W. (1985). Pooling of unshared information in group decision making: Biased information sampling in group discussion. *Journal of Personality and Social Psychology, 48*, 1467–1478.

Steele, C. M., & Aronson, J. (1995). Stereotype threat and the intellectual test performance of African Americans. *Journal of Personality and Social Psychology, 69*, 797–811.

Strack, F., Schwarz, N., Bless, H., Kübler, A., & Wänke, M. (1993). Awareness of the influence as a determinant of assimilation vs. contrast. *European Journal of Social Psychology, 23*, 53–62.

Swim, J. K., Aikin, K. J., Hall, W. S., & Hunter, B. A. (1995). Sexism and racism: Old-fashioned and modern prejudices. *Journal of Personality and Social Psychology, 68*, 199–214.

Tajfel, H. (1957). Value and the perceptual judgment of magnitude. *Psychological Review, 64*, 192–204.

Tajfel, H. (1959). Quantitative judgment in social perception. *British Journal of Social Psychology, 50*, 16–29.

Tajfel, H., & Turner, J. C. (1986). The social identity theory of intergroup behaviour. In S. Worchel & W. G. Austin (Eds.), *Psychology of intergroup relations* (2nd ed., pp. 7–24). Chicago: Nelson Hall.

Tajfel, H., & Wilkes, A. L. (1963) Classification and quantitative judgment. *British Journal of Social Psychology, 54*, 101–114.

Tesser, A. (1978). Self-generated attitude change. In L. Berkowitz (Ed.), *Advances in experimental social psychology* (Vol. 11, pp. 181–227). San Diego, CA: Academic Press.

Thagard, P. (1989). Explanatory coherence. *The Behavioral and Brain Sciences, 12*, 435–467.

Trope, Y., & Bassok, M. (1983). Information-gathering strategies in hypothesis testing. *Journal of Personality and Social Psychology, 43*, 22–34.

Trope, Y., & Liberman, N. (2000). Temporal construal and time-dependent changes in preference. *Journal of Personality and Social Psychology, 79,* 876–889.

Trope, Y., & Thompson, E. P. (1997). Looking for truth in all the wrong places? Asymmetric search of individuating information about stereotyped group members. *Journal of Personality and Social Psychology, 73*, 229–241.

Turner, J. C., Hogg, M. A., Oaks, P. J., Reicher, S. D., & Wetherell, M. S. (Eds.). (1987). *Rediscovering the social group: A self-categorization theory*. Oxford: Basil Blackwell.

Vallacher, R. R., & Wegner, D. M. (1987). What do people think they're doing? Action identification and human behavior. *Psychological Review, 94*, 3–15.

von Restorff, H. (1933). Über die Wirkung von Bereichsbildungen im Spurenfeld. *Psychologische Forschung, 18*, 299–342.

Waldmann, M., & Hagmayer, Y. (1995). Causal paradox: When a cause simultaneously produces and prevent an effect. *Proceedings of the Seventeenth Annual Conference of the Cognitive Science Society*. Hillsdale, NJ: Lawrence Erlbaum Associates, Inc.

Wallach, L., & Wallach, M. A. (1994). Gergen versus the mainstream: Are hypotheses in social psychology subject to experimental test? *Journal of Personality and Social Psychology, 67*, 233–242.

Walther, E. (1997). *Der Einfluss von Wissensstrukturen auf konstruktive Prozess der sozialen Urteilsbildung*. Lengerich, Germany: Pabst Science Publishers.

Walther, E., Bless, H., Strack, F., Rackstraw, P., Wagner, D., & Werth, L. (2002). Conformity effects in memory as a function of group size, dissenters and uncertainty. *Applied Cognitive Psychology, 16*, 793–810.

Walther, E., Dambacher, U., Dias, N., & Reich, M. (1999). *Erkenne das Opfer in der Not. Der Einfluss von situativen Hinweisreizen und Priming auf die Identifikation von Hilfsbedürftigkeit*. [Recognizing a victim in need: The effect of situational cues and priming on the identification of need for help]. *Zeitschrift für Experimentelle Psychologie, 47*, 50–71.

Walther, E., Fiedler, K., & Nickel, S. (2002). *The more we know the better? Influences of prior knowledge on constructive biases*. Paper submitted for publication.

Walther E., & Trope, Y. (2002). *How temporal distance changes your mind: Assessing the valence of future activities*. In preparation.

Wänke, M., Bless, H., & Igou, E. (2001). Next to a star: Paling, shining, or both? Turning interexamplar contrast into interexemplar assimilation. *Personality and Social Psychology Bulletin, 27*, 14–29.

Wason, P. C. (1960). On the failure to eliminate hypothesis in a conceptual task. *Quarterly Journal of Experimental Psychology, 23*, 445–459.

Wason, P. C. (1966). Reasoning. In B. M. Foss (Ed.), *New horizons in psychology*. Harmondsworth: Penguin.

Wason, P. C. (1968). Reasoning about a rule. *Quarterly Journal of Experimental Psychology, 20*, 273–281.

Wason, P. C., & Johnson-Laird, P. N. (1969). *Quarterly Journal of Experimental Psychology, 21*, 14–20.

Watson, D. (1982). The actor and the observer: How are their perceptions of causality divergent? *Psychological Bulletin, 92*, 682–700.

Weber, R., & Crocker, J. (1983). Cognitive processes in the revision of stereotypic beliefs. *Journal of Personality and Social Psychology, 45*, 961–977.

Wegner, D. M. (1994). Ironic processes of mental control. *Psychological Review, 101*, 34–52.

Wegner, D. M., Wenzlaff, R., Kerker, R. M., & Beattie, A. E. (1981). Incrimination through innuendo: Can media questions become public answers? *Journal of Personality and Social Psychology, 40*, 822–832.

Weinstein, N. D. (1980). Unrealistic optimism about future life events. *Journal of Personality and Social Psychology, 39*, 806–820.

Wells, G. L., & Bradfield, A. L. (1998). Good, you identified the suspect: Feedback to eyewitnesses distorts their reports of the witnessing experience. *Journal of Applied Psychology, 83*, 360–376.

Wells, G. L., & Gavanski, I. (1989) Mental simulation of causality. *Journal of Personality & Social Psychology, 56*, 161–169.

Wigboldus, D. H. J., Semin, G. R., & Spears, R. (2000). How do we communicate stereotypes? Linguistic bases and inferential consequences. *Journal of Personality and Social Psychology, 78*, 5–18.

Wilson, T. D., & Schooler, J. W. (1991). Thinking too much: Introspection can reduce the quality of preferences and decisions. *Journal of Personality and Social Psychology, 60*, 181–192.

Wittenbrink, B., Judd, C. M., & Park, B. (1997). Evidence for racial prejudice at the implicit level and its relationship with questionnaire measures. *Journal of Personality and Social Psychology, 72*, 262–274.

Wittenbrink, B., Judd, C. M., & Park, B. (2001). Evaluative versus conceptual judgments in automatic stereotyping and prejudice. *Journal of Experimental Social Psychology, 37*, 244–252.

Zebrowitz, L. A., Voinescu, L., & Collins, M. A. (1996). "Wide-eyed" and "crooked-faced": Determinants of perceived and real honesty across the life span. *Personality and Social Psychology Bulletin, 22*, 1258–1269.

Zuckerman, M. (1979). Attribution of success and failure revisited, or: the motivational bias is alive and well in attribution theory. *Journal of Personality, 47*, 245–287.

Zuckerman, M., Knee, C. R. Hodgins, H. S., & Myake, K. (1995). Hypothesis confirmation: The joint effect of positive test strategy and acquiescence response set. *Journal of Personality and Social Psychology, 68*, 52–60.

Author index

Subject index

For Product Safety Concerns and Information please contact our EU
representative GPSR@taylorandfrancis.com
Taylor & Francis Verlag GmbH, Kaufingerstraße 24, 80331 München, Germany

www.ingramcontent.com/pod-product-compliance
Lightning Source LLC
LaVergne TN
LVHW010602110826
845149LV00003B/743